Ships'Cats

in war and peace

by
Val Lewis

Ships'Cats
in war and peace

First published 2001
This revised, expanded edition 2010

Jointly published by Nauticalia Ltd and G2 Entertainment Ltd.

G2 entertainment

**Nauticalia Ltd, The Ferry Point, Ferry Lane,
Shepperton-on-Thames, Middlesex TW17 9LQ,
England. Tel 01932 244396.
www.nauticalia.com. email: val.lewis@nauticalia.com**

**G2 Entertainment Limited 2010
West Barn, Westwood Farm, High Cross Road, Southfleet,
Kent DA13 9PH Tel 01474 834986 www.G2ent.co.uk**

A catalogue record for this book is available from the British Library

ISBN 978-1-907803-28-4

Printed and bound printed in Croatia
Typeset in Cheltenham BT Roman 11pt

This book is affectionately dedicated to three jewels,
Sapphire, Ruby and Emerald, and a Princess Charlotte.
also with equal love, to Dan, Ben, and Tobias.
(They are my grandchildren, not my cats)

With grateful thanks to Charmian Barttelot (daughter of Capt Kerans of the *Amethyst*) who kindly loaned us the painting of Simon - which she inherited from her late father - for the front cover. Although it is signed 'C.C.', neither Charmian nor her mother, Stephanie Kerans, knows the artist's full name. We are hoping that a sharp-eyed reader will be able to identify 'C.C.'.

Author's Note: In writing this book I have tried to be thorough in my research and consulted authoritative sources worldwide. But we are all experts in our own field and there will be many an old sea dog with sharper wits than me who will inevitably spot nautical gaffes and historical blunders. I hope there won't be many, but I would be so grateful if I could be put right so that next time I can make corrections.

Apostrophic Apology

The words **ship(s)** and **cat(s)** appear together frequently in this book and I have sometimes been uncertain about where to place an apostrophe. As a devout supporter of the Apostrophe Protection Society, I apologise for any inconsistencies. I decided that the rule should be that if there was only one cat it could only be aboard one ship at a time, so it should be referred to as a **ship's cat** singular. When there is more than one cat aboard a particular ship, I have written **ship's cats**. And when, as in the title, there are many cats and many ships, I have written **ships' cats.** Sometimes, though, when there is uncertainty about how many cats relate to how many ships, I have abandoned ship, cat and punctuation and called them simply ships cats! I also had difficulty deciding whether cats are **'who'** or **'that'**. I've been inconsistent, depending upon how close I felt to each cat.

List of Chapters and Stories

List of Chapters and Stories

Illustrations

Acknowledgements

With grateful thanks to Cdr Stewart Hett, MBE, RN, who was on the Amethyst in 1949, for his patience and assistance to the author, above and beyond the call of duty.

Jean Young, Archivist, SS Great Britain , Bristol

Stuart Nourse, Archivist, Royal National Lifeboat Institution

Lieutenant Commander K.S Hett, MBE RN Rtd

Bob Headland, Scott Polar Research Institute, Cambridge

Shirley Sawtell, Scott Polar Research Institute, Cambridge

Hugh McKnight, photographer and writer

Imperial War Museum, London

British Library, London

Claire Francis and Naomi James, inspirations to women sailors worldwide

Julia McLaughlin Cook, National Museums & Galleries on Merseyside

Baden Norris QSO & Kerry McCarthy, Canterbury Museum, NZ

Paddy Mummery, of Sunbury-on-Thames, for some old salt's guidance

Emily Nicholson, for story of the Siamese cats on HMS Vanguard

Ian Thomson, Laura Boyes and Peter Fryer, Nauticalia

Aileen Dalton and Peggy Hay, for the Sideboy story

National Maritime Museum, Greenwich (Trim)

Leading Marine Engineer Francis Clark, RN Rtd

Molly Tuck & Mike Nevitt, aboard Watwind

Gill Hubbard, People's Dispensary for Sick Animals

Sally Grimwood, Hope Services

Andy Balchin, technical wizard, Biddles

Alex Wake, Turkish Van Swimming Cat breeder

Stephen Courtney, Royal Naval Museum, Portsmouth

Anna Bowman, Royal Naval Museum, Portsmouth

Warwick Hirst, State Library of New South Wales

Jenny Brookhead, State Library of New South Wales

Lindsey Shaw, Australian Maritime Museum, Sydney.

Evelyn Wilde Mayerson for her wonderful bubbemeiser (grandmother's tale)

Jeanine Hardcastle, for her mother's story

Tania Abei, the plucky teenager who sailed the world alone

Alvah Simon, for his inspiring book, North to the Night

Jennifer Broomhead and Warwick Hirst, State Library, New South Wales, Australia

Vanessa Bond, State Library, New South Wales

Catherine Smith, National Maritime Museum, Greenwich

Lisette Flinders Petrie, descendant of Matthew Flinders

Annette Macarthur-Onslow, illustrator and writer

Vanessa Bond, State Library, New South Wales

Charmian and David Barttelot

Stephanie Kerans, widow of the Amethyst Captain

Boarding Noah's Ark. Tradition says that the animals went in 'two-by-two' but, typically, the cat seems to walk alone in this Victorian drawing.

The Owl and the Pussycat went to sea in a beautiful pea-green boat, wrote Edward Lear – and then sketched it as well

The Evolution of Ships' Cats

All cats, at heart, are really ships' cats. These graceful, enigmatic creatures have been sneaking aboard ships for thousands of years, which is how they managed to spread themselves around the world so abundantly, in all shapes, colours and sizes. Traditionally they have been welcomed aboard by seamen for a number of good, practical reasons - the most obvious being that they are so extraordinarily skilful at catching the rats and mice that plague sea-going vessels.

Although when they have to, they are able to swim, they are not by nature partial to water so it is strange that they should even contemplate venturing on ships that sail the high seas where there's "water, water, everywhere". It may seem foolhardy of cats to put themselves at risk in an unnatural and often perilous environment, but those that become seafarers do so inadvertently, if not intentionally, for their desire to explore is far greater than their dislike of water. Cats are notoriously curious creatures and will pry and snoop at just about anything that arouses their interest. There's many a cat who, unable to resist walking up a gangplank just to find out where it leads to, has unwittingly curled up in some cosy corner in the depths of a ship, only to wake up far out at sea, to the sound of crashing waves and howling winds.

It all began in Egypt 5,000 to 8,000 years ago, in the Nile River Valley. There the first cats to **choose** to be domesticated were members of the species *felis sylvestris libyaca*, also known as the African wildcat. They were drawn to domesticity by the human shift from nomadic to agrarian living. Once people learnt to farm they began to store their harvest crops, which attracted rodents which in turn attracted wild cats. As the cats demonstrated their usefulness by controlling the mouse and rat population, they were given food and other comforts to encourage them to stick around.

They soon earned tremendous respect from their Egyptian "owners" to the point of worship. If a pet cat died, the whole household observed a week of mourning. The Greek historian, Herodotus, describes how all the inmates, including slaves, would shave their eyebrows as a sign of respect and the beloved cat would be mummified and buried in a sacred place. Cats managed to retain the unique independence that is characteristic of all felines, condescending to be pampered and treated with reverence by the Egyptians but never, never agreeing to stay on a permanent basis and frequently wandering elsewhere, perhaps to search for new mates.

The tradition of having ships' cats originated when, in ancient times, sea traders visiting Egyptian ports noticed, and were impressed and fascinated by, the efficiency and grace of these strange, mysterious animals that guarded the nation's grain. It seemed an excellent idea to recruit Egyptian cats for their ships, to keep their own food stores on board free of rodents. As the trading vessels travelled from port to port, cats jumped ship and adapted easily to foreign environments, breeding with other types of wild cat. This is how domestic cats arrived in Greece in 500 BC, in India about 300 BC and in China about 200 BC.

As they settled in their new countries, they gradually developed characteristics to help them cope with harsh or extreme climates. Norwegian Skogatts, for instance, might have resulted from interbreeding between shorthaired cats left by the Vikings and longhaired cats brought back in ships by returning Crusaders. These cats developed specific physical qualities necessary for their survival in the harsh northern environment, such as thick, water repellent outercoats to shield them against rain and snow and woolly undercoats to insulate them from the cold. Thick ruffs and full bibs protected neck and chest, long tufts of hair on their wide paws served as natural snowshoes and three to four inch hairs in the "nether regions" of their ears protected them against frostbite.

Ships carrying the first settlers to the New World had cats on board and when passengers disembarked so did the cats. Maine's state cat, the Maine Coon, resulted from interbreeding between domestic shorthaired cats and free-running longhaired cats. Longhairs may have been seafaring cats that jumped ship or cats the Vikings introduced to the New World. Natural selection and Maine's harsh climate created this large rugged breed with its long shaggy water-resistant coat and large paws to make it easier to walk on fresh snow.

Some cats were smuggled aboard by sailors as pets to keep them company during long voyages. The Abyssinian cat is a distinctive, dog-like animal with short orange brown hair, a slender body, a ticked coat and almond shaped eyes. According to a Gordon Stables, writing in 1874, the first Abyssinian cat arrived in England on a ship as a gift for the Captain's wife, who called her Zula. Zula is the name of the northern Abyssinian port where Britain established its first base.

The Abyssinian is one of the most popular cats in the western world. It probably originated, not in Abyssinia (now Ethiopia) but in countries near the Indian Ocean or in Southeast Asia. When British sailors left Abyssinia in 1868 they brought some of these cats home. They were attracted by their pure grace and intelligence. With long, slender legs and neck and soft silky fur lying close to the body, each hair alternated between dark and light bands, tipped with a darker colour, giving the coat a ticked effect. These clever cats are easily trained to do stunts and Abyssinians often appear in television commercials and movies. They love company and will follow their owners as a dog does.

The blue-eyed, white-coated Angora cat was supposed to have developed its long, soft fur coat as a protection against the intense cold of its native Russia. They were first brought to Asia in trading ships and gradually found their way by sea to Europe.

The Burmese cat is muscular, athletic and compact with short hair and a glossy rich brown coat and golden yellow eyes. One of the first of its type was brought west to New Orleans from Burma, by a sailor who sold her to a local pet shop. The sailor described her as a Burmese cat. She was bought by a retired ship's doctor, who bred from her.

Cats are highly sensitive to atmospheric changes. In days of old, when all vessels were made of wood, which provided a perfect environment for rodents, few ships would set sail without at least one cat on board.

The slightest sniff in the air of bad weather will make a ship's cat restless and nervous, and set him walking about the deck with tail erect and fur standing on end. In cold weather salt ingrained in the wood, crystallised and forced its way out in hard globules, which made it easier to get at. Therefore sailors would look on nervously when a cat was noticed licking the wooden decks, to see if he licked against the grain to get at the salt, which was a sure sign of an impending snow or hail storm or a drop in temperature.

On the whole it was lucky as well as useful to have a cat on board a ship. If the vessel needed wind, all the crew had to do was place a cat under a pot on deck, which would encourage the wind to seek it out. A cat sneezing indicated mild rain and frisky behaviour meant a favourable wind was on its way and the crew could look forward to billowing sails and a smooth passage.

Cats, being such mysterious creatures, were often considered by superstitious sailors to be bewitched. At other times they were regarded as mascots or charms to protect the ship and the crew against ill fortune. Black cats were tolerated but treated with caution as they were deemed to be occasional companions of the devil.

A cat that was thrown, or even fell, overboard would be revenged by the rapid approach of a terrible storm and often nine years of bad luck for ship and crew. Throwing a **black** cat overboard was to be avoided at all costs, for this would be sure to incite the devil's wrath. In fact, any unnatural action by the ship's cat, such as licking its fur in the wrong direction, or scratching the legs of a table, was a sign that storms were expected.

In Medieval Europe, when a suspected witch was persecuted and burnt at the stake, her cat was regarded as her evil familiar and was usually burnt with her. The last recorded execution of a cat for witchcraft was in England in 1712.

When Crusaders returned home from the holy wars, the holds of their vessels carried disease-ridden black rats that swarmed off the ships and spread the plague. If there had not been such a drastically diminished cat population as a result of persecution of witches, these rodents might have been rapidly dealt with and consequently saved Europe from the horrors of the Black Death.

All-black cats were considered to be personifications of the Devil, or the Prince of Darkness and were repeatedly put to death, which why **totally** black cats are so rare even today.

Those with even a tiny patch of white were reprieved because the white was considered to be a sign of innocence, placed there by God and referred to as "God's Finger".

Recognising the significance of ships' cats, in 1275 King Edward I of England introduced a strangely contradictory law which stated that "if any living being, be it man, dog or cat, escaped from a stricken vessel, then it could not be considered a wreck". In other words, it was only a wreck if all aboard perished, in which scavengers were free to forage the vessel's cargo and contents. The law was probably intended to protect the owner of a vessel who, having escaped a watery death, would want to return in calmer weather to try to salvage his ship and contents before the scavengers did. Perhaps King Edward had in mind the ancient proverb: "Never was a cat drowned that could see the shore."

Ships cats are wonderfully adaptable. They will snuggle in the hold if it's cold, and if the decks are wet they will walk on tiptoe so that the pads of their paws hardly touch the ground. They'll cheerfully eat whatever is going – an odd fish head, a sliver of raw seal or penguin or even a raw egg, but aren't too worried if they are left to fend for themselves and have to make do with the unsavoury looking body of a dead rat or mouse which they will gulp down whole, fur, bones and all.

Being vain creatures, perhaps what they like most of all about life at sea is the attention they get. Sailors are often away for months and, in ages past, even years. Cats provided them with tranquil companionship and gave them a sense of home and security. And, when the ship was in the "doldrums" the crew whiled away the hours teaching them clever tricks, which the cats were happy to perform over and over and over again. If foul weather closed in and things got tough they merely sought out a warm cosy niche in which to curl up and sleep until it was calmer.

This book relates true tales of courageous cats that have undergone hardship and amazing adventures on the high seas. Some of them and their experiences are well chronicled but most are only briefly recorded. There are probably many not yet told. But one thing is certain! Most cats that go to sea invariably have stunning experiences.

One exotic cat, appropriately named Princess Truban Tao-Tai, logged more than 1.5million miles as a crew member of the British merchant ship, *Sagamore*. Doodles, a regular aboard the ocean liner *Cedric*, also travelled more than a million miles in **his** seafaring career.

Simon, of HMS *Amethyst*, was badly wounded when he was caught up in naval warfare on the Yangtze River in 1949. He was awarded a medal for bravery. Then there is Mrs Chippy, who travelled on the *Endurance* with Sir Ernest Shackleton on his legendary expedition to the Antarctic in 1914/1915, and Matthew Flinders' cat, the amazingly entertaining Trim who, early in the 19th century, circumnavigated the globe and twice circumnavigated Australia with his besotted master.

Bubbles, a large black fat cat, was living a life of luxury sailing the Mediterranean on his own yacht, crewed by Molly Tuck and Mike Nevitt. After six years at sea, he had sailed over 5,000 miles.

Some of these tales are scary and will "shiver your timbers". Others are sad and will soften the souls of the toughest of seafarers. Some are long, some are very short. They are not just about ships nor just about cats. They are about **ships' cats.** Some tales are even about cats' tails!

Cats were trained by the Egyptians to catch birds hiding in the thickets which grew along the edge of the Nile. In this fowling and fishing scene Mutsa, third priest of Amen, is seen with his favourite cat poised to jump out.

World War II Cats

At a conference of naval chaplains held in the early days of World War II, it was decided to encourage the presence of animals on board ship as the best cure for a "browned off" ship's company. It was pointed out that many of the boy seamen were homesick, seasick and frightened. Pets reminded them of home, particularly cats, who had only to purr contentedly to create a feeling of normality.

Several instances were cited of seamen who had become real "hard cases" and had been miraculously transformed by the simple companionship of a puppy or kitten. The theory was that, by caring for an animal and receiving its warmth and love in return, the sailor forgot his own grievances and fears and was able to relax. As a result of the conference, the Allied Forces Mascot Club was formed and servicemen from the Army, Navy and Air Force were encouraged to apply for membership for their pets.

Apart from those formally registered, ships in particular were prepared to take on board a menagerie of creatures, from pet monkeys, parrots, dogs, rabbits and even geese, as illustrated by George Wilby, serving on HMS *Delphinium*, Flower-class corvette ship, in a letter dated 22 May 1944, which he sent to his mother and father, living at Hilary Road, Westway, London.

George was clearly not cut out for the Navy but was a talented young artist whose ambition when he was demobbed was to have his own studio. In his letter he draws an amusing picture in words of pets at sea.

"We have quite a few pets on board. A goose, three dogs and a cat. We did have two geese, they belonged to the Petty Officers, but they killed one for their dinner one day when we were short of meat. I don't expect the other one will live long. We shall have to get rid of one of our dogs, as three is too many for a ship of this size. We used to have three cats at one time, but they keep on walking off and other cats walk on. At the moment we have another kitten on board, a tabby and white one. He came aboard tonight. I don't know if he will stay or not. I hope he does."

Few cats joined the Army and Air Force because they disliked changing addresses whereas life at sea seemed to suit them. On a ship a cat could always rely on sleeping in the same familiar snug spot and know exactly where its food would be placed each day. There was a feeling of permanence on board a ship, despite the rolling motion. The immediate surroundings remained constant and the cats were able to form affectionate bonds with selected members of the crew and still satisfy their natural instinct to travel and explore. And yet they retained the option, if the ship didn't suit them, of transferring to some other vessel at the next port.

But there were cats and cats! Anonymous ships' cats with fiercely independent spirits who came and went at will and Mascot Cats with names and distinct personalities who had their own complex social system on board ship. Cats that took the fancy of a member of the ship's company for instance, might find themselves adopted as mascot of some particular part of the ship, such as the wardroom, the gunroom, the engine room or a special mess-deck. Sometimes they earned this honour by impressing the crew with their hunting skills, or being particularly amusing, companionable and affectionate.

An outstanding cat could rise from the ranks to become the mascot of the entire ship, spending several years on the same vessel. Whether as casual travellers or as official members of the crew, ships' cats would go about their business hunting mice and rats and otherwise pursuing their personal lives unperturbed by the roar of naval guns. In some instances, where toms and queens shared the same ship, they became so absorbed in their own affairs that they produced families under gunfire!

One sailor, Charles Hodgson, remarked, "a ship's cat can create an oasis of peace and serenity even amidst the noise and clamour of war". Despite this obvious truth, in the interests of hygiene, in 1975 the British Admiralty dismayed sailors everywhere by banning **all** animals from HM ships.

The Cat that Sailed the World But Walked By Itself

Minnie was one of the best known and most travelled naval ship's cats of World War II. She joined the crew of the cruiser HMS *Argonaut* in 1944, at Hebburn-on-Tyne, and for two and a half years sailed the world unruffled by the savage exchanges of gunfire the ship was frequently involved in. One of her shipmates, Able Seaman Curtis, described her fondly as having "rendered excellent service as a mascot, a pet and rodent controller".

A "handsome tabby with white paws and breast and always immaculately clean", Curtis said she was the epitome of Rudyard Kipling's immortal cat in his delightful "Just So Stories" who refused to be owned by anyone and insisted: "I am not a friend and I am not a servant. I am the cat who walks by himself."*

Minnie didn't care to attach herself to anyone in particular and was impervious to rank. She was very particular about who she allowed to stroke and pet her and, whether it was the Captain or the cabin boy, she expected them to do so with proper respect. The whole ship was her domain and she would sleep equally at ease in the Captain's cabin or on the mess decks, with no loss of dignity.

The first action she saw was on D-Day and she was "one of the first of the Allied cats to arrive at the Normandy beachhead". Although the ship's guns were firing almost continually and an occasional bomb or mine exploded too near for comfort, Minnie took not the slightest notice. It was not *her* war, not *her* concern. Her daily routine of sleep, food and prowling round the ship looking for mice went on uninterrupted. The *Argonaut* saw action in the invasion of the French Riviera. Then at Palermo, in Sicily, where the ship was based for several weeks, one of the crew rescued from the shore a woolly brown puppy and brought it aboard. Minnie gave it the evil eye and, despite much pampering, it died after only a few weeks at sea.

In December 1944, the *Argonaut* sailed east of Suez, to Colombo and then to Trincomalee. She was involved in three operations against the Japanese in the East Indies, when the ship was part of the escort for British aircraft carriers and the *Argonaut* claimed at least one Japanese bomber. Minnie retired below decks and appeared, unperturbed, when all the fuss and noise was over.

In February 1945 they sailed to Fremantle and Sydney, followed by the monotony of Pacific Ocean warfare with long months at sea without sight of land and endless steaming under the scorching sun. But by May they were back in Sydney, preparing for the next operation. During this period most of the larger groups of islands in the Pacific were visited – the Admiralties, the Carolines and the Philippines. The Formosa and Takashima group was amongst the targets of the attacks.

It was whilst the *Argonaut* was anchored off Tokyo that news came of the Japanese surrender and they returned to the Philippines. Able Seaman Curtis noted: "The first peace-time voyage Minnie experienced was to Formosa and then to Shanghai, through some foul China Seas weather, during which Minnie proved that even a hurricane and the tail end of a typhoon couldn't upset her."

In November 1945 the *Argonaut* returned to Sydney via Hong Kong. Minnie by now was showing signs of restlessness. It was much too quiet for her. Life at sea in peacetime was pretty tame after all she'd experienced. The ship visited Adelaide, Port Lincoln and Fremantle again before steaming northwards to Singapore and Hong Kong, where Minnie spent her second Christmas.

Early in 1946 the ship went further north, leaving the warm China Sea for the snow and cold of a Japanese winter. The *Argonaut* was in Japanese waters for three months. Minnie was able to go ashore only in Nagoya, for at Yokohama and Kure the ship lay at anchor.

The ship returned to Hong Kong in March, and made a trip to Singapore and back before finally beginning the long voyage home in May. It was in Singapore that Minnie decided to abandon ship. Perhaps she'd had enough of shipboard life, or fallen in love with some Singapore tomcat.

The crew of the *Argonaut* was convinced Minnie had been kidnapped. This theory was based on the fact that, a few weeks before, Minnie wandered aboard a water boat in Hong Kong harbour and was reported missing. After many frantic exchanges between wireless operators and signalmen, she was eventually located aboard one of the destroyers in the harbour and the *Argonaut's* motor boat was sent to bring her home.

Someone, they now reckoned, had taken such a fancy to the cat that the next time an opportunity occurred to capture her, they were more cunning and cautious. The entire ship's company searched ship and shore looking for Minnie but, although a search party remained ashore up to the last possible minute, they returned empty handed.

As *Argonaut* sailed with "one of the best-known and best-loved members of her crew adrift", this signal was sent to the Commodore Superintendent at the Singapore Naval Base:

"Minnie, Argonaut's famous cat, was absent on sailing. If found request she may be sent to UK by next ship."

Alas she was never found. However, during her time on board she had given birth to "a large number of charming kittens". Two of these carried on the family tradition by serving on the *Argonaut* in her place.

*Note: This fable epitomising the personality of the domestic cat is by Rudyard Kipling (1865-1936) in his "Just So Stories" (1902). After the dog, the horse and the cow had agreed to become domesticated, the cat finally appeared at the human den and said: "I am not a friend, I am not a servant. I am the cat who walks by himself and I wish to come into our cave." Some hard bargaining followed in which the cat promised to catch mice "for always and always and always, but still I am the cat that walks by himself".

Winston Churchill stoops to stroke the ship's cat on board HMS *Prince of Wales*, so preventing him from deserting the British ship for an American ship, the *Augusta*. The cat was immediately renamed Churchill by the crew.

(by kind permission of the Imperial War Museum, London)

The Cat that Winston Churchill Stopped From Deserting Ship

Winston Churchill had a lot of things on his mind when, in August 1941, he and President Franklin Roosevelt met for a three day conference at sea with the intention of drawing up the "Atlantic Charter", a statement of international peace aims. The historic meeting took place in Placentia Bay, off Newfoundland. Churchill was aboard HMS *Prince of Wales* and Roosevelt was on the *Augusta*.

Despite having all these important issues to contend with, the Great Man was distracted by the sight of the enormous black ship's cat of HMS *Prince of Wales* on the verge of deserting the British ship for the American vessel. Churchill swiftly bent down and stopped the cat in his tracks, for he was fond of cats and had one at home called Nelson.

The poignant moment was photographed for posterity. The cat was, of course, immediately renamed Churchill by the crew and became a favourite mascot. When the *Prince of Wales* was later sunk by the Japanese a few of the crew managed to swim to safety, including Churchill. Churchill settled down with the other survivors at Sime Road RAF Station, sharing the men's rations and thoroughly at home on dry land. When they were moved to another camp, he went with them.

In February 1942 orders came to evacuate Singapore immediately. This meant within hours, and poor old Churchill had gone off on one of his frequent hunting trips. The last fourteen men left at the station hunted vainly for Churchill but he could not be found and he had to be left to whatever fate finally befell him.

Chief Petty Officer Edward Stupple's Secret Mission with Churchill

When, under great secrecy, in 1941 Winston Churchill sailed aboard the Battleship *Prince of Wales* to meet USA President Frank Roosevelt, Chief Petty Officer Edward Stupple was one of the crew. His son, Vic Stupple, told me that his father often went on secret missions before and during the war.

"When he was demobbed from the Royal Navy, my father had a job as watchman. He was very fond of cats and used to bring home stray cats from various ships and sheds in the navy dockyards. One of his favourites was a jet black cat called Nigger, not a name you can use today. When my father went to the pub she would, on most occasions, follow him and sit by the door, then return with him when he came home for lunch.

"She came off one of the boom defence ships that were laid up in Stangate creek, as the reserve fleet on the river Medway after the war. I think she missed the sailors' company and had enough of the sea life. As the ships were moored up with no crews for company she jumped ship for a life ashore."

When serving on the HMS *Prince of Wales*, (shipmate's snap and also in artist Gwynn Hughes's painting of the incident on the back page of the cover) he was there, watching with amusement, as Winston stroked the ship's cat and prevented him from leaving the ship.

Winston later thanked the crew and handed to Chief Petty Officer Edward Stupple one of his famous Havana cigars as a gift.

Still in its original metal container, it has become a treasured Stupple family heirloom.

Aboard HMS Scarborough 1936.
Chief Petty Officer Stupple on the right is holding
the black and white cat.

Lucky and Tommy, the D-Day Heroes

The steam rescue tug *Empire Winnie* had two mascot cats aboard, Lucky and Tommy, a black female and a black and white tom. Both excellent sailors, they made continuous trips to the Normandy and Channel ports on D-Day and for weeks afterwards.

After working the tug so hard, the crew were ordered to sail the *Empire Winnie* to the Tyne for a general refit and the crew were given leave to spend the Christmas of 1944 at home. A shore watchman was employed to keep an eye on the ship and look after the two cats.

Lucky was particularly affectionate and missed the attentions of the crew. Three days before the men returned, Lucky decided to abandon ship. On their return one of the ship's sailors described in a letter home, how he and the rest of the crew hunted for her all over the shipyard. "We are all sad and broken hearted, as she made us cheerful at moments when everything seemed dull and wrong. We hope that little Lucky found as good a home and was admired as much as she was by the lads of the *Empire Winnie*."

To the relief of the crew, Tommy had not been tempted to leave. The same seaman continued: "He was a cat that many people would love to possess. He did great deeds aboard by catching many rats that somehow or other got on our ship. One night, however, we were ordered to sea suddenly as often is the case with rescue tugs and it was discovered that Tommy was missing. A search of the ship took place but no trace of our dear cat was found. We all thought he had been washed overboard. You can guess how we felt, as everybody aboard from the captain down to the cabin boy thought the world of Tommy as his walks aboard the ship took him regularly to the bridge and the saloon.

"On returning to the same port enquiries were made and we were told he had gone aboard another rescue tug. But we all believe the other crew took a liking to our Tommy, as he was a beautiful animal, and coaxed him aboard to keep him.

"The last news we had of Tommy was that he was still at sea. Believe me, if ever we see our Tommy, none of us will hesitate in fetching him back to his own ship, and to the seamen who thought so much of him."

The Captain and the Rose

One February night in 1941, Ruby Peates, a pretty 26-year-old London girl, was working part time arranging a library for the Forces, at an Eaton Square hostel which was being used as a club for foreign servicemen awaiting orders.

Ruby noticed a group of Belgians, amongst them a talkative, impetuous looking young man in his thirties. Their eyes met and there was an instant spark. He came over and introduced himself as Chief Officer Robert Pierre Van Damme, of the Belgian Merchant Marine. His ship, the *Gerlinger*, had been abandoned by her owners in Casablanca, leaving the crew stranded. Now Van Damme was passing through London to join another Belgian merchant ship, ss *Julia*.

The young couple corresponded throughout the war years. When on leave, Van Damme would visit the Peates family in London, telling them amusing tales (and drawing delightful sketches) of two mascots on board ss *Julia* - Peggy, a nervous black and white cat, and her best mate, a plucky, lively dog called Mireau. Peggy followed Mireau everywhere, seeking protection, comfort and security. These tales lifted the family's spirits, taking their thoughts away from the dangers of war, and the risks that their new friend, the Chief Officer, and his crew, were facing daily.

In 1944, the Allies prepared for invasion and the ss *Julia* set sail for Normandy, one of only a few Belgian ships carrying ammunitions and US troups.

Later Van Damme wrote: "It was a windy day when we received the historic order to head for Omaha beach. The coast of France after three years is still familiar. The crew has confidence in the Captain, as the guns of the Navy open. Just our little dog Mireau is shivering at the sound of the gun-fire. We have made little lifebuoys for him and Peggy the cat."

Ruby and her family waited anxiously for news of their Belgian Chief Officer. "We all knew in England, that we would have the greatest defeat or victory. We always hoped for news of the invasion. Every day and in the evenings behind the black-out curtains, we talked at length trying with our poor military knowledge to find out more. We longed to see our Chief Officer again because, over the war years, he had become a jolly companion and brightened up the daily life of an ordinary English family. On D-Day, the 6th of June, Churchill gave a speech on the BBC saying '… let us pray and wait…' and we did!"

On the 9th of June, the Chief Officer appeared on the family's doorstep. He had disembarked at Southampton after the invasion of Normandy, in order to deliver an important gift. Still in battle dress, he presented Ruby with an old cardboard box. Within was a single red rose, still fresh.

He explained he had found it growing on a ruined wall in Normandy, surrounded by the bodies of German soldiers sleeping forever, far away from their homeland. The Chief Officer told Ruby: "This is the first rose of France. It is also the red rose of England. You can still smell the perfume of France. I have to return to my ship but I hope you will keep this rose forever".

Ruby was by now enamoured by the Chief Officer, but was not sure if he felt the same. Nevertheless, she began to keep a diary. "We were deeply moved" wrote Ruby. "It was such a poignant thought amidst all the suffering he had witnessed. I put the *Rose of Normandy* in water and later framed it under glass, so that one day my grandchildren could see it and hear the story."

When ss *Julia* finally safely reached the South Coast, after the Normandy landings, not only did the Chief Officer disembark, but the normally plucky Mireau was so frightened he jumped ship without a second thought for Peggy the cat. He was found shivering with fear at the dock in Southampton, where a lady called Mrs. Dugdale rescued him and took him home.

Despite having let down the shy cat Peggy by deserting ship and leaving her to fend for herself, the two were eventually reunited, and Van Damme took them under his wing. They were awarded membership of the Armed Forces Mascot Club, which had been initiated by the People's Dispensary for Sick Animals.

According to Captain Van Damme's daughter, Jeanine Hardcastle, Peggy the cat became a family pet. Mireau went to live in the Belgian Ardennes with a new owner. It should have been a peaceful retirement for him, but sadly a local farmer mistook him for a fox and shot him. A tragic end for the plucky little sea dog.

After the war, the Chief Officer came back as a Captain to claim his Ruby, his own true English rose. They were married on 13 November, 1947 in London. From then on, each year on D-day, he would send Ruby a bouquet of red roses - wherever he was.

Ratcatcher Off Watch on HMS *Cossack*

Buster Stumpy (D57), like all good sailors, slept in his own hammock, slung up in the Forward Mess Deck. And, like all good ships' cats, when he wasn't prowling around hunting mice, he spent most of his time sleeping instead of entertaining the crew.

Once, when the Captain was carrying out his early rounds, he came across Buster Stumpy curled up asleep. A note was pinned to his hammock: "Stumpy, Ratcatcher Off Watch. Do not Disturb".

Members of the crew who have the Middle Watch (0000-0400) are entitled to "Guard and Steerage" meaning they are permitted to lie in for an extra half hour in the morning when the rest of the crew have to get up. The crew felt that it was necessary for Buster Stumpy's lazy habits to be drawn to the attention of the Captain.

Stripey the Cat Born Aboard HMS *Warspite*

Stripey was a tabby and white cat born aboard HMS *Warspite* about 1939. She did not leave the ship once until 1947 when *Warspite* left Portsmouth to be broken up. Little is known of her early career, but for over a year after *Warspite* was paid off, she was the sole crew, remaining on board with seaman George Waters, who was left in charge.

George had become very attached to the ship's cat. They had shared a lot together. He wrote: "I have no intention of letting Stripey go with *Warspite* when she leaves to be broken up. This cat is one of the most faithful pets anyone could have. No rats can exist where she is. She always escorts me when I set the lights for safety in the evening. I don't think Stripey would settle down to shore life as she knows no other than life than on shipboard and seems a little wild. I am very fond of her and shall see she is never abandoned."

When the sad day came to say goodbye to *Warspite*, Stripey and George were transferred to HMS *Malaya* and, hopefully, sailed together happily ever after.

Susan of *Landing Craft T166*, Who Was Scared of Grass

Another ship's cat who was happy to share the honour of ship's mascot with a dog, was Susan, who served on HM *Landing Craft T166* with her mate Bosun, a bumptious, friendly mongrel.

Susan was hastily given to Lieutenant M. Sproull just as *Landing Craft T166* was due to sail. Susan was in a pretty poor state, probably a starving stray from the streets and, being a real cat lover, Sproull was happy to accept responsibility for her and hastily shut her in his cabin while he attended to his immediate duties.

After the ship was well on its way, he returned to his cabin. To his horror he realised that the new recruit was infested with fleas. Lieutenant Sproull knew he would not be popular if the wardroom became infested too. Since there was no insect powder available, the harassed naval officer soaked the violently protesting cat in strong disinfectant. The treatment seemed to work and, after a gentle rub with a dry towel and some warm milk to revive her, Susan seemed none the worse.

She developed into an attractive, lovable cat and settled happily into the ship's daily routine, quickly making friends with Bosun. The two shipmates were adored by the crew and one or the other was often to be found tucked cosily in the duffel coat of a sailor.

The two ship's mascots took part in a number of engagements in the Channel and were present at the Normandy landings. After her early life as a street cat, abused and starved almost to death, the ship seemed a snug, safe world. Susan became so completely a sea cat that nothing could ever induce her to leave the ship.

Bosun died of heart failure just before the war ended and Susan was even more wary of leaving the ship. When Lieutenant Sproull was demobilized he had difficulty getting her ashore. She was particularly terrified at the sight of the green grass. In the end, however, she adjusted to life on land and settled in Ireland, where she soon enjoyed playing on the lawn in the garden with her companions, two blue Persian cats, a Yorkshire terrier and her own son, named Bosun after her late shipmate.

Nigger of HMS *Orion*

Nigger, of HMS *Orion*, was an intrepid cat famous for insisting on remaining on the bridge while *Orion*'s guns shelled Salerno, in Italy. He then promptly joined another ship. A letter written in October 1943 by the ship's Commander, records: "Unfortunately Nigger is not with us at present. He wished to remain in active service in the Mediterranean, so he was allowed to transfer temporarily to one of His Majesty's battleships in the sphere of operations. We hope, however, to have him back before long."

They never did! Nigger never turned up on any of HM ships - presumably preferring to spend the rest of his life on land basking in the Mediterranean sunshine.

Thomas Oscar of HMS *Scorpion*, Who Signed His Own Letter

Thomas Oscar was the tomcat mascot of No. 3 Mess on HMS *Scorpion*. He really was the cat that got the cream and was spoiled atrociously. The crew provided him with his own special hammock, a mattress, a pillow, a blanket, a kit bag, an HMS cap ribbon for Sundays and a rabbit's tail to play with.

In October 1944, the crew wrote to the Allied Forces Mascot Club and asked if he could be enrolled. It was recorded that his full name was Thomas Oscar and he was born on April 2, 1944 and held the rank of Able-Bodied Cat. He had been on several convoys to Russia and a raid to Norway and saw service on D-Day during the beachhead offensive. Throughout he was always cheerful and a big source of comfort to the men. He was never seasick and spent hours being rocked gently to sleep in his custom-made hammock.

The letter of application was signed collectively by all the crew of No. 3 Mess and countersigned by Tom's inky paw mark.

Smokey of HMS *Bulldog*

On 9 May 1945 an advance party of two British warships sailed across the Channel for a stirring ceremony when the Germans unconditionally surrendered the Channel Islands after five grim years of occupation. Hundreds of islanders lining the waterfront went wild with delight as HMS *Bulldog* & HMS *Beagle* entered St. Peter Port, Guernsey. The islanders had been surviving on near-starvation rations and were out of touch with the mainland and desperate for news of loved ones with whom contact had come to an abrupt and cruel end when the Germans seized control.

On board HMS *Bulldog* was the ship's mascot, Smokey. As she sat watching the excited crowd with some interest the BBC commentator, reporting the event to captivated listeners world wide, described her presence on board "as a symbol of the importance Service men and women attached to their animal friends, and of the intimate part such animals played on board". This brief reference to Smokey caught the imagination of millions of eager listeners who wrote in their thousands to enquire about her. For a brief period, Smokey became a celebrity.

By coincidence, two war correspondents - the author's father Harry Procter of the *Daily Mail* and *Sunday Dispatch*, Victor Lewis of the *Daily Sketch* and *Sunday Graphic* were "embedded" with the Relief Forces on Deliverance Day. Harry had a pass for Guernsey and Victor for Jersey. Victor Lewis's in-laws were Guernsey business people and had remained on the island throughout five years of the Occupation and he was anxious for news of them, so he asked Harry to swap passes. They later became bitter rivals in Fleet Street and were a bit miffed when 14 years later they met again for the wedding of their two offspring, Val Procter and Lynn Lewis, both, by then, rival junior reporters in Kent. But that's another story…

Ginger & Fishcakes of HMS *Hood*

Launched in 1918, HMS *Hood*, was once regarded as the pride of the Royal Navy, but her usefulness deteriorated due to changing technology in the naval armour and weaponry.

She was scheduled to undergo a major rebuild in 1941, but the outbreak of the WWII resulted in her being pressed into service without the upgrades she needed.

This grand old battle cruiser was therefore sometimes referred to as *Noah's Ark*, particularly as she had so many mascots aboard, including a goat, a possum, a squirrel, a monkey, a marmoset, beavers, a variety of birds, a wallaby and a bull terrier.

The favourites were two inseparable cats, Ginger and Fishcakes. Ginger was huge with an orange brown coat and a bulging white front. Fishcakes was neat with black fur, smart white 'tuxedo' front and white paws.

In May 1941, HMS *Hood* and HMS *Prince of Wales* were ordered to intercept the German battleship *Bismarck* which was en route to attack convoys in the Atlantic.

This picture of the two cats aboard the *Hood* was taken in the early part of 1941, so it is presumed that they were on board when, on 24 May 1941, in the Battle of the Denmark Strait, *Hood* was destroyed in an explosion that split the battlecruiser into two pieces.

The loss of mighty *Hood* had a profound effect on the British, resulting in orders from Prime Minister Winston Churchill to the Royal Navy to 'sink the *Bismarck*' culminating in a naval battle on 26-27 May that ended in the sinking of the *Bismarck*.

Annie of HMS *Anson*

Annie Anson was an amazingly fertile ward room cat, famous for increasing the cat population on board HMS *Anson* after a particularly long commission. Her rate of reproduction and the number of kittens born at each confinement was astounding. No sooner had she given birth than it seemed she was pregnant again. At the end of the voyage a check of cats recorded there were over fifty kittens on board the ship, all looking remarkably like Annie.

Beauty of HMS *Black Prince*, Who Gave Birth In the Midst of D-Day Gunfire

Another female cat mascot was Beauty of HMS *Black Prince*, who chose the moment when the guns of the ship were blasting the coast of Normandy on D-day to present the ship with three fine kittens. The Commander of the ship was impressed and said she "carried on with magnificent indifference to her surroundings".

Whiskey of HMS *Duke of York*, Who Slept as an Enemy Ship was Sunk

Cats are creatures of routine and will not allow outside events to interfere with their own personal arrangements if they can help it. Whiskey, a fine tabby cat serving on HMS *Duke of York*, missed seeing her ship's guns help sink the formidable German battleship, *Scharnhorst* on Boxing Day 1943. She was taking her afternoon nap and was determined not to let anything disturb her and remain curled up fast asleep oblivious to the noise. It must have been a dreadful battle for, out of the German crew of almost 2000 there were only 36 survivors.

Nontheless, when she was awake she had a reputation as a formidable ratcatcher.

Oscar of the *Bismarck*

Oskar, a mysterious black cat with tabby markings, was only one year old when he was recruited to the German battleship *Bismarck* as official rat catcher. He rapidly developed an uncanny bond with the crew who regarded him as a manifestation of their "Iron Chancellor's" soul. With the distinguished Admiral Gunther Lutjens as commander, it seemed Oscar's future was assured for all of his nine lives.

Admiral Lutjens, sometimes referred to as 'The Black Devil', had a strong sense of destiny and it was no secret that he felt that Bismarck's career would end in tragedy and that he himself would not survive. His fatalistic attitude was unnerving at a time of war, and it is no wonder that the crew latched on to the ship's cat as a symbol of fortitude.

On 26 May 1941, Oskar was aboard when the *Bismarck* dramatically sank the British battleship HMS *Hood* in the Atlantic, with the loss of over 1,400 lives. British ships went into action and relentlessly pursued the German ship. On May 26 a torpedo from a Swordfish air craft which had taken off from HMS *Ark Royal*, hit the German battleship, jamming the rudder and rendering her unmanoeuvrable Now an easy target, next day the crippled vessel was attacked again by the British, and sunk. Out of a crew of 2,090 there were only 110 survivors.

Admiral Lutjens courageously went down with his ship but the same fate did not befall Oskar. Because of the cat's strong bond with the crew, it is said that he took on a mystic mission to avenge the victims of the *Bismarck*. As the ship keeled over, Oskar gambled on one of his nine lives and took to the water. According to Janus Piekalkiewicz, the Polish war historian, he was picked up by the British destroyer, HMS *Cossack*.

The *Cossack* had earlier been withdrawn from the scene of conflict and was crossing the same waters on her way home when one of the crew spotted the bedraggled black cat clinging to a piece of wood floating amongst the debris and dead bodies of the *Bismarck* crew.

The half-drowned black cat was hauled aboard and revived. In its pitiful state, it seemed harmless. The few *Bismarck* survivors, finding some solace in his escape, identified him as their mystic mascot Oskar. The *Cossack* crew made a huge fuss of him and adopted him on the assumption that any creature fortunate to have survived such a dramatic sea battle was bound to bring them luck. He was renamed Oscar. At a later stage he was also occasionally referred to as 'Unsinkable Sam'.

But this dauntless feline survivor's good luck was not to last. Five months later the Cossack itself was sunk. Oscar fearlessly jumped into the ocean and again managed to swim to a piece of wood and was apparently calmly cleaning himself as he bobbed up and down on the waves when one of the crew of the aircraft carrier, HMS *Ark Royal*, spotted him and hauled him aboard. Another of his lives used up!

But it was becoming painfully obvious that Oscar was a serious jinx. Instead of bringing luck to the *Ark Royal*, the ill-fated ship was torpedoed by a U-boat in November 1942. By then Oscar knew exactly what to do. It was almost a matter of routine for him to jump into the water and swim to the nearest piece of floating debris. Deciding not to wait for orders to abandon ship, crewman Tom Blundell also jumped into the ocean from the stricken vessel and, on surfacing, was amazed to find himself swimming alongside the invincible Oscar. HMS *Legion* rescued 1,487 officers and men – and Oscar. Another of his nine lives forfeited!

It could be argued that he did bring *some* good fortune to the ship, for only one rating died in that disaster. But HMS *Legion*, hearing of the cat's previous poor record as a lucky mascot, wisely resisted the temptation to recruit him. He was compulsorily retired. Official records state that as a precaution he was taken ashore at Gibraltar as a 'suspect jinx' and handed over to the harbour master and from there was duly posted to an Old Sailors' Home in Belfast.

But this precaution proved futile for HMS *Legion* which didn't escape Oscar's mysterious powers of vengeance. She was also sunk on 26 March 1943, when she was attacked from the air in Malta. Perhaps Oscar's sixth sense had warned him to seek a permanent base on dry land before his own luck ran out. After all, he only had four lives left.

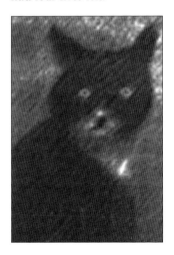

British psychic animal portrait artist, Georgina Baker Shaw, believed she had a powerful spiritual relationship with Oscar. She hadn't heard of him before he made spiritual contact with her and apparently he passed on to her information about his mystic mission. In 1960 she did a pastel portrait of him, which is now at the National Maritime Museum, Greenwich.

Turkish parapsychologist, Aziz Evliyaoglu, describes Oscar as a 'deathless' spirit who took on all the negative energy of Bismarck's tragic end, which he subsequently discharged towards the British ships that unwittingly adopted him as their mascot. "Perhaps he was a substance, like the ancient Egyptians' Ankh, designed to bring bad luck to Bismarck's foes".

Deathless or not, Oscar found life as a landlubber much to his liking, for he died peacefully at the Old Sailors' Home in Belfast, in 1955, at the grand old age of 15 years. He certainly earned his reputation for being one of the luckiest ships' cats of all time, or the unluckiest according to how one looks at it. And there are some who believe he lives on, as a feline spirit with uncanny powers.

Wren Figaro, the Cat That Might Have Graced a Catwalk

Wren Figaro was a dainty black and white cat adopted by a Wren Depot. She was described by Wren Jane Garrett as extremely graceful, "who wore her outfit with elegance". It was "a black coat with white shirt front and knee stockings, not to mention whiskers". The Wrens adored her and said she was most affectionate, an excellent mouser and altogether a "most convenient cat" as she preferred dried milk to fresh. It was recorded that "the morale of the depot has gone up since we adopted her, even though she devoured part of the Chief's lunch when he was out of his office". One day Wren Figaro just walked off into the night and was never seen again but was "sincerely mourned".

When HM Ships' Cats Were Ordered to Wear Collars

Although the Royal Navy actively encouraged cats on board their ships during the Second World War, they were never officially listed as part of the ship's crew. Then, aware that cats were hopping on and off ships at random it was decided to try to regularise the situation. An order went out that "all cats in naval establishments must wear collars at all times". The collars were to be embroidered with the name of their ship to ensure that no moggies tried to enlist without permission.

The order was signed by the Lords Commissioners of the Admiralty with the ominous warning that "all cats found in naval establishments without collars are to be summarily dealt with".

The ship's cat at HMS *Vernon*, the shore establishment at Portsmouth or 'stone frigate' as it was fondly called, was swiftly supplied with his own smart collar emblazoned with the name of his ship. Who paid for it is not known, but it must have been more expensive than the navy had funds for because, as a result, the tricky question was raised about where the money was to come from to pay for the thousands of ships' cat collars which would undoubtedly be required. Since neither the Admiralty nor the Treasury was prepared to cough up, the order was discreetly put on hold and not mentioned again.

Convoy, the Cherished Cat
On HMS *Hermione*

The crew of HMS *Hermione* must have been inordinately fond of their black and white mascot cat, Convoy, to go to all the trouble of making this special hammock for him shortly after the 5,450 ton anti-aircraft cruiser was launched in May 1939. A few months later World War II was declared and the *Hermione*, her crew and the cat, all went to war. Convoy had full kit and was listed in the ship's records. He was called Convoy because of the number of times he had accompanied the ship on convoy patrol.

The picture below was given to the Royal Naval Museum at Portsmouth with no other information beyond the name of the ship and the date. Despite all the pampering, the cat with no name didn't bring much luck to the ship. The 485ft *Hermione* was sunk in June 1942 by the German submarine U-205 in the Eastern Meditteranean.

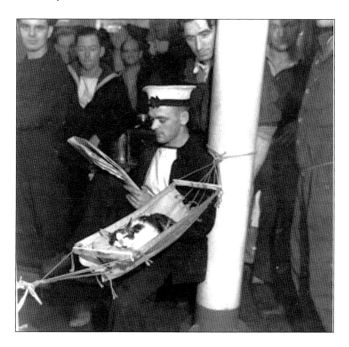

(By kind permission of the Royal Naval Museum, Portsmouth)

Able Seaman Simon, Hero of HMS *Amethyst*, proudly
wearing his newly engraved name tag and collar.

World War II was Over, but Conflicts Continued: Able Seaman Simon, Hero of HMS *Amethyst*

Simon was the last of a litter of kittens born in the armaments supply store on Stonecutters Island, Hong Kong. In the spring of 1948, Lieutenant Commander R.G.Griffiths, DSC, RN, called there to pick up supplies for his ship, HMS *Amethyst*, a 300-foot frigate of the Royal Navy.

Cats of Stonecutters Island have the sea in their blood. They are born and bred within the sound and smell of the sea and are accustomed to the noisy bustle of the dockyards, ship's horns, Customs and coolies, smart officers in uniforms and loading and unloading of containers carrying goods such as sugar and spices.

All Simon's siblings had been found jobs as rat catchers on various ships. But Simon had been unlucky. Perhaps it was because he was mostly black – not a colour regarded as a good omen on a vessel. True he had smart white paws resembling a pair of naval officer's gloves and a stylish white fur bib on his chest. But nobody had found these features endearing enough to offer him regular employment. He'd been hanging around the supply store now for two years, begging for snacks and seeking affection wherever he could.

There was a bit of a rat problem on the *Amethyst*. The weather was hot and steamy and, to escape the oppressive heat rodents had been seeking relief in the cooler regions of the ship, where there was no shortage of food. They raided the galley and food storage areas and grew fat and strong. Fleas nested in their fur, biting their flesh, sucking their blood and injecting them with deadly viruses - harmless to rats and mice, but not so kind to humans. With rodents roaming the food areas of the ship, indiscriminately distributing their body wastes, there was a serious danger that these viruses could be passed on to members of the crew

They had to be got rid of. And a good ship's cat was the best solution.

Captain Griffiths was partial to cats and it just so happened that there *was* a vacancy for a ship's cat on HMS *Amethyst*. The Captain took an immediate liking to the friendly black tom that purred contentedly round his ankles, desperate for affection. The sharp green eyes revealed intelligence and cunning essential in a rat hunter. Also, the clerk of the supply stores revealed to Griffiths that he came from a long line of ship's cats. So the Captain recruited Simon as a member of his crew. The armaments supply clerk, relieved at finding Simon a job at last, provided him with a stylish red collar and a metal identification disc, on which he roughly etched the name 'Simon and underneath HMS *Amethyst*'. Mercifully the cat had no inkling of the horrific adventures that lay ahead of him, which were to make him one of the most publicised ship's cats ever.

Simon boarded HMS *Amethyst* sitting proudly aloft on the Captain's shoulder. From the start, he was indisputably Captain Griffiths' cat. He allowed Able Seaman Simon to sleep not only with the Captain, at the bottom of his bunk, but also to curl up in the Captain's smart white cap decorated with gold braid. Guests who sat at the Captain's table for dinner were rather disconcerted when Simon sprang up unexpectedly and nonchalantly strolled from one set of knees to another, begging for titbits. A particular nuisance was his habit of sitting on the chart whenever a course was being laid.

A drawing by War artist, John Worsley, of Simon curled up in the Captain's cap.

He wasted no time proving he could earn his keep, turning out to be a resourceful hunter, diligently prowling the depths of the ship, sniffing every nook and cranny for prey, from the bulwarks and gunwales to the utmost depths of the engine room, the wheel house, the washhouse and the various ships' messes.

The crew spoilt him shamelessly, discreetly dropping scraps to him under the tables in the mess. Ship's cook, Petty Officer George Griffiths (not related to the Captain), fed him tasty morsels, so he had no need even to eat his own prey. Instead he would lay the dead rats he'd caught at the feet of the Captain, as dubious gifts of love and grateful thanks. Sometimes, as cats do, he went too far and deposited them on his master's bunk, which was not appreciated.

The Captain had only to whistle and Simon would instantly come running from whatever depths of the ship he had been hard at work rat hunting. And, as the Captain patrolled the ship each evening, inspecting the ship and the crew, Simon was always close at his heels.

However, the affectionate bond that had developed between Simon and the Captain was soon to be severed. In December 1948 Lieutenant Commander Bernard Skinner succeeded him to command of HMS *Amethyst*. Captain Griffiths appreciated that it would be cruel to try to take Simon with him but fortunately the new captain was also a cat lover and was pleased to adopt him, allowing him all the special privileges he had with Griffiths.

At first Simon was wary of his new master. It took him some time to accustom himself to a new voice, a new smell, a new manner. Tactfully, Captain Skinner allowed the cat to get used to him at his own pace. But Simon couldn't bring himself to respond to Skinner's whistle, nor would he follow loyally at his heels.

It was a pleasant, cushy life Simon led aboard the *Amethyst*. But it was not to last. The ship was scheduled to sail up the Yangtze River to Nanking before the truce between the Chinese Communists and the Nationalists expired. The Chinese Communists, fighting to overthrow the Chinese Nationalist government, had established troops on the north side of the river, facing the Nationalists on the south side.

The Communists were winning and had called a truce. They had given the Nationalists until midnight to accept their terms for ending the war. If they didn't accept, the fighting would begin again. Meanwhile, the destroyer *Consort* had been guarding the British Embassy at Nanking for several weeks. The plan was for the *Amethyst* to relieve the *Consort*. If the Communists *did* capture Nanking, the British in the city would have to be evacuated.

On April 20, 1949, the *Amethyst* lay at anchor at Kiangyin, on the muddy Yangtze River, 100 miles upstream from where it emptied into the China Sea. Captain Skinner had been advised to wait until daylight before sailing further upriver. The Nationalists had forbidden all night traffic.

In theory it was a straightforward exercise. Since the truce was to last until midnight there would be plenty of time for the *Amethyst* to reach Nanking and for the *Consort* to sail downstream to safety at Shanghai. Nonetheless, they were entering a war zone and it was risky. Britain had not taken sides in the war and so no trouble was expected from either side, as long as the ship flew a White Ensign to indicate she was neutral and on a peaceful mission, and displayed two very large Union Jacks for identification.

The crew numbered 183. There were about fifteen boy seamen on their first voyage, aged from 17 years plus, and the sight of the friendly cat prowling round the ship reminded them of home and eased their homesickness.

With hands at 'Action Stations' as the ship approached a stretch of the river where Communist batteries were thought to be sited, the ship proceeded cautiously at a speed of 11 knots. Without warning, several salvoes landed in the water near the ship. *Amethyst* prepared to return the fire, but the British Ensigns and the Union Jacks were visible from shore, the firing ceased and it was assumed the ship was now recognised as British. An hour or so later, when passing another Communist battery, shells were again fired at the British ship. This time the bridge and the wheelhouse were both hit. In the confusion it was not possible to regain control before the ship turned in the narrow river towards the bank and ran aground.

In such a serious crisis, a ship's cat becomes of very little significance. Nobody looked out for Simon. Captain Skinner had been on the bridge battling to save his ship. Simon, traumatised by the explosions, instinctively bolted. But he wasn't swift enough. A piece of exploding shrapnel pierced his leg and back, and he fell to the deck. Before passing out, he managed to crawl into a dark corner, lucky to be alive.

Twenty-five other members of the crew were not so fortunate. They lay dead or dying on the decks, some of them boy trainees. Captain Skinner had suffered a fatal blow and now lay dead amongst the debris on the bridge.

When Simon came to he was in severe pain. He lay there for several days, weak and too frightened to emerge from the comparative safety of his dark refuge. There was damage to his back and his front paws and he was badly dazed. Hunger and thirst eventually drove him into the open, where he lay exhausted on the deck. It was daylight and the ship should have been a hive of activity, but the engines had stopped and there was a deathly hush.

Simon was not to know that after being ruthlessly shelled, the frigate had gone aground on Rose Island. The *Consort* had sailed from Nanking and proceeded down the river to assist *Amethyst* in her predicament. When *Consort* came within range of the Communist guns, they opened fire at her too. She desperately tried to silence the batteries and tow off *Amethyst*, but suffered severe damage and casualties and had to continue down the river leaving *Amethyst* badly damaged aground on the mud bank. The crew remaining on board struggled for sixteen fraught hours to refloat her and she was able to come off the bank and anchor in the river during the night.

In his shocked state Simon was found by ship's cook, Griffiths, who picked him up and tenderly felt him for injuries. His whiskers had been singed off and there was a lot of dried blood on his back and leg. Griffiths set Simon, badly dehydrated and close to death, on the galley counter, and gently squeezed a few drops of water into his mouth.

The ship's medical officer, Surgeon Lieutenant J. M. Alderton, who had also been fond of Simon, had been killed. Griffiths took Simon to the sick bay, where he was examined by the replacement medical officer, Flight-Lieutenant Michael Fearnley from the RAF. Chinese Nationalists, from the South Bank of the River, sent medics to the ship to treat the seriously wounded, who were then taken off the ship and ferried ashore on sampans. They then had to make the tortuous journey to Kiang Yin and be put on the train to Shanghai before being transferred to a

US Navy Hospital ship. So the sick bay was clear for the time being, and so a space was found for Simon.

A thorough examination revealed that Simon's heart had suffered and was very weak. He had shrapnel wounds in four places and a badly burned face. Despite this, Dr. Fearnley felt he had a fair chance of survival. The wounds were tenderly cleaned and stitched and he was prescribed rest and tender loving care.

Lieutenant Commander John Kerans, RN, the Assistant Naval Attaché in Nanking, joined *Amethyst* and was ordered to assume command of the ship. He immediately made it clear he didn't like cats and certainly didn't relish sharing his bunk or even his cabin, with a cat. So Griffiths selected a cosy corner of the petty officers' mess and prepared a bed for Simon. Then he returned to the sick bay. Simon could now sit up. He looked pathetic, even comical. His whiskers had been burnt off, and patches of his fur shaved away to expose his wounds, which were now stitched and bandaged. Griffiths gently took him to his new quarters and laid him in his box.

But Simon's curiosity soon got the better of him. Within days he was ready to explore and, not knowing anything about death, to seek out his master. He jumped out of his box and climbed painfully onto the deck, where a tragic scene was being enacted. The bodies of the men killed in the shelling had been sewn into their hammocks. Each was weighed down with two live shells so that it would sink to the bottom of the river, and laid out on the deck ready for "burial at sea".

While the crew stood in silent sorrow, Captain Kerans read the Anglican service for the dead, followed by Psalm 90. He then led the men in the Lord's Prayer. Then, one by one, each hammock-wrapped body was brought forward and Captain Kerans read out the name of the dead man, each time declaring: "We commit his body to the deep, looking for the resurrection of the body and the life of the world through our Lord Jesus Christ". The boatswain piped his whistle and two crew men lifted each tragic bundle over the rail and let it slip into the muddy water. In total seventeen men died in the gunfire. Two men were missing, presumed drowned. Two of the wounded died after being landed.

Simon sat silently observing the proceedings, as cats do, perhaps sensing the sadness as he occasionally licked his own wounds. He followed Griffiths, his new protector, to the galley where he managed a few morsels of minced chicken then, feeling stronger, went to look for his old master. Captain Kerans was annoyed when he found Simon curled up in his officer's cap, mistakenly thinking it was Captain Skinner's. Captain Kerans had too much on his mind to be bothered by a cat. He certainly didn't want him in his cabin, spreading cat hairs everywhere. He promptly kicked the surprised cat out and then dealt with a radio message from Vice Admiral Madden in Hong Kong:

LATEST NEWS JUST RECEIVED BY TELEPHONE FROM NANKING INDICATES THAT COMMUNISTS HAVE CROSSED IN SOME STRENGTH FIFTEEN MILES EAST OF NANKING. YOU ARE THEREFORE NOT REPETITION NOT TO PROCEED TO NANKING.

The only alternative was to stay put until further orders. But the ship had 260 tons of fuel oil and sufficient food and water for two months. The situation looked grim.

A message came from the Communists that they wanted to speak to someone in authority either on board the *Amethyst* or on shore. Captain Kerans selected Petty Officer William H Freeman for the duty. He was ordered to don Lieutenant Stewart Hett's uniform and pose as a senior officer. Freeman and But Sai Tin, the Captain's steward and interpreter, were put into a boat with two ordinary crewmen, and they rowed ashore.

They reported afterwards that the Chinese were fairly cordial to them and took them in a truck for about four miles to a peasant's house where they waited an hour for a Major Kung, who claimed that the *Amethyst* **was** to blame for the whole tragic scenario because her men fired the first shot. Freeman maintained firmly that it was the Chinese who were the first to fire.

However, Kung was prepared to admit that the Chinese knew full well it **was** a British ship but again said that, since the *Amethyst* fired first, then the British were responsible for what had followed. Freeman then asked permission to allow the *Amethyst* safe passage down the river. Kung said he had no authority to grant such a request and only the General in Nanking could grant safe passage. With that he strode out of the room and left them to them to make their own way to the *Amethyst*.

Next day another request came for a talk and this time Lieutenant Stewart Hett himself was sent, but again it was stalemate. It looked as though the *Amethyst* would have to remain where it was until the war ended.

Life on the ship settled into a dull, hot, humid procession of boring days consisting of bouts of furious activity in the heat, repairing the damage to the ship, and hours and hours of unadulterated tedium. Tempers became frayed as temperatures rose to 110 degrees Fahrenheit below decks. In the sick bay, some of the boy seamen lay sick and shocked from the trauma of the battle. As they tossed and turned uncomfortably, Dr. Fearnley had the bright idea of using Simon as therapy treatment to cheer the lads up and soothe their frightened souls. He encouraged the wounded cat to sit on the end of their bunks, or even on their chests, where he would knead away with his paws, purring contentedly.

Simon was still not an appetising sight. His wounds had gone scabby, and there were bald patches where his fur had been shaved and anyway, a cat without whiskers looks positively bizarre. Many of the boy seamen carried superficial scars of battle.

In one bed lay 16-year-old Seaman Mark Allen with his eyes closed. In the shelling, the boy had lost both legs below the knee. For four days since he had regained consciousness, he had refused to talk or eat or even open his eyes.

Dr. Fearnley lifted Simon on to the boy's bed. The cat sat looking at him intently. But Mark Allen's eyes remained closed. The doctor moved Simon onto the boy's chest, placing his limp hand on Simon's back. The boy half-opened his eyes and saw Simon looking at him steadily.

"I have a cat at home," he said. "But I'll never see him again." He pushed Simon away and buried his face in the pillow. Simon instinctively crawled back on the boy's stomach and began kneading away persistently. After a while Mark weakly reached out and stroked Simon's rough fur, and then began to sob.

From then on Simon visited the sick bay every day, seeking out Mark but also comforting the other wounded sailors in the same way.

So Simon progressed from being not only Chief Rodent Controller to Chief Counsellor and Comforter. The sight of him, worse for wear because of his own injuries, brought immense pleasure to the whole crew. But he didn't neglect his day job. His rat catching skills were needed more than ever. Stores were low and therefore precious and had to be safeguarded from contamination by rats. He worked tirelessly, usually managing to kill at least five rats a day.

Captain Kerans was unimpressed by tales of Simon's prowess. He still didn't like cats and was struggling to keep life on board his ship on an even keel. Then, one day, Simon brought him a gift of one dead rat, and laid it at his feet. The Captain asked Griffiths in astonishment what on earth did the creature think it was doing, bringing him a dead rat?

Griffiths explained patiently that it was a gift. Intrigued, Kerans cautiously stroked Simon as a gesture of thanks. But even so – what was he expected to do with a dead rat? When Simon wasn't looking he gingerly picked the rat up by its tail and threw it overboard, not wanting to hurt the cat's feelings by openly rejecting his gift. The Captain was beginning to mellow.

One particularly vicious and frightening rat had been plaguing the food storage quarters. It was huge - almost as big as Simon himself. The crew nicknamed him Mao Tse-tung and set traps for him, considering Simon in too weak a state to tackle such a monster. All attempts to catch it had failed and the men were beginning to despair. Mao Tse-tung had a gang of smaller rats who followed him around as he ruthlessly raided the stores, knowing that where he lead them there would be plenty to eat. Then one day cat and rat came face to face. Simon leapt at the rat's neck and sank his teeth in. Within seconds Mao Tse-tung was dead. Simon was hailed a real hero by the delighted crew, and promoted to Able Seaman Simon. From then on Griffiths kept a record of every rat Simon killed, and where.

Captain Kerans fell ill and sent for the doctor. Nothing too serious – just a virus brought on by the excessive heat and humidity, but he was ordered to stay in bed for a few days. Simon sneaked in to visit him and jumped onto the bunk like in the old days. This time the Captain didn't push him away. From then on Simon was allowed to sleep there whenever he chose.

The days of tedium continued and the crew became weak and debilitated from shortage of food and water. As they lay about, trying to keep up their spirits, Simon patrolled the decks, visiting the sick, dispensing of rodents and cheering up the men.

Admiral Sir Patrick Brind, Commander in Chief of the Far East Fleet, became irritated with the situation on the Yangtze. He decided to speed things up by negotiating with General Kang Mao-chao, the Communist commander, using Captain Kerans to deliver messages between them. On July 14 - over two months since the initial incident – a message came, which the Captain read out to the crew.

"It is clear that the Communists have been holding you hostage to wring admissions from the British Government, which would not only be untrue but would harm the cause of free nations in the future. For the present, therefore, you are in the forefront of the cold war in which the cause of freedom is being attacked. I know it is a pretty hot war as far as you are concerned and our stand is widely recognised and greatly admired."

How much of a consolation this message was to the crew, who were being driven to distraction by the extreme heat, is debatable. On 19 July the temperature reached 110 degrees on the decks and 118 degrees in the engine room. To save fuel, the boilers were shut down and there was no power in the ship for periods of up to three days. This meant there was no ventilation and no domestic refrigerators which made the heat even more intolerable. Even Simon began to wilt. It helped a little when a few essential medical stores and mail were delivered overland from Shanghai.

As if things couldn't get worse, a message came that a typhoon called Gloria was expected to hit the Yangtze Valley on the Sunday night. The ship was anchored by two cables. Should the cables not hold, the ship would have to be taken down river in the storm or else risk being wrecked by the typhoon. Captain Kerans needed to get permission from Madden to make a dash down river. He tried to write a message he hoped Madden would understand but not the Chinese.

WOULD BE GRATEFUL YOUR ADVICE ON MY ACTIONS IF MENACED BY THE TYPHOON.

An apparently meaningless reply came back:

TYPHOON UNLIKELY REACH YOU IN SERIOUS STRENGTH AND YOU ARE IN GOOD HOLDING GROUND. THE GOLDEN RULE OF MAKING AN OFFING AND TAKING PLENTY OF SEAROOM APPLIES PARTICULARLY.

So the crew of *Amethyst* battened down the hatches and made tight, and then sat around waiting for Gloria to strike. Sunday came and went and nothing happened. It got hotter and more humid. Next day, a hot wind began whipping up waves on the river's surface. The order "all hands below decks" went out. Simon was shut in the Captain's cabin to ensure his safety. He was now such a valuable member of the crew, nobody wanted to lose him.

For hours the *Amethyst* strained at her anchor cables. The rain came down like stair rods, and poured along the decks. The wind lashed at the ship with a gale force eight. Three stalwart officers donned their oilskins and stayed on the bridge ready to act should the cables snap.

By noon there was a gale force nine, or 55 miles an hour, and waves rolled over the decks and crashed against the sides of the ship. Three hours later it had turned into a hurricane, with winds at 75 miles an hour. Below decks the men were in a poor state, particularly the inexperienced boy seamen. Simon remained curled up on the Captain's bunk, and slept through it all. Then the rain eased and the storm subsided. It was clear that the *Amethyst* had survived yet another crisis.

But the *Amethyst*'s position became more desperate. Food was seriously short. The yeast had gone bad and there was only a limited supply of flour. The crew had been on half rations for two weeks. Soon they'd be on quarter rations.

More serious was the fuel supply. On July 30 there were only 55 tons of fuel in the tanks. If Kerans tried to make the 120-mile dash down the river, a considerable amount of fuel would have to be used just to turn the ship around, and the tanks were already seriously depleted. They would need all the fuel they had to steam the 160 miles from the anchorage to the open sea. This meant that there would be no fuel available for daily use to provide electricity for ventilation, communications and light, if the ship remained at anchor. Within a few more days the men and the ship would be totally at the mercy of the Communists.

Kerans decided he had no option but to make a dash for it that night, as soon as the moon set. There were eight Chinese crew members aboard. Kerans wasn't prepared to rely on any of them remaining loyal including But Sai Tin, his own steward and interpreter, so he took the precaution of locking them in a cabin.

He called seventeen officers and seaman together and assigned them tasks for camouflaging the ship. Her superstructure had to be painted black, black canvas rigged from the bridge to the funnel and around the guns to make the ship look like a Landing Ship Tank rather than a frigate, her bridge had to be protected from possible shrapnel damage by wrapping hammocks and mattresses around the bridge railing and piling up bags of precious flour.

Empty fuel tanks were flooded to lower the ship in the water. Kerans planned, in case the worst happened and the ship was damaged beyond hope, to beach her, get the men ashore and then blow the ship up. Then it would be up to the men to get to Shanghai by whatever means they could.

For the next hour, furious activity took place on board. There was a period of tension when, at 8.30, a sampan was seen approaching with contractors. They had come to take an order for fresh food. The men were told to stop their emergency tasks and act normally. The store crew met the contractors on the gangway and explained that it was too late to make arrangements that evening and they must return the next day. In the meantime some crewmen hurried down to the quarterdeck with campbeds and pretended to settle down for the night. The sampan was waved away, tension eased and the crew returned to their preparations for flight.

They were all aware they faced a dangerous mission, but it was a relief to be doing something positive. Kerans told his men, from the ladder on the bridge, that they should prepare for the fight of their lives. It was planned to slip the anchor at 2200 hours. As this time approached, a river ferry, the Kiang Ling *Liberation*, was seen proceeding down river. Kerans decided to wait until she passed, slip anchor and follow cautiously in her wake in the hope the ship might escape undetected.

Perhaps it was a foolhardy plan, but the Captain felt there was more hope for his men if they made this mad dash for freedom. If they stayed, they might well be killed by the Chinese Communists.

Predictably, perhaps, they were soon spotted and a Communist battery on shore shot an alarm flare and the *Liberation* replied with a siren. Shells were fired and one hit the *Amethyst*. She tipped precariously to starboard. For a while it looked as though she'd had it. Kerans decided to bring plan B into force. Black smoke poured from the funnel, which successfully hid the ship from the shore batteries.

At once Kerans sent a message to his Admiral:

AM UNDER HEAVY FIRE. BEEN HIT.

But miraculously the ship righted itself and steamed defiantly ahead, screened by dark smoke. There was life in the old girl yet. Kerans found time to order Simon to go below decks.

Amethyst sped along the murky river, through the dark. Hett who was navigating the ship, listened intently for the depth soundings which were reported up to the bridge, and advised Kerans on the course to steer and the position of the ship in the river. Soon they passed Rose Island, where they had gone aground three months earlier. After midnight it was found that the ship was taking in water through one of the old shell holes. The pumps worked hard and just about managed to keep up.

As the ship neared Kiangyin, the port from which they had sailed 101 days previously, a flare from the shore lit up the ship and she suffered another a battery of gunfire. The Captain ordered another smoke screen.

At this particular stretch of the river there was a boom composed of a row of sunken ships with only a narrow passageway for a ship to get through. This passageway, according to the charts, was marked by two lights, pointing to the opening through which a ship could safely pass. But only one light appeared to be functioning. The Captain had to decide which side of it to go. If he chose the wrong side, then the *Amethyst* risked joining the sunken wrecks below.

He chose to pass to starboard and prayed. Miraculously the ship slipped through the boom without a scratch. She steamed on down the river at full speed. But the danger still wasn't over. Guns waited for them on both sides of the river further down.

As the *Amethyst* made her way in the darkness, along what were the closest guarded stretches of river, with batteries on both sides, their bow hit a junk broadside and sliced it in two, knocking those aboard into the water. The Captain decided he could not risk stopping to rescue them and went on, reasoning that his first responsibility was to save his own men.

They steamed on, through the heavily guarded shores of Woosung without further mishap. As dawn broke, a lookout shouted excitedly that there was a destroyer in sight and she looked uncannily like the *Concord*. Euphoric with relief, Kerans bent down, where Simon was rubbing himself against his ankles and lifted the cat above his head in triumph, for all the crew to see. A message was relayed to the commander.

NOW HAVE REJOINED THE FLEET. AM SOUTH OF WOOSUNG. NO DAMAGE OR CASUALTIES. GOD SAVE THE KING.

Admiral Brind replied in a radio message:

WELCOME BACK TO THE FLEET. WE ARE ALL EXTREMELY PROUD OF YOUR MOST GALLANT AND SKILFUL ESCAPE AND THAT ENDURANCE AND FORTITUDE DISPLAYED BY EVERYONE HAS BEEN REWARDED WITH SUCH SUCCESS. YOUR BEARING IN ADVERSITY AND YOUR DARING PASSAGE TONIGHT WILL BE EPIC IN THE HISTORY OF THE NAVY.

By Sunday, 31 July, after 101 days, the long, perilous ordeal was over. King George VI sent a message from Buckingham Palace to "splice the mainbrace" meaning that each member of the crew should receive an extra ration of grog (rum), the traditional reward for sailors who performed the tough task of splicing the heavy rope brace attached to the main yard on sailing ships.

Next morning the crew assembled on deck for a special presentation – a symbolic representation of what they had all been through. Officers and crew stood to attention and one boy seaman held Simon in his arms, as Petty Officer George Griffiths faced them and announced solemnly:

Able Seaman Simon for distinguished and meritorious service to HMS Amethyst, you are hereby awarded the Amethyst Campaign Ribbon.

Be it known that on 26 April 1949, though recovering from wounds, when HMS Amethyst was standing by off Rose Bay, you did single-handedly and unarmed stalk down and destroy Mao Tse-Tun, a rat guilty of raiding food supplies which were critically short.

Be it further known that from 22 April to 1 August you did rid HMS Amethyst of pestilence and vermin with unrelenting faithfulness.

The People's Dispensary for Sick Animals Headquarters, in England present a special medal to any creature who exhibits great courage. It is called the Dickin Medal, after the founder of the PDSA, Maria Dickin. Up to this time, it had regularly been awarded to dogs and pigeons but *never* to a cat. Captain Kerans decided to nominate Simon for the Dickin Medal.

The frigate sailed down the Chinese coast to Hong Kong, arriving just before noon on Wednesday, 3 August. News of what they had been through and the valour they had shown, had got around. They were hailed as heroes. Hundreds of British citizens waited on the docks to cheer the ship and its crew.

By now news of Simon's valiant behaviour during the ordeal had also been broadcast on the radio and in the newspapers. This "human interest" story captured the imagination of a nation still recovering from the horrors of World War II. It was a welcome relief from what the country had been through. And the British do love cats.

Two weeks later the PDSA delivered a message to the ship in dock, saying that they were unanimous in conferring the Dickin Medal on Simon, the *Amethyst's* ship's cat, pointing out that he would not only be the first cat to hold the Dickin Medal, but it would be the first time it had gone to the Royal Navy. A presentation ceremony would be arranged as soon as the *Amethyst* returned home.

The PDSA sent a tricolour ribbon collar for Simon to wear and released the news of Simon's unique award to the media. Almost overnight he became not only a hero but a star. There were photocalls aboard the ship and his photo appeared in hundreds of newspapers, magazines and movie news reels, worldwide. He revealed a natural talent for posing for the camera, looking suitably rakish, winsome or proud almost on demand. After the blasts of gunfire he had faced, the flashlights were a doddle. He stared unblinking at the cameras' lenses and the world fell in love with him.

The ship of heroes didn't mind being overshadowed by a cat. They were proud of him and basked in his reflected glory. Letters arrived on the *Amethyst* from all over the world. Poems praising Simon's bravery, and gifts of food and cat toys,

Simon being given a saucer of milk by the skipper, Lt Cdr John Kerans

came in every mail. He received more than 200 pieces of mail a day – fan mail any Hollywood star would envy.

Suddenly all the attention became too much for him. He was just a ship's cat, after all, trying to get on with his job of keeping his ship clear of rats and safeguarding food supplies.

It was difficult for a chap who just wanted a quiet life after such a hairy adventure. It seemed he couldn't move without a photographer jumping out and taking a snap of him. He simply had no privacy at all.

One day, maybe to escape all the attention, he strolled down the gangplank onto dry land. A photographer, delighted to come face to face with the star himself, snapped his camera and later told the Captain, who he'd come to interview, how pleased he was with his shot of the cat. Alarm bells rang in Captain Kerans' head. Simon had never been known to step onto dry land and never even ventured near the gangplank. Out went an order for the crew not only to search the ship for Simon, but to go on to search every street, road and alley in the city. The men were told to leave their duties and went off in all directions, looking for Simon. It seemed certain he had abandoned ship. Captain Kerans had grown fond of him and felt a distinct sense of loss.

Three hours later, to his extreme delight, Griffiths, from the top of the gangplank, saw Simon stroll out of an alley and nonchalantly climb aboard. Even with all the irritating attention he was getting, it seemed life on the *Amethyst* with all his mates was preferable to life as a mere alleycat of whom nobody took the slightest bit of notice.

Visitors and the press continued to flock to the ship every day and Simon was plagued by requests to pose. Reporters interviewed crew members about him. They even took his pawprints. Simon coped as he had done during the Yangtze incident, with dignity and endurance.

The ship's repairs finally completed, the *Amethyst* sailed home to England. Every port the ship stopped at, in the Indian Ocean, the Suez Canal and the Mediterranean, cheering crowds gathered and more reporters and photographers came aboard. The ship finally reached Plymouth on 1 November 1949.

But a prophet, or even a hero, is rarely honoured in his own country. Despite his courage and fame, Simon suffered the indignity of being treated just like any other cat returning to Britain after a spell abroad - and was ordered to enter into quarantine for six months, at Hackbridge, Surrey. He was treated well, but missed the crew and ship life. Solid ground seemed strange after swaying decks and the smell of the sea.

He was visited regularly by members of the crew, including Lt. Cdr Kerans and his original owner, Lt. Cdr R.G.Griffiths. Four cats in Chelsea sent a poem of dubious merit, written by their owner:

Hero of HMS Amethyst, sneaks down the gangplank. After being absent being absent without leave, resulting in panic amongst the crew as they searched high and low for him, aboard and ashore, he returned three hours later.

Simon being held aloft by Petty Officer John E Webb

O Simon of the *Amethyst*,
Stout member of her crew,
We fill our saucers high with milk
And drink a health to you;
What though cannon roar and thunder,
Your courage ne'er went under.
For England, home and beauty
You are steadfast in your duty
As terror of the rats!
So here's a greeting and congrats
From four admiring Chelsea cats.

Miss Louise Edwards, who looked after the hotel cats at Arden Hotel, Birmingham, sent a tin of sardines, and said it was from her three cats, Smoky, Peter and Kit. There were hundreds of similar messages and presents. Admiring fans queued up to visit Simon and he got the VIP treatment he deserved from the quarantine kennels staff. Joyce Ballack, his personal maid, brought him a toy mouse on a stick to play with, and kept him company for hours at a time each day.

The presentation of his medal was set for 11 December 1949. Seventy-nine year old Maria Dickin, founder of the PDSA, planned to be there, as did the Lord Mayor of London. The medal was to be presented with much pomp and ceremony.

Shortly before the presentation Simon fell ill. Kennel maid, Joyce Ballack, was worried that he seemed listless and his nose felt unhealthily warm. She sent for the vet, who came within an hour, having being told an important patient needed his attention urgently. He took Simon's temperature – it was 104 degrees Fahrenheit. The vet said Simon must have picked up a stomach bug and gave him an injection and some

This huge pastry was baked by the cook on HMS Newcastle at Malta in 1949 in honour of Simon of the Amethyst. Left to right: AB Aldridge. AB Murphy. Boy Seaman K.J.Morton. PO Faceman (holding Simon). LS Mullins. CD Harris. OD Delue

tablets. The vet then left, promising to call again in the morning.

Joyce stayed with Simon all night. For several hours he lay on his side and seemed to sleep. Then she noticed he was cold and going stiff. She felt his poor, weak heart. It had stopped beating. The vet arrived to examine him. "It wasn't just the virus."

he said. "He should have been all right. But his heart was weakened by his war wounds. It couldn't cope."

Not only was Captain Kerans, and the rest of the crew heartbroken, it seemed the world was too. As the news spread, via radio and newspapers and the newsreel, cards, letters and flowers arrived by the truckload at Hackbridge. Time Magazine featured his picture on its obituary page, with the headline "In Honoured Memory".

There were some rousing verses from T.R.Phillips, of Shaftesbury Avenue, Norwood Green, Southend, Middlesex, dated 1 December, 1949.

> Brave Simon – Nelson of the cats
> The terror of those naval rats
> Trafalgar with its victory blast
> Has claimed you to itself at last.
>
> Though shot and shell did singe your fur
> Your milk you greeted with a purr
> And with the curling whiskers lost
> You did not stop to count the cost
> But true to the Navy's own traditions
> Carried out those expeditions.
> 'Gainst those communistic rats
> A warrior bold among all cats
>
> Or perhaps your war wounds gained a hold
> Or did you mourn the shipmates bold?
> And fretting thus from them apart
> Did break your salty pussie's heart?
> I do not know, I never shall
> But *Amethyst* bids you – Farewell!

Simon was buried at the PDSA animal cemetery at Ilford, in a specially made casket, draped with a Union Flag. Father Henry Ross, the rector of St. Augustine's Church, in London, conducted a suitable ceremony. It seemed the right thing to do!

A little group of mourners gathered round the grave and, after a short service, the earth was scooped over the casket which had been laid down in the little grave, at the head of which a PDSA officer placed a temporary wooden marker which read:

**"In honoured memory of
Simon, DM. HMS Amethyst
Died November 28 1949."**

Later the little wooden marker was replaced with a specially designed stone monument, which can still be seen today.

In Memory of Simon
Served on HMS *Amethyst*
May 1948 – September 1949
Awarded Dickin Medal
August 1949
Died 28ᵗʰ November 1949.
THROUGHOUT THE "YANGTZE
INCIDENT" HIS BEHAVIOUR
WAS OF THE HIGHEST ORDER.

The medal was presented to him posthumously and received on his behalf by Captain and Mrs Kerans. The medal was held on board HMS *Amethyst* as a Naval trophy. When *Amethyst* was scrapped the medal was transferred to the Naval Trophy Store on HMS *Nelson*, in Portsmouth.

Eventually it was put up for auction and sold to a private collector in Canada. In 1993 it again came up for auction at Christies and was expected to fetch between £3,000 and £5,000. The Eaton Film Company, in London, which made a TV film called Animal Heroes, in which Simon is featured, bought it for £23,467. It is usually kept in the company's safety vault.

At present it is on permanent loan at HMS Collingwood, the land based training establishment at Fareham, Hants.

HMS *Amethyst* with holes in her hull caused by shellfire.
From a painting by War Artist, John Worsley

The Cat on ss *Hjalmar Wessel* That Always Came Back.

A black and white cat known only as Puss, who served as chief rat catcher on the Norwegian cargo vessel, ss *Hjalmar Wessel*, during World War II, had incredible homing instincts and was able to walk off her ship at any new port and be back before the ship sailed. She would stroll nonchalantly up the gangplank with minutes to spare, as if she had all the time in the world.

Part of a convoy, HX84 ss *Hjalmar Wessel* was once attacked by the German pocket battleship *Asmiral Scheer* in the North Atlantic, from which she survived.

Built in 1935 of 1,712 gross tonnage, she was owned by A/S Bauuegsard Sarpsborg.

Having survived, at the end of September 1943 ss *Hjalmar Wessel* was sent to the Mediterranean as part of a convoy, used to ferry war goods between North Africa and Italy.

Serving aboard as ship's cook was a British sailor, George Barrat who, like all the crew, was devoted to the ship's cat. Puss had a fiercely independent nature and made it clear from the start that she needed to be free to wander ashore whenever she fancied. A particularly strong mutual affection built up between her and the Chief Engineer, who she followed round the ship and down into the engine room.

When arriving at a new port, she was always ready when the gangway went down, eager to go ashore but always returning promptly to the ship before it sailed.

In Italy the local population was at starvation level so Puss, to her disgust, was often confined to a cabin when at anchor, because the crew feared that if she was allowed ashore she might be stolen and turned into a tasty stew.

Seaman George Barrat recalled: "We did many trips between North Africa and Italy and our cat always returned safely at sailing time. But the day came when we were due to sail from Algiers and our cat hadn't returned from her trip ashore. We waited until the very last minute, hoping she would turn up. But as the whole convoy to Italy was being delayed, we had no option but to leave without her."

After losing Puss, the *Hjalmar Wessel* made a number of crossings from Algiers to Italy, calling at Brindisi, Bari, Barletta and Ancona.

After about four round trips between the two countries, in Algiers they loaded a cargo of high octane aviation spirit bound for the port of Bari.

The day before arrival in Bari there was a raid and the port was bombed and 17 ships sunk. Many crew members and local population lost their lives. Consequently ss *Hjalmar Wessel*, with her sensitive cargo, was diverted north to the port of Barletta.

George Barrat described how, on arriving at Barletta he was leaning over the ship's rail with a shipmate "when to our astonishment our cat came crawling weakly up the gangway looking exhausted and very much worse for wear. We were amazed she had survived the onslaught of war.

"Somehow she had managed to travel across the sea from Algiers, where we last saw her, to Italy. The most probably explanation was that she hitched a lift on another ship in Algiers and came ashore at Barletta. How she knew we were there is a mystery.

"It was only by chance that we went to Barletta. Had we arrived at Bari on the day we were due, because of the explosive cargo we were carrying we would have been blown to smithereens.

"Puss made it up on deck and collapsed against the bulkhead. On examining her, she was found to have a nasty back wound. We had no idea what we could do for her, so I sprinkled some talcum powder on the wound. She still made no attempt to move and the Chief Engineer picked her up and took her to his cabin.

"She died the next day and we solemnly trussed her up as one would with any dead shipmate, weighed down with stones, and committed her body to the sea with a prayer."

After the war, on 21 January 1962, while sailing from Oslo to Rotterdam, a fire broke out in the engine room and ss *Hjalmar Wessel* was damaged beyond repair and scrapped.

ss *HjalmarWessel*

The Cat that got drunk on Rum on his birthday.

HMS *Snowflake* was a 'Flower' class corvette, launched in 1941, on Atlantic convoy duties, and the ship's cat, U-Boat, was spoiled rotten by the crew. He was described by a crew member as 'an incredible little animal' who taught himself how to be smart and keep things ship-shape. Fastidiously clean, he was careful to discreetly do 'his business' on the upper deck, knowing it would be cleaned up promptly by the crew

Like many other Royal Navy cats, U-Boat had his own little hammock and lifejacket, and he was formally listed on the ship's complement. When 'action stations' was called, U-Boat would make a beeline for the flour bin in the galley and would stay on top of it until the action was over.

At the end of a voyage, U-Boat went ashore as soon as the ship had tied up in harbour - but knew instinctively when it was due to sail again and reappeared shortly beforehand. On one memorable occasion he hadn't returned by sailing time, and half the crew were talking of jumping ship. It was considered extremely unlucky to sail without the mascot; but then, just as *Snowflake* was casting off, a little grey shape came hurtling down the jetty, made a flying leap across the widening gap of several feet between ship and shore, just made it onto the deck and then calmly sat down to wash himself.

After U-Boat had been on board a year, someone decided he should have a birthday and, as was customary on such an occasion, they celebrated with rum. U-Boat had his share of rum mixed with evaporated milk, in a saucer and lapped it all up with gusto. It made him quite drunk, and he ended up with a terrible hangover! He eventually slept it off, and from then on would never touch rum again.

The next day he was caught short and didn't make it in time to the upper deck, where he normally did his toilet. He accidently made a mess on the captain's wardroom chair. The captain, being fastidious about hygiene, put him on report and decided the disgraced U-Boat was to be put ashore when the ship reached Newfoundland and was not to be allowed back on board.

The crew felt this judgement was 'over the top' and were not at all happy about it. But the proud U-Boat, rather than waiting to be dishonourably discharged, made a decision to take his leave of his own accord. When *Snowflake* tied up at St John's he went ashore, as was his custom - and didn't return. The crew never saw him again.

'That Bloody Cat' on HM SBB7

On a bitterly cold winter's night, the crew members of the steam gunboat HM SBB7, which was launched on the Clyde in Scotland in 1941, were unloading boxes of ammunition from railway wagons and carrying them to the vessel. It was a foul night and snowing heavily. The crew were anxious to get the job done as quickly as possible and return to the warmth of the ship.

Grumbling and cursing as they worked, one crew member suddenly heard what he thought was a baby's whimper. They promptly stopped work and listened, trying to locate the source of the cry. Shining a torch under one of the wagons, they found a tiny frightened kitten, shivering with cold.

A crew member picked the kitten up and said: "poor little bugger" and tucked it into his jersey. Back on board on the mess deck, the near-frozen kitten was gently thawed out in one of the galley's warm ovens, with the door open, and then on top of a bulkhead heater. It was offered a bowl of warm milk with a dash of rum, which it lapped up gratefully.

From then on he was known as *That Bloody Cat*, or *TBC* for short and became a part of the crew. He soon recovered from his wretched start in life and proved himself a stalwart sailor. Whenever the Action Stations alarm sounded he would rush towards the bridge, along with the rest of the crew. And he made sure he was around when the rum ration was issued - his was served in a dish with warm milk added.

TBC was always the first ashore and last aboard in port and used the forward torpedo tubes as his launch pad for disembarking and returning. He would often come flying down the jetty at the last minute, intrepidly leaping aboard as the vessel started to move off. Sadly on one occasion he misjudged his departure when coming into port, and slipped on the rounded surface of the torpedo tube and fell into the sea. A sailor dived in after him, but TBC had disappeared and was presumed to have drowned.

The Cat on HMAS *Perth*
Who tried to desert ship

Red Lead was a little black kitten, the much revered mascot of the warship HMAS *Perth*. At the beginning of 1942, HMAS *Perth* and her crew were famous across Australia. Only the year before she had been fighting the Italian Navy in the Mediterranean Sea. HMAS *Perth* also evacuated thousands of war-weary Australian troops from Greece.

HMAS *Perth* and its crew of over 600 men were returned to Pacific waters where they were needed for a very important task - to stop the Japanese advance across south-east Asia.

They left Sydney in January 1942, stopping off at Fremantle on the way. It was here that Red Lead probably crept aboard the ship. The inquisitive little kitten meticulously explored the ship before deciding to make it his home. It was the perfect kitten's playground. In the sailors' quarters were swinging hammocks for him to jump on, the wide, wooden deck and the towering masts for him to hone his claws, and the round signal lamps and, deep in the bowels of the ship, the growling engines. Red Lead's chose his favourite spot to curl up in, the captain's cabin. The new captain, Hec Waller, found it a welcome diversion to spare a moment or two for the playful kitten.

But Red Lead had little time to settle in. On 27 February, HMAS *Perth* joined a fleet of British, Dutch and American ships to stop a Japanese naval convoy from landing on the island of Java. The fleet was hopelessly outnumbered and one by one, the Allied ships were crippled, sunk or forced to withdraw.

The sound of firing *ack ack* guns and the shouting of the men deafened the delicate ears of the kitten! As Japanese planes zoomed overhead he escaped to the place he felt safe - in Captain Waller's cabin. There he remained until the Captain gave orders to withdraw from the battle and the warship steamed back to harbour.

In the safety of the harbour, Red Lead was having second thoughts about life on the ocean wave. Instinctively perhaps, he knew he would not survive another battle like that. It was time to find a more peaceful way of life.

Quietly determined, Red Lead crept down the gangway. "Where do you think you are going?" yelled out one of the sailors and scooped up the little kitten, returning him to the deck. Foiled, Red Lead tried again three times to abandon the ship but to no avail. Each time he was brought back by some well-meaning sailor.

The crew eyed the unhappy cat with foreboding. This was a bad omen. The official log at the end of the day read: "Red Lead, ship's kitten, endeavoured to desert, but was brought back on board, despite vigorous protests."

Red Lead sensed that things would not improve, and sulked below decks. The next day HMAS *Perth* and USS *Houston* sailed for the south coast of Java and met a large fleet of Japanese ships. After a desperate battle, the *Perth* was sunk. More than 350 men (including Captain Waller) and one little black kitten went down with the ship.

Maizie, the Cat that mothered American Sailors adrift on a life-raft.

After their merchant ship was sunk in the North Atlantic in March 1943, ship's cat Maizie and six crew members spent 56 hours on a life raft before they were rescued.

Crewman Eugene Clancy of New York said, 'If Maizie hadn't been with us, we might have gone nuts. We completely forgot our personal discomfort and almost fought for the privilege of petting her.' Maizie took her turn at eating malted milk tablets and condensed food with the men, and even comforted those suffering from exposure or seasickness by going from one to another licking them tenderly 'almost like a mother'. It was reported that the cat had spent only about ten days on shore since America entered the war in December 1941.

The Mascot Kitten on HMS *Belfast*

As HMS *Belfast* leaves harbour, a member of the crew snapped this newly recruited kitten looking wistfully out of one of the portholes as if wondering if it was such a good idea, after all, to go to sea. He was probably thinking, like many of the crew, that it was too late now to change his mind. Launched on St. Patricks Day, 1938, HMS *Belfast* was one of the most powerful large light cruisers ever built and is the only surviving vessel of her type to have seen active service during WWII. Today HMS *Belfast* is moored on the Thames near London Bridge, as part of the Imperial War Museum and is the first ship to be preserved for the nation since Nelson's *Victory*.

The Sick Cat That Wasn't Allowed Ashore

Because of quarantine laws, cats were usually not allowed off vessels in Britain even if they wanted to land. When the cargo ship ss *Coulbeg* arrived at London's Surrey Commercial Docks in January 1951, an emergency call was put out to the People's Dispensary for Sick Animals for a vet to be sent to examine Paddy, the ship's cat, who had been badly injured during the voyage.

The strict rules prevented Paddy going ashore to see a vet – so Mr Donald Fossey, of the PDSA, and his staff drove to the docks in their ambulance to examine and treat the cat aboard the ship. Luckily Paddy made a good recovery and lived to sail another day.

Tiger who Chose His Own Ship And Joined the Crew

Ships' cats don't stand on ceremony, as illustrated by Tiger who, in March 1960, casually ambled aboard a British cable ship in Djibouti, French Somaliland. The Third Officer on the ship described how, to the amusement of the entire ship's crew, he just walked up the gangway of the ship as if he owned her.

"He paid no attention to anyone in the way of greeting, but got straight to work catching rats and eating them with relish," wrote the officer in a letter to the Times. "No cat-and-mouse games but serious business. *We* had the rats – *he* wanted them and he went ahead and caught them and ate them. That suited us all right, so we allowed him to stay."

Tiger would probably have argued it was the other way round and it was he who graciously decided to join the crew only because it suited him. And maybe because of the abundance of rats on board!

Carlsen who Refused to Abandon His Threatened Ship

A cat who was determined, if necessary, to go down with his ship was a fiery feline nicknamed Carlsen, after the gallant skipper of the *Flying Enterprise* who had also famously refused to leave his post.

On 17 January 1952 the Liberian freighter *Liberty* went aground near Land's End and was abandoned by her 38-man crew. But for the next 48 days, the ship's cat refused to leave, despite frantic efforts by the salvage workers to lure him ashore. He cleverly avoided all the traps they set him and soon the story of his courage and obstinacy became news.

When fire broke out on the bridge of the *Liberty*, the chief salvage officer, in the excitement of the moment and before the fire was quenched, skillfully managed to capture him. A furious Carlsen showed his resentment by niftily biting his rescuer on the hand to teach him that what a cat had to do a cat had to do, and no mere man should try to interfere.

Sarah of HMS *Shropshire* who Slept in a Hammock

Sarah, the ship's cat on HMS *Shropshire*, had the crew running around for her as though she was royalty, slavishly bowing to her every wish and whim. Every sailor knows that the best way to get a good night's rest is in a hammock and, fearing that the *Shropshire*'s precious mascot might be finding the going tough they made her 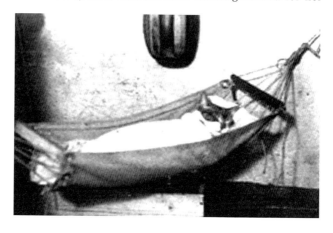 a tiny, personal hammock with her own blanket, pillow and mattress. One crew member remarked that it could be said she lived the life of Riley.

Beeps who Refused to Leave Scott's *Discovery*

A ship's cat who decided to cock a snook at authority and take the law into his own paws was Beeps, who enlisted as part of the crew on Sir Robert Falcon Scott's famous former old ship, the *Discovery*, when he was a mere kitten. At the time the historic ship was owned by the Sea Scouts but by 1953 it was decided that they couldn't afford the £3,000 a year it cost to maintain her. So they enquired around for a buyer.

The Admiralty liked the idea of buying her and restoring her to her former glory, as an historic Museum ship, but they insisted on a formal structural survey. The decks and cabins had to be stripped and properly cleared of all fixtures and fittings, but Beeps refused to abandon the ship that had been his home all his life. Indeed, he had never set foot on land and was not prepared to do so now just because the powers that be wanted him to do so. So he stuck to his guns and the Admiralty finally surrendered and Beeps stayed put while the refurbishments went on around him.

Charlie's Last Post

There is no doubt that sailors become inordinately attached to their feline mascots, particularly when the ship's cat in question has served for a decade or more. After the Admiralty decided in 1975 that it was too difficult to adhere to the strict quarantine laws and banned cats on Her Majesty's ships, some were allowed to continue their duties on shore. Having served at sea for many years Charlie, whose service number was C1111115, was transferred to HMS *Pembroke* offices at the Chatham naval base in Kent and listed as a full member of the staff. He even had his own Navy pay book.

When Charlie was tragically run over by a car, everyone at the base were distraught with grief. Determined to demonstrate the extent of their respect and affection for Charlie, the officer-on-the-watch conducted a funeral service complete with full naval honours, including lowering the flag to half-mast while a bugler played the Last Post. Some of the hardened seamen who attended, it was said, were reduced to tears.

Fred Wunpound, of HMS *Hecate*

Fred Wunpound was rated so highly by the crew of HMS *Hecate*, that when the forms for the 1971 census arrived with orders that the entire ship's company had to be meticulously listed, the crew took it literally and entered Fred as: **Able Seacat Fred Wunpound, Mouser (Second Class).**

But canny Mr A. Rennie, Registrar General for Scotland, spotted the cunning hoax and was not the least bit amused. He stiffly wrote back to say that he regretted that Fred, not being an actual sea**man**, could not be included in this very important census of the population of Scotland.

Able Seacat Fred Wunpound spent eight years and covered a quarter of a million miles on board HMS *Hecate* and built up a reputation as the cat who never missed a single voyage. Instinctively he always seemed to know when the ship was about to sail. After a night on the tiles, he would appear from nowhere and scurry up the gangplank with seconds to spare. Then one day, when the *Hecate* was about to set sail from Plymouth to the Hebrides, his sixth sense let him down and he missed the boat.

The worried crew had no option but to sail without him. It soon became clear that it was an unfortunate decision to make. During the voyage the ship's computer system broke down, one of the engines developed a fault, the ship's washing machine packed up and a second engine blew up. Even the potato peeler in the ship's galley snapped and became useless.

HMS *Hecate* finally limped into Stornoway, having covered the voyage on a wing and a prayer. All the bad luck was attributed to the fact that the ship's lucky mascot, Fred Wunpound, was not on board. The captain immediately sent two of his sailors on an urgent mission to Plymouth to find Fred and bring him back before he was prepared to set sail again. Having located him and reinstalled him on the *Hecate*, from then on the crew took the wise precaution of locking Fred in one of the cabins the night before sailing to make sure he didn't get left behind ever again.

The Siamese Cat of *Sagamore*, Listed in the Fixtures and Fittings

One exotic Siamese cat, named Princess Truban Tao-Tai, logged more than one and a half million miles as a crew member of the British merchant ship, *Sagamore*.

The Siamese Princess had been recruited, and given her imperial name 16 years earlier by a former captain while on his travels to the Far East. Since then she had never set a paw ashore because of quarantine restrictions. But she was perfectly content on the *Sagamore*, happy to leap about on deck, from one ship's instrument to another, with total confidence. Her favourite perch was on top of the bridge telegraph

where she could keep a close eye on her men.

In 1975 the *Sagamore's* owners, Furness Withy, one of Britain's largest shipping groups, decided to sell the 15,500-ton ship to an Italian group for half a million pounds.

Furness Withy included Princess Truban Tao-Tai in the extensive list of fixtures and fittings, pointing out that she was "coming to the twilight of her life and we don't want to see her destroyed – so we appealed to the Italians to take her and look after her."

At first the Italians declined the offer, and for a while it seemed the proud nautical princess would have to be put down. Then Furness Withy insisted and inserted a special clause in the sale contract specifying that the new owners had to "guarantee to keep the cat happy".

Since it was a case of losing the deal or taking on the cat, the Italians finally agreed and Princess Truban Tao-Tai was able to live out her days on the ship she regarded not only as her home, but as her entire world.

Her only problem was learning to respond to the Italian language instead of English.

Siamese Cats of HMS *Vanguard*

There was not one, nor two, nor even three but eleven ship's cats for members of the Girls Nautical Training Corps to cuddle in 1951 when they met for classes on board HMS *Vanguard* at Chatsworth, in Plymouth.

The cats, all Siamese, belonged to the girls' commanding officer Monica O'Donnell, who remarked at the time: "I teach the girls how to tie knots, do naval drill and seamanship. But since there is invariably a cat aboard a ship, I felt it was important for them to learn how to get on with a ship's cat too."

Count von Luckner (The Sea Devil) bedecked in his many medals, with his beloved countess, Irma. He revered ships, women and cats and it was his proud boast that he never took a man's life nor that of a cat during his buccaneering days on his pirate ship the *Seeadler*, in the First World War

The Benevolent Buccaneer who Sank Ships and Rescued Cats.

Count Felix von Luckner was a benevolent German buccaneer who, during the First World War, sailed the oceans of the world capturing Allied ships. Before sinking them he first transferred all the crew, including the ship's cats, to his pirate ship the *Seeadler*. At one point he had 400 prisoners and 140 cats aboard.

Born in Dresden on 9 June 1881, this legendary figure was from an old and famous military family who were friends of the German Royal Family. As a baby he boasted he once sat on Queen Victoria's lap. But he was determined to "sail before the mast" rather than follow family tradition and become a military officer.

When only 13 he ran away to sea and for seven years learnt his trade the hard way, roaming the oceans under an assumed name as a common jack-tar, suffering beatings, starvation, shipwreck and other appalling hardships and ruthlessly exploited by unscrupulous, cruel sea captains.

He developed into a swashbuckling brawny sea rover with a blustery manner and a booming foghorn of a voice. A powerful charismatic man, 6ft 4 ins tall with a massive frame and huge shoulders, he became known as the Sea Devil. He eventually achieved a position as a respected German naval officer, was reunited with his family and became a favourite of the Kaiser who was fascinated by tales of his adventures.

His pirate ship, the *Seeadler* (the Sea Eagle) was originally a 1,570-ton, three masted American Clipper, built in Glasgow in 1888 and captured early in the war by the Germans. Luckner had her converted into an auxiliary cruiser, heavily armed and equipped with two 500 horse power engines and skilfully disguised inside and out as a Norwegian timber-carrying sailing ship which he called the *Irma*, after his sweetheart. The guns and ammunition were cunningly concealed and there were hidden cabins – sufficient to accommodate all prisoners in comfort. Luckner and his crew posed convincingly as Norwegians. One slender, beardless officer, Schmidt, was even provided with a blonde wig and an outfit of women's clothes so that he could, when necessary, pose as the captain's wife.

The plan was that when an Allied vessel was spotted, Luckner would signal to the captain to "heave to" and the true name of the ship, the *Seeadler* would be dramatically revealed as his crew donned their German naval uniforms. He sank a total of 16 ships, French, British, Italian and American. Each ship he sank had at least one and often several cats aboard and it was his proud boast that he never took a life nor drowned a cat.

The *Seeadler* left Germany on 21 December 1916, intent on breaking through the British blockade. They were stopped by an armed British merchant cruiser, the 15,000-ton coal-carrying *Avenger*. The British officers who came on board meticulously examined the ship and its papers and were totally taken in by the Germans' fake

Norwegian accents and the charms of the captain's "wife". To the Sea Devil's glee, despite a thorough inspection they failed to find the hidden cabins, guns and ammunition and the *Seeadler* was allowed to sail into British shipping lanes.

On 9 January the buccaneers sank their first ship, a British steamer, the *Gladys Royal*. The Norwegian flag disappeared and so did the Norwegian clothes. The men changed into their German naval uniforms and then fired a warning shot across the steamer's bow. All the steamer's crew were rescued and safely brought on board the *Seeadler* before a bomb was planted in her hold and she was blown up.

The next day they captured another British steamer, the *Lundy Island*, and repeated the exercise. Then followed the exquisite French sailing barque, the *Charles Gounod*. The sight of a sailing ship with a fine hull could move Luckner to tears and it hurt him to have to sink this graceful vessel with its three tall masts.

"One should never have to sink a sailing ship, for the shipyards aren't building them any more," he noted regretfully, having the presence of mind to first commandeer the *Charles Gounod's* store of fine French wine and three fat hogs before exploding the ship.

Because of his daring adventures he had become a legend in his own life time and early in his career had earned the nickname "The Sea Devil". Despite his rough and ready manner he revered above all things ships, women and cats. He was particularly in awe of women and cats, regarding them as beautiful, delicate mysterious creatures meant to be cherished and even worshipped.

When he was an incongruously romantic apprentice sailor, he dreamt he was destined to meet a fairy tale princess. Years later, as an officer on board a German steamship the *Panther*, the ship stopped at Fuerteventura, an island in the Canaries. There he met Irma, his princess-come-true, a "dainty slip of a girl" with blonde curls and blue eyes. With his massive frame and huge shoulders he could have crushed her in one bear hug, but he treated her like a piece of Dresden china. They became engaged and agreed to marry after the war.

Luckner next bagged a three-masted Canadian schooner, HMS *Percy* bound for Nova Scotia with a cargo of gaberdine. The newly married captain had his bride on board. When informed that the captain of HMS *Percy* and his bride were on their honeymoon, Luckner gallantly allotted them the best cabin on the *Seeadler*. The lovely bride was delighted and regarded her stay aboard the *Seeadler* as an unexpected and exciting part of her honeymoon. After the war, she wrote that it was "like being on a luxury holiday cruiser or a floating hotel".

HMS *Percy* was so light that it was not necessary to use bombs, but some shots into her hull were sufficient to sink her. After having taken her crew on board, Luckner prepared to give the order to sink the ship by gunfire. As he did so, one of the captured ship's crew, who was standing behind him, was heard to say, "too bad about the cat". It turned out the *Percy's* mascot was still aboard. Luckner immediately told the gun crew to hold their fire and ordered the rescue boat crew to row across the distance of half a mile to the stricken ship with orders not to return until the cat had been found.

Their next conquest was the four-masted French brig, the *Antonin* followed by an Italian ship, the *Buenos Aires* "a fine vessel but filthy dirty" whose captain came aboard the *Seeadler* during a hurricane, incongruously carrying an opened umbrella, which the Germans thought hilarious. Then they nabbed a magnificent French barque, *La Rochefoucauld*.

The biggest capture of all was the 9,800-ton British steamer, the *Horngarth*, loaded with fine champagne and cognac. On board also were a Steinway grand piano and other valuable musical instruments as well as magnificent paintings and expensive furniture. Luckner managed to haul most of it aboard the *Seeadler* before giving the order to open the sea cocks to sink the ship.

From then on each night there was music, dancing and fine champagne. The Canadian captain's bride became the reigning queen and prisoners and crew made a huge fuss of her. The war seemed far away as they sailed beneath the stars.

They went on to capture another French ship, the *Dupleix*, whose captain couldn't believe his eyes when he came aboard the *Seeadler* and was offered a welcoming glass of champagne. His ship was sunk as the prisoners on *Seeadler* continued to make merry. None of them wanted the voyage to end although they all knew it had to eventually.

One ship that broke Luckner's heart to sink was the British four-masted sailing ship the *Pinmore*, on which he had made the longest and most harrowing voyage of his life as a teenage sailor. For 285 days the ship had sailed from San Francisco around Cape Horn to Liverpool. They had rations for only 180 days and seawater got into the fresh water tanks. Between half rations and brackish water, six men died of scurvy and beriberi. Massive storms overwhelmed them but the crew was too weak to climb the riggings to adjust the sails.

On this voyage on the *Pinmore*, Luckner had a curious and cunning little cat called Sinbad, who got up to all sorts of amusing antics. At night he curled up with the young Luckner in his bunk and brought him warmth and comfort from the misery of the trip. The captain's wife, who was sailing with them, took a fancy to the attractive little cat and ordered the steward to bring him to her. Naturally Luckner was upset.

"I told the steward that if he did not bring Sinbad back, I would go to the Captain. The steward laughed so I determined to go to the Captain and complain about the steward and demand my cat back."

Wrathfully he strode across the deck to the Captain's cabin. But he was still an apprentice sailor and painfully in awe of the ship's master. He described how he trembled for a moment outside the door before mustering enough courage to push the door open a crack.

The *Seeadler*, in full sail as she struggles in a squall. From a sketch made from a photograph taken by the captain of the French ship *Antonin* just before she was captured. Noticing the Captain had a camera in his hand, Luckner audaciously delayed raising the German flag to reveal the *Seeadler's* true colours, because he wanted the photograph for his picture library.

"The skipper was sitting there, reading a paper. My bravery suddenly oozed away and I turned and tiptoed back to my bunk. I never did get my cat back and forever held a grudge against the steward."

Although his time on the *Pinmore* had been a terrifying experience, it had also been a significant phase of his life when he had hardened into a proper, seasoned sailor. The old ship had a special place in his affections.

Nonetheless she was a British ship and she had to be sunk. Luckner said he gave the fateful order and then went and shut himself in his cabin while the dirty deed was done. It was, he said, like blowing up an old and faithful friend.

Meanwhile, said Luckner, no group of passengers on a liner ever enjoyed such happy comradeship as they all did aboard this bizarre buccaneering craft. "The fact that we were captors and captives seemed to make it all the jollier," he said. "We took great pleasure in making time agreeable for our prisoners with games, concerts, cards and story telling. We served special meals for all the nations of those ships we captured. We were a happy ship."

When the Canadian captain's bride complained of lack of female company, Luckner promised he would see what he could do. Sure enough, in the South Atlantic one day a large British barque came into view and on the deck stood the white, slender figure of a woman. The ship was the *British Yeoman* and the girl, it turned out, was the Captain's fancy woman. The entire crew, including two cats, a couple of pigs, some rabbits, doves and three dogs, were duly taken on board the *Seeadler*. Luckner then gave orders to sink the British ship by gunfire. He insisted that the woman should be treated with as much respect as his other woman passenger.

Luckner took the two pigs on board to ensure that the crew had fresh meat. But they were allowed the freedom of the ship and became like pets and in the end the burly sailor couldn't bring himself to slay them.

On 21 March they captured their 12th and last vessel in the Atlantic, the French sailing ship the *Cambronne*. "Our floating hotel was about full," wrote Luckner. "If we wanted any more guests aboard we would first have to get rid of our present company."

So instead of sinking the French ship, Luckner ordered the masts to be cut off to slow down the ship's progress and Captain Mullen, the English officer from the *Pinmore*, was put in charge. Luckner made sure the ship was well stocked with provisions.

That night a farewell party was held aboard the *Seeadler*. Champagne and cognac flowed and music played on the salvaged grand piano echoed across the moonlit water. The ship's cats crept stealthily round the feet of the revellers seeking scraps. The little dogs yapped and the pet pigs probably thanked their lucky stars that they hadn't been slaughtered and eaten as part of the festivities. Crew and captives were genuinely sorry to be parting. It had been like a holiday cruise.

Next day the prisoners were all given the wages they might have earned if their ships had not been captured and sunk. With great sadness, the prisoners and most of the cats were transferred to the *Cambronne*. Captain Mullen was asked not to tip off any other ship until they reached Rio de Janeiro. He kept his word and did not inform the authorities about the *Seeadler* until they reached Brazil ten days later.

The *Seeadler* then headed for the Pacific. There they sank four more vessels. Three were four-masted American schooners, the *A.B.Johnson*, sunk on 8 June, 1917; the *R.C.Slade*, sunk 18 June 1917, *Manila*, sunk 8 July 1917 and an English cruiser.

On 29 June 1917 the *Seeadler* crashed upon some reefs off the Island of Mophelia, where its wreck can still be seen today. Some of the men and animals, including the pet pigs, swam for the shore and were beset upon by a group of sharks who, luckily, seemed to prefer pig flesh to that of humans.

Everything useful was salvaged from the wreck and the men built themselves a shantytown, which they called Seeadlerburg (Sea Eagle Town). The Americans were in their element in this tropical paradise, but it was too tame for the Germans who soon missed their exciting, buccaneering life. So they devised rigging and sails for one of the lifeboats from the *Seeadler* and prepared her for the sea, loading her with provisions for half-a-dozen men for a long voyage. She was only 18ft but they found room to store not only food and water, but machine guns, rifles, hand grenades and pistols.

She was christened the *Kronprinzessin Cecilie* and Luckner, with six of his men, set sail on what must have been the smallest auxiliary cruiser in the war. Their aim was to capture a ship then sail back to Mophelia and pick up their comrades before continuing their raiding missions. The old Sea Devil and his crew sailed 2,300 miles in 28 days in their tiny open boat, wandering from atoll to atoll seeking a ship to capture.

They found a suitable vessel to commandeer in Wakaya, but their plans were foiled by the untimely arrival of a British officer and four Indian soldiers. Lacking the German naval uniforms in which to fight chivalrously, they surrendered and were interned in New Zealand for the remainder of the war.

As the war drew to an end, the reputation of this extraordinary "Boy's Own Hero" spread far and wide. Amazing stories of his adventures as a youth came to light. As a 13-year-old runaway, he was befriended by an ancient Dutch mariner called Peter who was impressed when Luckner told him he was a count and tried to persuade him to go home.

When it became clear the lad's mind was made up, old Peter got him his first position as a cabin boy on board a mean, dirty old craft called the *Niobe*. He gave him his old sea chest and some wise advice. "My boy, always remember, one hand for yourself and one for the ship."

This meant, of course, that when aloft a sailor must hold on with one hand and work with the other but old Peter pointed out that the motto had a deeper meaning and "in every channel, sea or backwater of life you should keep one hand for yourself and one for whichever ship you sail through life in".

Alas, Luckner didn't heed the warning. On the *Niobe* Luckner was treated like some sort of galley slave. Not only was he not paid, he had to eat the scraps from the table and swill out the pigpens and the latrines. Determined to prove his worth, one day during a storm he intrepidly climbed the mast to help unfurl the sails and he forgot old Peter's advice and a gust of wind knocked him 90ft to the deck. As he lost consciousness a huge wave swept him overboard.

When he came to in the water, he could see that a boat had already been launched to rescue him but he realised that, in the high waves, it was unlikely that anyone would spot him. Two or three huge albatross hovered above him, thinking they had found a tasty morsel. One swooped down menacingly and viciously attacked him. To the bird's surprise Luckner retaliated by grabbing hold of its talon and holding on for dear life. Watched by the other circling birds, the bird frantically tried to rise but was hindered by the weight of the boy. It began to strike at the boy's hand with his beak until blood flowed into the sea. The lifeboat men saw the commotion and realised what it was about and rushed to the spot and pulled the boy out of the water.

On another ship, the *Caesarea*, he broke a leg in a storm when some timbers crashed down, bending his leg into an L-shape opposite to its natural position. His shipmates tied him to the bulwarks and with a block and tackle, pulled slowly but painfully until the leg was straight and the bones in place. After which the ship's carpenter made him a crude pair of splints. Consequently forevermore the old Sea Devil walked with a curious lurching limp which nicely fitted his image.

Between the two world wars he and Irma, his fairy tale princess who was now his countess, travelled extensively through Europe and the USA. Tremendous crowds greeted them wherever they went. A real showman sailor, he revelled in his fame. But he remained a warm, humane, if somewhat eccentric, man. In Germany he was acclaimed a hero and awarded the rare honour of being placed above the scope of German law, the prerogative of only the German Royal family. He was even summoned to Rome by the Pope who called him a "great humanitarian". The United States gave him the freedom of many of their cities.

When Luckner was too old for active service in World War II, Adolf Hitler tried to use him for propaganda purposes. Luckner refused to co-operate. In 1943 he saved the life of a Jewish girl by giving her shelter and providing her with a passport. Hitler was furious and made life difficult for him by stopping his bank account. But because of his international renown, Hitler could only confine him to the remote town of Halle. The town received relative immunity from air raids, which they firmly believed was because the Count lived in their midst. In April 1945 the Mayor asked the Count to meet approaching American troops and seek clemency. Luckner succeeded in negotiating with the Americans who agreed not to bomb Halle.

He admired and respected the British and the Americans but seemed contemptuous of the French. He said he loved his Fatherland and believed the constant wars in Europe were due to the fact that it was a continent consisting of so many different countries with different cultures and languages, all of which were bound to clash.

"As a sailor who has sailed the world under many flags and whose friends are the citizens of many countries and climes, it is my dream that one day we shall all speak the same language and have so many common interests that terrible wars will no longer occur."

But he added this advice: "Keep your bodies fit and if your country needs you, just remember the motto of the sea: **Don't jump overboard! Stay with the ship**!"

He died aged 85, in Malmo, Sweden on 14 April 1966.

Side Boy of HMS *Neptune*

Sideboy was the handsome black mascot cat on board the battleship, HMS *Neptune* during the First World War. The crew believed he brought them good luck and sent this postcard of him home to their wives and sweethearts to reassure them.

The *Neptune* was a sturdy ship, an impressive 20,000-tonner. Whether the ship's good luck was due to Sideboy or her own impressive seaworthiness is questionable, but nonetheless the *Neptune* survived the war and was eventually sold in 1922.

"SIDE-BOY" H.M.S. NEPTUNE

Cats That Braved the Frozen Wastes

The Cat that Ate a Biological Specimen

One anonymous, swift-moving ship's cat rather let the side down when, on an important scientific voyage to the Antarctic in 1842, it pounced on a rare fish specimen and gulped it down before the dismayed eyes of the biologist who was about to pop it into a bowl of preserving liquid.

The ship, HMS *Terror*, was under the command of Sir James Clark Ross who, in 1831, discovered the North Magnetic Pole. From 1839-1843 he was sent on an expedition to the Antarctic – commanding two illustrious ships, HMS *Erebus* (skippered by himself) and HMS *Terror* (skippered by Captain Francis Crozier) and mentions this incident of the thieving cat in his book "Voyage of Discovery".

The scientists on board the two ships were not only mapping out new territory but also collecting valuable information relating to new species of animal life and plants. Each specimen would be methodically sketched, measured and then preserved in alcohol for later scrutiny.

On 21 February 1842, during a particularly savage storm, James Clark Ross made notes about a "remarkable circumstance which occurred on board the *Terror* during this storm, which may help to convey a better idea of the intensity of the cold we experienced than a mere reference to the state of the thermometer."

All hands were on deck, desperately chopping away thick coats of ice from the *Terror*'s bows. Each wave the ship plunged into formed a fresh layer of ice as it smashed onto the frozen deck. One vast wave lifted with it a particularly curious species of fish, and dashed it against the mast, where it instantly stuck, frozen fast.

Dr. Robinson, the ship's biologist, was excited at the prospect of adding this strange specimen to his collection. After he'd prised it away from the icy mast, he laid it down on the deck and sketched and measured it. Having made a careful note of the dimensions, he was about to pop it into a dish of preservative when the ship's cat pounced.

"The strange fish was unfortunately seized upon and devoured by the ship's cat," Ross noted with exasperation.

James Clark Ross also described how he sent out a party to cut firewood on Enderby Land. His men found a cat's nest with two kittens in it, still blind. For some extraordinary reason they decided to destroy the kittens, but the terrified mother cat escaped and found refuge on one of the ships.

A few years later Sir John Franklin took command of the *Erebus* and the *Terror* (again skippered by Captain Crozier), when he made a brave attempt to discover the North West Passage.

It is believed that the *Erebus* and the *Terror* were crushed by thick ice in the

Victoria Strait in 1846 and that Franklin was eaten by polar bears. The 105 survivors, led by Captain Crozier, attempted to reach safety but died of starvation and scurvy. In 1848 Sir James Clark Ross made a voyage to Baffin Bay in search of the remains of Franklin and his men.

HMS *Erebus* (HMS *Terror* in the background)
(National Maritime Museum, Greenwich)

Nansen of the *Belgica*, the First Cat to Winter in the Antarctic

Nansen was a loveable black and white kitten and is reputed to have been the first cat to spend a whole winter in the Antarctic on the Belgian Sailing Ship, the *Belgica*. In August 1897, under the leadership of the Belgian Captain Adrien de Gerlache, the *Belgica* headed for the Antarctic with a multi-national crew of 23. It was the first Antarctic expedition of a purely scientific nature. Although they never actually reached the Pole itself, they became the first humans to winter on the Antarctic ice when the ship became trapped in the ice off Alexander Land on the Antarctic Peninsula region.

The pretty little kitten was brought aboard the ship by the Norwegian cabin boy, Johan Koren. He named him after one of his own country's heroes, a previous great Antarctic explorer, Fridtjof Nansen (1861-1930), described by many as a Norwegian demi-god.

Nansen and four others were the first to cross the Greenland ice cap from east to west on skis in 1888 and it was he who demonstrated that the North Pole was an ocean covered with close packed ice and not an open sea.

The cat Nansen became the *Belgica's* good luck mascot. He was spoiled and petted by the entire crew and, when the long dark winter night descended, Nansen provided not only amusing entertainment but, with his kittenish antics, brought a touch of homely warmth to the depressing cold dark days and nights.

Second Officer on the Belgica was Norwegian, Roald Amundsen, who over ten years later was to snatch victory from Captain Robert Falcon Scott by reaching the South Pole a few days ahead of him. In his diary on 27 September 1897, he noted with delight:

"There are a lot of flying fish and dolphins near the ship and at night, in particular, they provide a very beautiful display with their rapid movement in the phosphorescent sea. Three flying fish flew over the rails tonight. Of course, they were given a warm reception, especially by Nansen, our small cat. When it is dark, she creeps round the deck and catches flying fish all night long."

In his book "Through the First Antarctic Night" the ship's doctor Frederick Cook, describes how Nansen had steadily worked his way into the affections of the entire crew:

"It is Sunday, the weather is warm, wet and too stormy to permit our usual Sabbath excursions. We are playing cards and grinding the music boxes and trying in various ways to throw off the increasing gloom of the long night. But something has happened which has added another cloud to the hell of blackness which enshrouds us.

"One of the sailors brought with him from Europe this beautiful young kitten. He is at home alike in the forecastle and in the cabin, but with characteristic good sense he did not venture out on exploring trips. A temperature thirty degrees below

Nansen, the ship's cat on board ss *Belgica,* captained by Belgian Captain Adrien de Gerlache in the 1897 Expedition to the Antarctic. As drawn by the Norwegian cabin boy, Johan Koren, who named him after one of his own country's sea heroes.

zero was not to his liking. The quarters about the stove and the bed of a favourite sailor were his choice.

"Since the commencement of the long darkness he has been ill at ease, but previously he was happy and contented and glad to be petted and loved by everybody. The long night, however, brought out all the bad qualities of his ancestors. For nearly a month he has been in a kind of stupor, eating very little and sleeping much. If we tried to arouse him, he displayed considerable anger. We have brought in a penguin occasionally to try to infuse new ambitions and a new friendship in the cat, but both the penguin and the cat were contented to take to opposite corners of the room.

"Altogether, Nansen seemed thoroughly disgusted with his surrounding and his associates and lately he has sought exclusion in unfrequented corners. His temperament has changed from the good and lively creature to one of growling discontent. His mind has wandered and from his changed spiritual attitude we believe that his soul has wandered too.

"A day or two ago his life departed, we presume for a more congenial region. We are glad his torture is ended, but we miss Nansen very much. He has been the attribute to our good fortune to the present, the only speck of sentimental life within reach. We have showered upon him our affections, but the long darkness has made him turn against us. In future we shall be without a mascot and what will be our fate?"

That day, 22 June, it was midwinter in the Antarctic and the temperature was -28 degrees centigrade. Poor little Nansen. Despite the efforts of Frederick Cook and Roald Amundsen to save him, he finally gave up the ghost. Did he die of the cold or was it the lack of sun and daylight that sent him a little mad? We shall never know! But he had the dubious honour of being not only the first cat to spend a winter in the Antarctic, but the first cat to die there.

Perhaps it **was** the lack of the ship's mascot that soon brought bad luck to the *Belgica*. Some time after Nansen's death one of the Norwegian sailors, August Wiencke, fell over board and drowned. Wiencke Island is named after him. Then the Belgian geophysicist, Emile Danco, died of heart failure and the coastline along that stretch of land is called the Danco Land in his honour. The rest of the crew returned home safely in November 1899.

Two Cats that Sailed on the *Discovery* With Captain Scott of the Antarctic

Ship's cats, Blackwall and Poplar, each spent two winters on the ice in the Antarctic when, in 1901, they sailed with Captain Robert Falcon Scott and his men on the revolutionary, brand new, 172ft steam ship, the *Discovery* – the first ship to have been specifically built for a scientific exploratory expedition. Built in Dundee the *Discovery* was launched in March 1901 and left England for the Antarctic in August with a team of scientists and loaded with expensive equipment.

Blackwall & Poplar basking in the sun on the *Discovery*

There were 38 men on board including a 27-year-old merchant seaman, the charming and charismatic Sub Lieutenant Ernest Shackleton. Scott, aged 33, was a Royal Naval Officer and rather resented Shackleton for having a mind of his own and not being prepared to obey orders without question. He'd rather his crew had been all Royal Navy men trained to do exactly as they were told in the best naval tradition.

Blackwall, a handsome black and grey tabby, immediately attached himself, as cats do, to Captain Scott and soon wormed his way into the leader's affections and his bunk, where he spent almost every night, despite having to compete for his attention with Scamp, Scott's small black Aberdeen terrier, which he brought with him.

Poplar was an affectionate little black cat belonging to an American, Arthur Quartley, leading stoker on the *Discovery*. The two ship's cats got on well together and would cheerfully share their favourite warm spot near the stove when the temperature dropped to below zero. A photograph of the two of them probably taken by Edward Wilson, the ship's biologist, illustrator and photographer, shows them crouched companionably on deck looking smugly confident that if they stayed there long enough, a tasty plate of left-overs would soon come their way.

Discovery's sponsors back in England were not unduly concerned when news arrived that their brand new ship had become embedded in the ice during that first bleak winter on the freezing white continent. After all, that was why she and her crew had been sent there – to map out new territory. As planned, the relief ship *Morning*, with a crew of 32 men, sailed from Lyttelton, New Zealand, with supplies to allow the *Discovery* to spend a second year on the ice. There was still a lot of scientific work to be done, new mountains and lands to be conquered and anyway, Scott and his men were enjoying the harsh life with gusto.

The *Morning* carried two ship's cats – a black female called Night and her pure-white kitten, Noon. Before the ship arrived in Lyttelton from Britain, there were three cats on board - Morning, Noon and Night. There is no record to explain how Morning, a grey tabby, came to be on the ship. But her trip didn't last long. She was recorded as having been lost overboard on the return voyage Captain Scott and his crew, healthy, full of confidence and with a real sense of well being, were pleased to welcome Captain William Colbeck and his ship, the *Morning*, the January after that first winter. They all felt as if they were on a sort of "Boys' Own Adventure" and they'd been hugely enjoying the hardship, the cold and the long treks in the snow to discover uncharted territory. A strong sense of comradeship prevailed.

The *Morning* carried fresh provisions and equipment and, most important, mail from home. On 2 March the *Morning* departed carrying a number of men discharged by Capt.

Scott from the *Discovery*. Amongst them was Ernest Shackleton who had been ill with scurvy and who Scott insisted was not fit enough to endure another harsh winter, even though Shackleton protested he was as fit as any of the rest of the men.

Rumour had it that Scott felt he compared unfavourably beside Shackleton who already showed signs of being a strong leader capable of inspiring immense respect and devotion. Shackleton excelled himself in 1914 by displaying considerable courage and leadership when his ship *Endurance* finally gave up the ghost after being crushed by the ice. He led his entire crew across the icy wastes to safety. Not a single man was lost! (*See story of Mrs Chippy, ship's cat on the Endurance*).

The Admiralty and sponsors were uneasy when the Captain of the *Morning* reported that the spanking new *Discovery* was embedded in ice ten feet deep. She had cost a fortune to build and was full of expensive scientific equipment, which they didn't want to lose, to say nothing of the valuable data that had been collected so far. So it was decided that two winters in the ice were quite enough and that the *Morning* should return the following winter to escort them all home.

This time a second relief ship, the *Terra Nova*, captained by Harry McKay, was to accompany the *Morning* as a back up. Famously known as the "Iceman", Harry was a hardy Dundee whaling captain and an expert at blasting his way through the ice with dynamite. Ironically, the *Terra Nova* was the ship used by Captain Scott on his second, ill-fated attempt to conquer the South Pole, in 1910 when he and four brave men died in such tragic circumstances.

The *Terra Nova* set sail from England with a large shipment of stores for both *Discovery* and *Morning*. and joined up with the *Morning* in Hobart, Tasmania. There was at least one white cat on board, probably belonging to Second Engineer William Smith. The two ships sailed in convoy, with orders to rescue *Discovery* from the ruthless grip of the ice and return with ship and men intact. If the ship could not be freed then Scott must abandon ship.

Scott was upset and resentful when the two relief ships arrived and he was told what their orders were. The *Discovery* was now embedded in fourteen feet of ice and there were twenty miles of solid ice between the ship and the open sea. And yet he was stubbornly confident that he had enough provisions to last another winter and he was sure his ship was in no real danger. When Capt. Colbeck of the *Morning* asked Capt. Scott what the prospects were of the *Discovery* being freed that year, he may have been inspired by the sight of Blackwall serenely curled up and unperturbed by the drama going on around him, when he replied defiantly: "Not a cat's chance".

Nonetheless men from all three ships began dynamiting away at the ice to try to free the *Discovery* so that they could escort her home. Scott and his men were depressed and distraught at the possibility that they might have to abandon their ship, to which they had become inordinately attached. The cat Blackwall had the dubious privilege of seeing the great hero in his moments of deep depression. Scott would retire to his cabin with his dog and cat and not emerge for days.

To add to the gloom, Poplar, the endearing black cat belonging to Stoker Arthur Quartley, was savagely set upon and killed by the ship's team of highly excitable and half-starved huskies on 2 February, 1904, at Hut Point, the *Discovery's* winter quarters off Ross Island. Quartley was devoted to his cat and was angry and distraught at his pet's gruesome demise

Nonetheless the *Morning* and *Terra Nova* went on battling through the frozen waters and eventually the *Discovery* was triumphantly released from the grip of the ice. Most of the credit for this went to Harry McKay of the *Terra Nova*. The three ships set sail and eventually arrived in Lyttelton, New Zealand on Good Friday, 1 April with Blackwall still on board having survived two winters on the ice.

Blackwall, the handsome black and white tabby who sailed on the *Discovery* with Captain Robert Falcon Scott (1901-04) risks getting frostbite in his paws by venturing onto the frozen deck

Nigger, the Swinging Cat
On Scott's *Terra Nova*

In 1910, while the *Terra Nova* was moored at the London Docks, a tiny black kitten decided that life on the ocean wave was for him. He sneaked up the gangplank and curled up in a warm dark corner and when he woke up he was far away at sea and it was too late to change his mind.

How was he to know that he was on the same famous relief ship that, along with the *Morning*, was sent to rescue Captain Robert Falcon Scott and his crew when their ship, the *Discovery*, became trapped in the Antarctic ice in 1903? On this occasion Captain Scott had resented being "rescued", stubbornly convinced that he and his men were perfectly safe. They had enough provisions to last them one or even two more winters, even though the *Discovery* was cut off from the ocean by 25 miles of frozen water.

The little black kitten had no inkling that this same ship was about to embark on yet another formidable voyage in a second attempt by Scott to conquer the South Pole. The ship's company numbered sixty-five, including twelve eminent scientists.

The *Terra Nova* had already proved herself to be a tough and powerful ship that could tackle the Antarctic winter. She was mainly responsible for smashing through the ice and reaching the *Discovery* - convincing evidence that she was the best ship for the job.

When the stowaway cat emerged from his hiding place, the men on board made a great fuss of him. Some sailors say black cats are lucky omens. Others say they are demons in disguise and bring bad luck. Sailors of old might have reflected on the wisdom of allowing a black cat on board but these early Antarctic explorers, although often deeply religious, were not prone to superstition.

The coal black kitten positively oozed appeal and purred his way into the affections of all on the *Terra Nova*. They called him Nigger and fondly dubbed him the ship's mascot. He became a great favourite with the entire ship's company, providing them with endless entertainment for three arduous years.

Nigger used up his many lives rapidly, falling overboard at sea on one voyage and being rescued by the ship's boat and revived with brandy on another. The crew even designed and fashioned a special hammock for him, which swung between the bulkheads. He'd lie there, snuggled under his warm blanket with his small black head resting on his very own pillow, swinging to and fro in his cat's cradle like a baby, oblivious to the fiercest of storms or the severest of weather.

It is difficult enough for even the most seasoned sailor to climb into a hammock – the most comfortable way to sleep whether on land or water most mariners would claim. Nigger became an expert, skilfully jumping in and waiting for the swinging to slow down before curling up under the warm bedding provided by the soft-hearted sailors.

Dr. Edward Wilson, the ship's biologist and illustrator, delighted in sketching and taking pictures of him. In a ship full of hardy men who were not too fastidious about washing, Nigger put them to shame by constantly grooming his sleek black coat, meticulously washing his face with his paws and delicately trimming his claws.

Prior to their journey south, the ship moored in Melbourne, Australia, between two huge ships – the *Powerful* (13,000 tons) and a White Star liner (12,000 tons). Dr. Wilson noted proudly that the *Terra Nova*, although only 700 tons in comparison, nonetheless looked smart and neat.

The night before the *Terra Nova* set sail, her ship's company was invited by the crew of the *Powerful* to dine with them on board ship, to give them a good send off. Wilson mentions (but doesn't name) a very important Admiral who, that night, dined alone with Captain Scott. Early next morning, he asked to be shown around the *Terra Nova*. Wilson said he asked the most intelligent questions and "seemed to go to the heart of every detail at once and was really pleasant".

"Our cat was inspected. We have a small muscular black cat called Nigger who came on board as an almost invisible kitten in London. He has grown stiff and small and very strong and has a hammock of his own with the "hands" under the forecastle. The hammock is about 2ft long with proper lashings and everything made of canvas. A real man o'war hammock with small blankets and a small pillow and the cat was asleep in his hammock with his black head on the pillow and the blanket over him."

Wilson wrote that the Admiral was very amused when Nigger opened his eyes and stared unimpressed at the Admiral, rudely yawned in his face and then languidly stretched out one black paw before turning over and going back to sleep.

"It was a very funny show and amused the Admiral and his officers as much as anything. Nigger has learned to jump into his hammock which is slung under the roof along with the others and creeps in under the blanket with his head on the tiny pillow."

When the bigwigs had left Wilson said that all the men relaxed and got into their old and dirty rig and prepared to sail. Bowing and scraping to VIP's was not their cup of tea. They were eager to get on with the voyage and the next adventure.

Wilson notes:"It was a funny coincidence that Lt. Edward Evans, now in the command of the *Terra Nova*, had been told in the old days when he was a midshipman by this very same man, now an Admiral, that he had better leave the service as he would never do any good in it. His manner was different now and Evans took the opportunity of a fair wind to show that he could manage the ship he was in charge of anyhow."

There was another cat on board the *Terra Nova*, a blue Persian kitten. But he must have lacked character and the men didn't find him as appealing as Nigger. Which is probably why there is no record of his name or his fate.

When they reached the frozen wastes of the Antarctic Nigger wisely spent practically all his time aboard the ship, usually snug in his hammock, while the shore parties went out with their sledges and dogs, mapping out new territory. Their most important mission, of course, was to reach the South Pole before anyone else. There was stiff competition from a rival party of Norwegians, lead by Roald Amundsen, whose plan to

Ship's cat, Nigger, in the hammock made for him by the crew of the *Terra Nova* captained by Captain Robert Falcon Scott for his 1910-12 expedition.

By kind permission of the Canterbury Museum, Christchurch, New Zealand

get to the South Pole was, Scott admitted, "a very serious menace to ours".

The five brave men who set off to conquer the South Pole on sledges pulled by huskies and ponies, were Captain Robert Falcon Scott, Captain Lawrence Oates, Lt. Edgar Evans, Lt. Henry Bowers and Dr. Edward Wilson.

After much hardship, half starved and exhausted from the cold, frostbite and other severe afflictions, when they did reach their goal on Friday, 16 January 1912, they were bitterly disappointed to find the Norwegians **had** got there first by a matter of a few days. "It is a bitter disappointment and I am very sorry for my loyal companions," wrote Scott.

After a few cheerless days camping, and trying to make the best of things, on the Wednesday, 17 January they grimly prepared for their wearisome return.

Scott determinedly kept his diary up to date. He wrote: "We have turned our backs now on the goal of our ambition and must face 800 miles of solid dragging – and goodbye to most of the daydreams."

The weather got steadily worse and the five men weaker. First Evans died on 17 February. Oates died on Saturday, 17 March of terrible frostbite in both hands and feet. He knew he was dying and becoming a burden to the others and one morning he stood up and said meaningfully: "I am just going outside and may be some time". They never saw him again.

The three surviving men knew there was little hope but bravely carried on for a while longer, Scott still valiantly writing his diary with painfully frozen fingers.

On 29 March, his last entry, he wrote: "I do not think we can hope for better things now. We are getting weaker and the end cannot be far. It seems a pity, but I do not think I can write more."

The dead heroes were found eight months later. Inside the stricken tent were the bodies of Captain Scott, Dr. Wilson and Lt. Bowers. The following January the *Terra Nova*, with the ship's cat Nigger still on board, returned to bring the survivors of the voyage home. A memorial was put up at Hut Point, their winter quarters, in memory of the brave men, inscribed with the immortal words from Alfred Lord Tennyson's Ulysses: "To strive, to seek, to find and not to yield."

The rest of the western world had been avidly following accounts of Scott's journey, and were shocked by the distressing circumstances of their deaths. They became national heroes. It seems almost flippant, in view of their tragic and courageous end, to mention in the same breath that the alluring little cat Nigger, after surviving three Antarctic voyages aboard the *Terra Nova*, was washed overboard during a storm as the ship approached the English Channel at the completion of the expedition. The weather was foul and, although the ship's boat was sent out to rescue him, it was to no avail. Sadly, he was swallowed up by the waves and died the death of the true sailor.

Poor little Nigger. Was it he who, in the end, inadvertently brought bad luck to the *Terra Nova*? Of course not! And yet! Strange things do happen at sea!

Mrs Chippy, ship's cat on board Sir Ernest Shackleton's *Endurance*, with steward Perce Blackborow.

(By kind permission of Scott Polar Research Institute)

Mrs Chippy, the Cat Who Sailed With Shackleton.

Mrs Chippy was not a female at all, but a hardy tomcat from Glasgow. In 1914 her owner Henry McNeish a carpenter and master shipwright, was recruited by Sir Ernest Shackleton for his third expedition to the Antarctic. The story goes that when McNeish joined the ship his cat followed him everywhere like a possessive wife and so the crew called it Mrs Chippy – wife of the 'chippy' as carpenters are inevitably nicknamed. By the time they found out the cat was male, the name had stuck.

Henry had been unsure about whether he should take his cat along with him. But as he was packing his tools he found the cat curled up in one of his toolboxes, as if hell-bent on coming with him. A cat, Henry reasoned, would be a great comfort on a ship as well as being useful.

Shackleton was more than pleased to include Mrs Chippy in his team of explorers. A good rodent controller was essential on a ship. He was an astute little cat, even-tempered, pleasant and with an affectionate nature. Tiger-striped with dark markings, a broad face and handsome whiskers, he was also a champion mouser and rat catcher – a skill no other member of the expedition could boast.

So, with Mrs Chippy established on board to guard the ship's valuable provisions, Shackleton's magnificent, three-masted ship, the *Endurance*, sailed from London's East India Docks on 1 August, 1914, calling on the way at Plymouth, Madeira, Tenerife and Buenos Aires, before heading for the remote South Georgia Island, where she remained for four weeks during research and scientific investigations and preparations.

There was a crew of 29 on the Imperial Trans-Antarctic Expedition, as it was officially called. At Buenos Aires, a young British lad, Perce Blackborow, stowed away on the ship. When he was found the ship had already set sail, so he was put to work. He proved such an asset, Shackleton allowed him to stay for the voyage and he was eventually promoted to steward. He became Mrs Chippy's second best mate, next to Henry McNeish.

On 13 September Mrs Chippy apparently changed his mind about the whole thing and jumped to what he thought was freedom, out of one of the cabin portholes. The officer on watch, Lt. Hubert T. Hudson, seeing him floundering in the water, niftily turned the ship round and picked him up, reckoning that he must have been in the icy water for at least 10 minutes. So that was one of his nine lives already used up. He was going to need all of the remaining eight to see him through the terrible ordeals he and the rest of the crew would have to face in the icy wastes, in the coming months.

On 5 December, 1914, the *Endurance* set sail southwards for a small whaling station, Grytviken. Mrs Chippy wasn't really interested in the ship's destination.

Nor was he impressed by the fact that the *Endurance* was a three-masted sailing ship, equipped with a powerful 350 horsepower steam engine fired by coal and, later, by seal blubber.

He was a very laid-back sort of cat, a real feline Sybarite who liked his comforts, took things in his stride and never got flummoxed in a crisis. As long as he was well fed and comfortable and close to his master, he was content. And his job, protecting the ship's valuable store of provisions from rats and mice, kept him occupied when he wasn't sleeping in the warmest, softest spot he could possibly find, or imperiously accepting titbits from the crew, who were all more than happy to indulge him in return for an appreciative purr.

He seemed instinctively aware that his job was vital to the success of the expedition, which depended on rations lasting out. A mouse nibbling into the odd flour bag or barrel of meat preserved in brine could spell disaster.

The biggest drawback to the whole project, from Mrs Chippy's point of view, was the unpleasantness of having to put up with the 69 sledging dogs on board. They were Canadian huskies, hungry for their freedom and maybe the odd cat as well. Although they were cooped up in kennels fore and aft, along the port and starboard sides of the main deck, it was a frightening situation for a cat to find himself in. True, they were restrained by stout chains. But Mrs Chippy didn't trust the frantic, bloodthirsty "wolfish wails" that they made in unison each evening. These poor animals received no exercise at all and they must have envied Mrs Chippy's freedom of movement. Who could blame them for exercising at least their lungs?

Far from being sympathetic to their plight, and grateful for his own pampered circumstances, at first he was uneasy that one might somehow escape and chase him round the decks in a mad, energetic frenzy. But as the voyage progressed, he became more confident. Flaunting the power he had to taunt them mercilessly, he pranced around on top of their kennels meowing, which sent them all into a state of near madness. Unperturbed by their wild wails, he'd sit there serenely cleaning his whiskers and sharpening his claws, arrogantly confident of his safety.

The main diet on board, for the crew as well as Mrs Chippy, was defrosted seal meat for breakfast, lunch and dinner. Though tedious, it was healthy and probably accounted for Mrs Chippy's sleek, shiny fur and robust good health. His own diet was, of course, supplemented by the odd rat and mouse - a luxury not enjoyed by other members of the crew, although Mrs Chippy dutifully presented dead rodents as gifts to his very best ship mates. These gifts of love were always cheerfully received but tactfully tossed overboard when his back was turned. Mrs Chippy also had milk and bread and butter from the plates of the men and the luxury of an occasional sardine, the best treat of all.

By the middle of January the *Endurance* was well on her way. She was enjoying fairly good sailing conditions after breaking through the main pack of ice. Mrs

Chippy spent his time strolling below decks, occasionally coming up to see how the men were getting on. Tension began to build up as it got colder and snow storms became frequent. But that wasn't the chief moan of the men. It was the ice, which limited the ship's movements, that put everyone in a fretting mood. Because there was a danger that the ice might damage the ship's rudder and engine propellers, Shackleton ordered the engines to stop and for the ship, when she could, to proceed by sail only.

On 18 January the *Endurance* entered loose "brash" ice, which was difficult to navigate. With what proved a fateful decision, the ship was made to lie to until a change in the wind direction opened up the ice again. Instead of opening, the ice closed round the ship, hemming it in. Heartbreakingly, she was only eighty miles from her destination, where she would have been assured of a safe harbour for the winter.

This was the beginning of their long ordeal. As the crew struggled to cut out a path in the ice for the *Endurance*, Mrs Chippy preferred to spend most of his free time curled up asleep, oblivious to his ice-numbed shipmates' futile attempts to free the ship. His duties, though, were not neglected and he regularly prowled around protecting the ship's precious stores from mice, who also preferred to stay below where it was warm.

One night a crack in the ice a quarter of a mile wide and a mile long was spotted some fifty yards ahead of the ship. By combining the steam power of the engine and sail, there was the hope that the ship could be forced into the open water through this narrow lane. But there was no beating the ice. The channel closed in again as the valiant ship was trying to battle her way through.

Eventually bored with all the activity, on 5 February Mrs Chippy decided the best thing to do in this icy cold weather was to hibernate. So he curled up somewhere warm and cosy and went to sleep. The crew searched the ship for him, fearing he had ventured onto the ice and frozen to death. To their relief, he nonchalantly rejoined them on 10 February, unaware of the fuss he'd caused. Everyone was pleased to see the warm, friendly cat and made a great fuss of him. As if the crew hadn't enough to worry about! They were now facing the dismal prospect of spending the entire winter in the pitch black of one continuous Polar night which normally lasted six months.

The ship was drifting dangerously northward in the icepack, which meant that the crew were not in control. There was a general feeling of isolation, of being cut off from civilisation. Even the seals and the birds were disappearing to warmer climes, leaving the men with a lonely sense of being abandoned even by nature. Food had to be strictly rationed, supervised by Thomas Orde-Lees, the store keeper, commonly referred to as Peggy.

On 26 February the *Endurance* officially became a weather station rather than an active ship. Resigned to being trapped there for a while, Shackleton decided that the dogs should be housed in kennels skilfully constructed from ice slabs, in

The ghostly white, ice encrusted _Endurance_
Photo by Frank Hurley

the manner of igloos, and aptly named dogloos. They were placed on the ice floe alongside the ship. At minus 2 degrees Fahrenheit, it was lucky the dogs each had a thick coat of fur to keep them warm. Mrs Chippy approved of all this and watched with satisfaction as a length of wire was tightly stretched between two posts and each dog was securely chained to the wire in a manner which enabled him to run short distances and back.

Now in the grip of the harsh Antarctic winter, the crew was restless with very little to amuse them, and painfully aware that, while they were there doing so little, a war was going on in Europe with thousands of lives being lost.

At least they were all fit and healthy. Inside the ship it was warm and there was enough food as long as it was strictly rationed. The staple food now was Pemmican, a mixture of dried ground meat mixed with fat. Pemmican, water and broken biscuits melted to the consistency of soup was called hoosh. The great enemy, apart from the ice, was boredom. But on the whole the ship's company was in good spirits.

The dogs themselves were not in such good health, because of a poor diet and lack of exercise, and were slowly diminishing in numbers. They had regular "sledging" practice, being harnessed to empty sledges careering and slipping over the ice to acclimatise themselves to what they would have to endure eventually. But there were now only fifty dogs, the rest having died from stomach ailments and worms – and general neglect. They did not rate the same sort of esteem as Mrs Chippy. Even Shackleton, who was so eager to "lead from the front" to demonstrate to his men that he was prepared to do any job they did, didn't show enough respect or interest in the dogs to take part in their welfare and training. He was not, it seemed, a "doggy" man.

One bone of contention was whether it was right to eat penguins. One crew member, Thomas McLeod, swore that penguins were the souls of dead sailors. Nonetheless, they were a valuable source of food and eaten dutifully by the rest of the crew. But even Mrs Chippy drew the line at penguin – especially when the meat was old, black and ropy. The dogs, of course, had no choice.

There was one frightening incident, at least from Mrs Chippy's point of view, when the Bosun, John Vincent, who was partial to dogs, accused Mrs Chippy of hanging round the dogloos provoking the already frustrated huskies unnecessarily. It was absolutely true, of course, but generally considered fair game. He picked Mrs Chippy up very roughly by the scruff of his neck and threatened to throw him to the dogs. Blackborow intervened and Mrs Chippy was delivered from an unpleasant fate. A formal complaint was lodged against Vincent and, as a result, he was demoted - to the delight of the rest of the crew who objected to his overbearing manner.

On 10 July, along with other members of the crew, Mrs Chippy was weighed. The good food and constant cosy naps he was enjoying below decks aboard the *Endurance* was patently visible. At nine pounds and 10 ounces, he was much heavier and much fatter than when they had first set sail. All other members of the crew had lost weight and were painfully thin.

On 14 July there was a howling blizzard, which lasted for several days with gales reaching a force of 60 or 70 miles an hour, setting the stricken ship trembling in the packed ice. The blizzard broke the solid pack of ice into many floes, which moved independently of each other, creating pressure capable of crushing the ship. The crew risked great danger if they stayed on board. Also, their precious stockpile of food on the ice, essential for their survival, was threatened.

A welcome diversion on 26 July was watching the top of the sun rise above the horizon. It only stayed for a minute or two, but the whole company who had assembled on the deck to watch, cheered. The spectacle signalled higher temperatures and the eventual breaking up of the ice.

Mrs Chippy frequently got ice on his paws, which he didn't enjoy and this was why he spent so much time below deck. Unlike the rest of the men, he washed fastidiously and constantly, grooming his fur and sharpening his claws on the main mast.

The ice showed signs of breaking up until on 10 October when it was warm and sunny and the crew gleefully stripped off their jackets and dispensed with their hats, enjoying a brief spell in the sun's warm rays. Four days later, the *Endurance* broke free from the ice and for the first time in nearly nine months floated clear on the open water – a situation which was potentially dangerous but at least lent hope for an early breakout. This significant change went unnoticed by Mrs Chippy, who preferred to stay below, being rather unsettled by all the noise and activity.

The next few days were fearful. The full horror of the danger that threatened them became patently obvious. The men didn't delude themselves about the possible fate that faced them, but their faith in Shackleton remained undiminished. He told them he was confident they would all survive. He took on a regular sea-watch schedule himself, four hours on deck and four hours below, watching for a break in the ice. The crew felt the thuds and shocks as distant floes drove heavily against those nearby. Mysterious grinding and scraping noises rose inside and outside the ship caused by large floes snapping as a result of their impact with the ship.

Yet Mrs Chippy slumbered on. One crew member commented admiringly fifteen years later: "Mrs Chippy's almost total disregard for the diabolical forces at work upon the ship was more than remarkable – it was inspirational. Such perfect courage is, alas, not to be found in our modern age."

There was a period of concern when the *Endurance* heeled at thirty-degrees to port, caused by the pressure of a floe on the starboard bilge and the collapse of the floe on which the port side was resting. But when the floes opened, thankfully the ship was righted.

On 19 October the boiler fires, which had not been lit since the ship had been trapped in ice nine months earlier, were lit.once more. Shackleton ordered all loose timber to be cut up to fuel the fires, so as to get up steam.

While the movement and break-up of the ice presented real danger to the ship, it also gave rise to the hope of an opportunity to steam through to freedom. The boilers were kept stoked in readiness to escape should a lane appear in the shifting ice.

On 24 October the men worked through the night at pumps trying to stem a dangerous leak that had sprung when the ship's stern had been savagely torn by the raging pressure of ice. Mrs Chippy's mate, McNeish, laboured in ice-cold water to build a cofferdam astern of the engines in an attempt to check the flood of water.

By 27 October great spikes of ice were forcing their way through the ship's sides. By degrees her prow was getting more deeply buried. It was a heartbreaking sight to see the proud brave ship, that had been home for so long to the crew, broken up in the relentless sweep of a thousand miles of packed ice.

The shipwrecked crew now camped in tents on the ice while Shackleton planned the next stage. They had to turn out of their tents three times in the course of their first night on ice, due to cracking of the floe on which they were camped. Mrs Chippy spent most of this time warming McNeish's sleeping bag - generously volunteering, whenever he also ventured into it, to cover his icy feet with his cosy furry body. As a result of Mrs Chippy spending so much time there, other members of the expedition jokingly complained that McNeish's bag was always nice and warm, unlike their own.

Shackleton had decided the best plan was to head for the nearest land, Paulet Island, some 346 miles away. His crew affectionately called him "The Boss". He was sometimes a stern master but they trusted him unquestioningly, admiring him for the hero he was. They would have loyally followed him anywhere, if he'd asked them. He assembled his men outside on the ice and addressed them with fortitude and courage.

"If you keep your spirits up and give me your loyalty, we'll all get home," he promised them.

He emphasised that to achieve this, the men must ruthlessly strip themselves of possessions to the barest minimum.

"The value of everything you carry must be weighed against your survival," he stressed firmly. "Anything that cannot pull its weight or is not useful to this Expedition, must be put down."

As an example, Shackleton threw some gold coins into the snow. Then he held up his precious Bible. It had been presented to him by Queen Alexandra, with a handwritten inscription on the flyleaf. It had sustained him during the nine months of hardship. Now he tore out a few pages and laid the Bible dramatically on the snow beside the coins. The pages he retained contained the 23rd Psalm and a verse from the Book of Job.

Out of whose womb came the ice?
And the hoary frost of Heaven, who hath gendered it?
The waters are hid as with a stone,
And the face of the deep is frozen.

As Shackleton spoke, the crew were stood stunned, deeply stirred by his words. There could be no doubting his meaning. Mrs. Chippy could be of little use a rat catcher in the grim journey that lay ahead of them. Those of the crew who were especially fond of Mrs Chippy, went quiet. Robert Clark, the biologist, picked the cat up and stroked him affectionately. One by one the men came up to him and gave him a tickle under the chin, a stroke or a meaningful caress. Mrs Chippy had been a great solace to them all.

Mrs Chippy accepted these displays of affection graciously, as his natural due. He was, after all, well used to being made a fuss of. One story goes that he was taken into McNeish's tent, where his master sat silently fondling him until Perce Blackborow came in with a rare treat in those hard times – a bowl of specially prepared sardines laced with something toxic.

Purring with delight, Mrs Chippy ate delicately, lingering over every mouthful with relish. A little while later Blackborow returned to see how he was getting on and picked him up and held him tightly, telling him how glad he was that Mrs Chippy had shipped along with them aboard the *Endurance*. Then, moist-eyed, he left.

Having finished his meal, Mrs Chippy stretched out luxuriously on McNeish's lap and yawned, ready now for his last long sleep. Outside it was cold, here it was warm and comfortable and Mrs Chippy didn't have a care in the world. Sleeping, after all, was his favourite pastime.

A conflicting report about poor Mrs Chippy's untimely end, which the author prefers not to dwell upon, is that Shackleton ordered McNeish to have his cat shot. Whichever is true, there is little doubt that, heartbroken by the loss of his beloved cat, McNeish harboured a festering resentment towards Shackleton and, during the long hard months that followed, became more and more difficult for Shackleton to control.

McNeish was allowed little time to mourn his beloved cat. As unrelenting as ever, Shackleton put him to work immediately on the three lifeboats, which had been lowered from the *Endurance* on to the ice floe. He was farsighted enough to know that the lives of all his men would depend on these three small boats, and was not prepared to allow the mere loss of a cat to interfere with the project.

First McNeish was told to build up the sides of the largest boat, a sturdy whaler, to increase her carrying capacity and make her more seaworthy. They later officially named her the *James Caird*, after the Scot who helped finance the expedition. The other two, both cutters, were named *Dudley Docker* and *Stancomb Wills*.

McNeish had been chosen to take part in the expedition because of his skills, his powers of endurance, his loyalty and his big, strong stature. Shackleton knew he wouldn't let him down despite the tension between them. Regardless of the harsh conditions, the newly fortified boats were placed on sledges and hauled through the ice and snow by men and dogs. It was exhausting work and after seven days they gave up and, for over two difficult months, they camped on the ice, waiting for summer. Their rations dwindled alarmingly, supplemented only by penguins and seals, which they shot.

They endured raging blizzards and as the ice dispersed, massive icebergs threatened to crash into their camp. On 9 April, after months of drifting on unstable ice, they decided to risk launching their makeshift boats. Led by the *James Caird*, they drifted in them for seven days before reaching Elephant Island, where they pulled the boats up on to the icy beach and set up camp yet again.

Food began to run out. Shackleton decided he had no option but to take one of the boats through the treacherous waters to seek help, and chose the *James Caird* as the most seaworthy. His aim was to reach South Georgia.

On 24 April 1916 the *James Caird* was again launched into the freezing waters. Shackleton was by now obsessively committed to getting all his men to safety. He wisely decided to take with him the most intrepid of his men - Frank Wild, full of energy and initiative; Frank Worsley, the Master of *Endurance*, exceptionally tough and a first rate navigator; Tom Crean, Irish and as strong as an ox; and Tim McCarthy, also Irish and an incurable optimist. Also included were Henry McNeish not just for his carpentry skills, but because he was now showing signs of becoming a troublemaker, and Bosun John Vincent, Mrs Chippy's sworn enemy, a difficult, aggressive man.

For 17 arduous days the Antarctic Ocean lived up to its evil reputation. The men endured immeasurable strife on those heaving, icy waters. Miraculously they finally reached South Georgia and hauled the boat onto the beach and set up camp at King Haakon's Bay on the south west of the island. But the likelihood of rescuing not only themselves but the men left behind on Elephant Island, seemed even more remote. To reach civilisation, they needed to cross the snowfields and mountains of South Georgia, to Stromness, on the north west coast where the whaling station base was. They were painfully ill-equipped in their Lapp reindeer boots – fine for ploughing through snow and ice but useless for climbing ruthless mountains. Shackleton and McNeish put aside their differences and together came up with the brilliant idea of taking brass screws out of the *James Caird* and fixing them into the soles of their snow-boots, to give them extra grip.

Shackleton, of course, took on the responsibility of this final ordeal, taking with him Frank Worsley. The two covered 40 miles in 36 hours. On May 20 they arrived at Stromness, welcomed by the astonished whaling station manager. Shackleton was in no mood to celebrate. He was determined to waste no time in getting his men back. He immediately sent the Norwegian steam trawler *Samson*, with Frank Worsley on board, back round the island to where they had left McNeish, Vincent and McCarthy, to rescue the men and bring back the *James Caird*. Meanwhile Shackleton set sail in the *Southern Sky* to rescue the twenty-two men left on Elephant Island.

The trip was unsuccessful. Undeterred he set sail in the Uruguayan trawler *Instituto da Pesca*, which failed to penetrate ice. By now, most men would have given them up for dead. But, undaunted, Shackleton tried a third time, in the schooner *Emma*, to no avail. Still he wasn't prepared to abandon hope. He again set sail in the steam trawler *Yelcho*. This time, on August 30, they penetrated the ice. All 22 castaways were hauled aboard, in comparatively good health and with morale still high.

And so, after three-and-a-half months of the most incredibly severe hardship, Shackleton kept his promise and rescued every single one of his men. Not a single life had been lost – except just the one hardy little feline soul!

Hauling the James Caird over the ice
Picture by kind permission of Scott Polar Research Institute

Lummo & Peter, of the *Penola*, on a Cheapy Expedition to the Antarctic

Two ship's cats sailed on the 130 ton *Penola*, a 103ft, three-masted schooner with auxiliary engines, which took a team of highly proficient scientists and ship's crew to the Antarctic for the 1934-37 British Graham Land expedition. The expedition was planned on a very low budget of only £20,000 (maybe £500,000 today) which had to include not only the cost of the ship and fitting it out for the Antarctic, but also an aeroplane and the *Stella*, a back-up sailing boat.

Lummo was a discerning and inquisitive white cat with black ears and crown, which rather resembled a warm black pixie hat above his white face. His tail and part of his hindquarters were also black. Lummo was a gift to the ship's Captain R.E.D.Ryder, VC, RN, from the Dean of the Cathedral at Port Stanley, in the Falkland Islands, when the ship moored there while loading up provisions for the voyage. There was already another ship's cat on board, a tabby called Peter but there was no animosity between them and the two cats seemed happy to share the task of keeping the ship free of rodents.

Lead by an Australian, John Rymill, the entire expedition consisted of only 16 men, all unpaid or else serving naval men. The main intention was to explore the passage through the Stefansson Strait to the Weddell Sea as an alternative to the eastern approach to the Antarctic which had proved so disastrous for Sir Ernest Shackleton over twenty years previously. It was also planned to carry out extensive scientific research.

This expedition had the advantage over previous expeditions in that they had not only a highly disciplined and competent scientific team, but also radio communication and the aeroplane, a De Havilland Fox Moth, capable of operating with skis or floats and used extensively for reconnaissance, aerial surveying and depot laying.

Perhaps the main drawback from the cats' point of view were the sledging dogs. At one time there were 65 on board. Fortunately for the cats, the dogs were unloaded at the expedition's first main base in the Argentine Islands. From then on Lummo and Peter had the *Penola* to themselves, except for the Captain and the ship's crew. Peter was a bit sickly and didn't care for the severe cold anyway and was relieved not to have to step on to the snow. Lummo didn't mind it so much and was even prepared to curl up in the soft white stuff, managing to give the impression he was lying on an extremely snug and comfortable cushion.

The expedition was so well organised and efficient that, compared to those ill-fated and highly eventful ones undertaken by Robert Falcon Scott and Sir Ernest Shackleton, nothing exciting or disastrous happened and as a result the expedition is today not widely remembered by the general public. In fact the team achieved most of what they set out to do and the voyage was considered highly successful.

Peter died during that first winter of 1934 but Lummo survived the expedition to the end and returned to England to live with the family of a member of the crew, at Woking, in Surrey. He survived to a reasonable old age, dying during World War II.

Lummo of the *Penola*, snuggled up in the snow
(1934-37 British Graham Land Expedition)

The Cat that Nearly Froze to Death in an Arctic Winter

In June 1994, an American adventurer, Alvah Simon and his New Zealander wife, Diana, set sail from Camden, Maine in their 36-foot steel-hulled cutter, the *Roger Henry*, intent on spending an entire Arctic winter embedded in the ice as far from civilisation as possible. Their quest was to test their powers of endurance and experience adventure of the rawest and harshest kind.

On the way they stopped at Halifax, Nova Scotia, to pick up supplies and, in the local flea market, they found two kittens for sale. One was placid and adorable, the other a wild little spitfire that scratched and hissed. They recognised this plucky little kitten as a natural fellow survivor and recruited her to spend the Arctic winter on the *Roger Henry* with them. Appropriately, they called her Halifax.

The intention was that Halifax could double up as a bed warmer and, with her keen feline senses, a bear detector. In fact she became their companion, their child and a vital member of their crew, braving months of total darkness, freezing cold temperatures and risking danger from bears, foxes and other predators.

As soon as they got her on the *Roger Henry* however, they began to question their own wisdom. She immediately tore up their charts and peed on their bunks, generally delighting in deliberately tormenting them. Nevertheless, they clung to the hope that she would calm down as the voyage progressed.

As they sailed up the coast to Greenland, at each port Halifax tried to escape onto the dock. Dog packs roamed freely, threatening to savage her, but she seemed to enjoy teasing them mercilessly before retiring to the safety of the *Roger Henry*.

Her first taste of what lay in store came at Melville Bay, where they anchored for the night and next day rowed to shore, with Halifax sitting on the bow poised ready to jump the moment they reach the black stone beach. Her leap proved ill timed and she ended up in the icy water and was fished out shivering with cold and shock.

Heading steadily north towards Quannaaq, they encountered foul weather and some dangerous icebergs. On one occasion, after Diana and Alvah had struggled to survive a particular vicious storm that raged for three days, Halifax decided to make a run for freedom. Exhausted but all set to sail, they saw her skipping happily over the ice, teasing them to chase her. Halifax was beginning to appreciate the power she had over these two over-indulgent sailors who clearly now doted on her.

Their first encounter with a bear came when one weighing about a thousand pounds started swimming round the boat and then climbed aboard intent, it seemed, on joining the crew. They managed to chase the bear back into the water and an amused Alvah noted wryly in his logbook: "Halifax, our bear detector, slept through the entire episode".

Alvah Simon with his faithful cat Halifax close at his heels, inspects their boat, the *Roger Henry*, as the ice melts and slowly frees her from its grip.

Snapped by Diana, Halifax surveys the icy wastes from the top of Alvah's thick fur hood.

Halifax (tucked in the right-hand corner of the shelf) curls up for a contented snooze while Alvah settles for a good read in the cosy cabin of the *Roger Henry*

By the end of September the *Roger Henry* was well and truly embedded in the ice in Tay Bay, 100 miles from the nearest settlement and surrounded by breathtaking views of mountains and glaciers. They prepared to settle in for the winter. They had plenty of provisions and fuel, the boat was well insulated and they had each other and they braced themselves excitedly for their harsh adventure in the icy white wilds. Their intention was to simulate, as closely as possible, life as experienced by native Eskimos. The word Eskimo means "eater of raw meat". In the Arctic they prefer to be called Inuits, which simply means the people.

On her birthday, 6 October, a message for Diana came over the radio, from her father in New Zealand. Apart from wanting to wish her a happy birthday, he said the doctors had just told him he had terminal cancer and had given him three months to live. Stunned by the news, all their grand plans paled in comparison. They discussed the implications. Both accepted that Diana had to get to him somehow. The crucial question was, should Alvah return with her? If he did, it meant abandoning their home to the mercy of the icebergs and possible pillagers. They would also have to leave Halifax. After much soul searching Alvah was determined he would stay, no matter how foolish and dangerous. Diana tearfully agreed, and within weeks an aeroplane arrived to pick her up, before the darkness of winter finally descended.

Alvah and Halifax watched the plane rise into the snow clouds and turn, until it was just a speck on the vast Arctic sky and they were alone. Alvah picked up Halifax and held her close. As well as being bed warmer and bear detector, Halifax had now replaced his wife as First Mate on the *Roger Henry*. "You've been promoted," he told her heavy-heartedly.

As they slowly adjusted to the strangeness of being without Diana, word got round the Inuits that they were there preparing to spend the harsh winter with only each other for company. It was foolhardy. No white man had ever done it and survived. There were bears to contend with and, being in total blackness for four months, he was bound to lose his mind.

Three Canadian Coast Guards turned up in a red helicopter and gave him one last chance to admit defeat. They brought him extra provisions and fuel, but what they wanted was for him to return with them to civilisation before the bad weather set in. Alvah refused. He was scared, he was lonely but he was adamant. This is what he had come for. To live like the Eskimo people. And anyway, he told them, he **had** to stay to defend his home. And he had Halifax for company. So they shook their heads and left them to their fate.

Dreadful nightmares plagued him almost immediately and he soon lost the ability to tell the difference between reality and his subconscious. He began by having delusions, imagining that his beautiful wife was being unfaithful to him. One night he dreamt that Diana was on his back pummeling him, scratching him, full of hatred because of his jealousy. He woke up to find it was only Halifax who, frightened by

Alvah's frantic thrashing, was struggling to get out of the sleeping bag they shared.

In a desperate attempt to recover his wits, he stomped off on a long hike across the bay, with Halifax close at his heels. Disregarding the danger of bears, he lay down on the snow, with Halifax clawing his chest trying to warm her frozen paws. They lay there for half an hour. Above them a huge lone raven soared, convinced they were almost dead and would soon make a tasty dinner. Sensing his intention, Halifax climbed fearfully into Alvah's parka hood for protection.

Alvah laughed dementedly at the raven and then turned to Halifax, to warn him that he might be going mad. When the darkness eventually came, it would be even more difficult for him to control his mind.

To counteract the risk of madness, he tells Halifax he is going to talk to him constantly. A man who talked to himself was likely to be locked up. But no one thought it odd to talk to a cat. Up here with no one to see him, it might even be OK to talk to himself. The real danger, he reasoned, was when he started talking **with** himself, a sure sign he had developed a split personality.

His plan was to keep clean and orderly, bathing regularly, airing their bedding, keeping the equipment, the boat and the galley in good order and making a nice environment for the two of them. Halifax was to be his companion, his sounding board, and his counsellor.

Halifax poked her face out her hiding place in his warm furry hood, as if understanding every word. "We're going to eat like bears, keep a keen interest in food and make it good and hot and varied. No more eating out of a can. You get Di's share of chocolate. I get her share of the whiskey. We're going to explore every foot of our new environment until it feels like home. This is not an emergency. This is an opportunity. Our boat is not a life raft. We do not need rescue. We are talking about survival and all we need for that is to be happy, because happy people are lucky people. And frankly, Halifax, we'll need some luck to live through this."

Feeling better, both physically and mentally, the two comrades hiked back to the boat, Halifax following Alvah like a faithful dog. At regular intervals she clawed her way up his back to thaw her paws. Then she'd leap down suddenly, hoping he would chase her, running ahead to hide in the snow and pouncing on him playfully as he passed. She loved their hikes. She was having fun. He reflected he had a lot to learn from her.

A man who introduced himself as Peter Semotiuk made radio contact with him, with a message from Diana to say she had arrived home and she was concerned about his safety. Arrangements were made to make contact two or three times a week.

Partly relieved at the news from Diana, yet strangely resentful at having his solitude interrupted by a total stranger, he slid into his sleeping bag with Halifax and read about another adventurer's experiences in this very region. He turned a page and his eyes lighted on a picture of a great friendly bear of a man. The caption informed him that it was Peter Semotiuk. He felt relieved to be able to put a face to the deep voice that was to be his lifeline.

They settled down to a routine as they waited for the long night to arrive. Sometimes, when he went on long hikes he felt would be too much for Halifax, he left her behind locked up below to stop her from following. He would go off in the sled, hearing the kitten whining and scratching, knowing she would be showing her resentment by peeing on his pillow or clawing at the woodwork.

These treks with only himself for company often drove him to the very edge of craziness. When Halifax was with him and he was able to share his thoughts with her, he felt he had less chance of losing his mind. One of his favourite treks, well within Halifax's capabilities, was to climb to what he called his Thinking Rock, overlooking the bay. The two of them would sit there for hours, at peace with the world and totally attuned to each other. Sometimes they were followed by the ever-hopeful raven who always made Halifax nervous. She knew she had to stay close to Alvah for protection whenever it hovered ominously above them.

Often they sat in the cabin in the dark for several days, to save fuel. Outside the temperature was -35 degrees below zero (Celsius). By comparison, inside was almost cosy. Halifax huddled deep in the sleeping bag, emerging only for sounds of her frozen milk being thawed out. Since Alvah slept in heavy hat, gloves and thick clothing inside the tightly tapered sleeping bag, space was at a premium. The two of them often had territorial disputes and Halifax usually won for she was better equipped to dig in with her sharp claws.

She became alarmingly thin. Alvah and Diana had expected her to eat what they ate and had brought with them only a little tinned cat food. But she proved more fastidious than they'd expected, and would not touch the smoked meats. Fearing she might waste away and die, he devised a unique way of making fresh bread which he soaked in butter and oily tuna. She settled down to her meal and Alvah was rewarded by the sound of a grateful purr. He breathed a sigh of relief. To lose Halifax would have been unbearable. Peter, his new radio friend, was as interested in Halifax almost as much as in Alvah. He had a cat of his own and was passionate about them. In their conversations over the radio, he always asked about Halifax.

On Thanksgiving Day they prepared a sumptuous feast. With Halifax watching critically as she hung onto his fur collar, he mashed canned turkey with dried vegetables and made a meat loaf shaped like a bird artistically surrounded with mashed potatoes covered in gravy and cranberries. He even baked a pumpkin tart and poured his last can of cream over it. Halifax ate her meal and then curled up contentedly on his chest, purring. Some of their precious battery power was sacrificed to play music on the cassette player. Finally, he tidied up, blew out the candle and crawled into the sleeping bag with Halifax, well satisfied with his day.

Alvah slept in the cave-like starboard aft cabin. The chore of constantly climbing in and out of the berth from the bed's head was offset by the cabin's opening porthole, which allowed him to let Halifax out to relieve herself, without getting up himself. In theory this was a considerable saving of precious heat because, if he did have to get up, it took a long time to reheat his sleeping bag. Halifax soon learnt that if she knocked down the hinged upper board beneath the main hatch, hypercold air would fill the boat. Alvah's nose would freeze and the cold air would choke his lungs so that, no matter how reluctant, he would have to reach out to close it.

He awoke one day and tried to roll over but felt only a dead tug. His legs were paralysed with cold. He tried to stay calm and soon worked out what must have happened. The cabin walls were glazed with half a foot of ice and he had fallen asleep with the lantern burning. In this confined space, the heat melted the ice, and consequently water had run down the cabin walls onto the berth, which had a waterproof sheet on the mattress. The water had flowed to the low spot beneath him. When the lantern went out, the cabin cooled and the water froze, trapping his legs in much the same way as the *Roger Henry* was embedded in the ice outside.

Aware he was in a life-threatening situation, he took all his clothes off and stood in the cabin stark naked. In the icy air, even his goose-pimples began freezing up as he crawled into insulated overalls. Then he put on boots, facemask, gloves and his parka. He had taken the wise precaution of keeping food stashed in the pockets of his coat, in case of an emergency such as this. Chewing at a piece of fatty sausage, he went for a long walk, knowing that the best way to get warm was exercise. With his feet still frozen, each step was unbelievably painful, but eventually the warmth returned. After some hours, he returned to the boat, where Halifax was waiting anxiously for him.

He changed his sleeping arrangements, by shutting off the aft cabin completely and restricting himself to the main cabin for sleeping, eating, cooking and reading. He made soup and beef stew in large quantities and stacked them outside to freeze so that, should he find himself too ill or without energy to cook, all he would have to do was hack off a slice of soup or stew and heat it up.

By now he had learnt how to sit for hours piercing the darkness with his ears. There was constant danger from bears and his great fear was of one finding its way below. Sometimes he heard the sound of a bear's feet prowling the deck and considered throwing Halifax out there into the dark, to test her keener senses. "But as our friendship and partnership grew, I could not bring myself to do that. Out here, my life has no more inherent value than hers," he wrote in his log book.

In this perpetual darkness he suffered terrible illusions. He was often not sure whether he was dreaming or if he was just going crazy or even if what he had dreamt had really happened. Halifax's behaviour was altering too. She whined and wailed a lot and appeared broody and petulant. Then they began to quarrel. She would wait for him to look at her and then deliberately destroy something, knowing it would rile him. Because he would often sit for hours oblivious of her, like any female she preferred to risk his wrath rather than be ignored. And when he did get angry, he admitted with shame that his temper was terrible and uncontrollable. One day he lunged at her in a blind fury. It was as though he was watching someone else in action, for he loved all animals and did not consider himself a cruel man. For a few days they were like husband and wife after a tiff. Every time he tried to pet her she rejected him, punishing him by hissing and scratching.

The next celebration was Christmas Day. For this he cooked a dubious dish of his own invention, which he called Bedouin beef, served over a plate of couscous. He gave Halifax a whole tin of tuna as a Christmas treat, which she slurped up greedily till not a drop of oil was left in the tin. He opened a small parcel from Diana containing his favourite Fig Newton's. Then the two lay in the warmth of the sleeping bag listening to the wind howling outside and the boat shuddering in the ice. As Halifax purred away on his chest, he felt content. Cats, he reflected, had that magic ability to create a sense of warmth and security, conjuring up images of home, cosy fires and family.

As he lay there reflecting about Christmas and its true meaning, Halifax suddenly decided she wanted to party. She escaped from the sleeping bag and started scratching the woodwork in order to provoke him into play. She was an intelligent animal, as proved by the way she often unscrewed the large lid on the water barrel. Her little paws would push the cap counterclockwise until it was loose and she was able to shove the lid to the floor so that she could stick her head down into the barrel for a quick slurp.

Too lazy to get up, he thought that since she was so smart she might understand the intonations of a little poem he had just composed for her in his head. He recited it aloud.

> "Halifax, my cat, was furry and fat,
> Oh, a finer companion could not be.
> I was trapped in the Arctic,
> My life was so stark it
> Had no other warm company.
> And so side by side,
> The dark months we did bide,
> Huddled as bleak blizzards blew.
> And when the food ran out,
> At eight pounds thereabout,
> She made a fine and filling meat stew."

The words stopped Halifax in her tracks. As if understanding every word, he wrote that she stared at him disdainfully, her lips curled in contempt.

A visit from an Arctic fox, who hung around for days, upset Halifax and bewitched Alvah. He regarded the visit as his Christmas present. The fox was pure white and fluffy, with emerald green eyes that stared directly into his with intense inquisitiveness.

Naturally Halifax objected to his presence and resented the fact that Alvah did nothing to protect her. Every time she went outside to do her business the fox was there, clearly with evil intent. Then Alvah read that there was a high incidence of rabies in Arctic foxes and it occurred to him that if Halifax **was** attacked, even if only slightly, she might become infected and pass it on to him. He saw himself foaming at the mouth and dying in agony. Reluctantly he chased his handsome Christmas present away, shooting to scare rather than to kill.

They had another party on New Year's Eve. This time Alvah baked a pizza, rashly turning on the lights and the stereo and opening a bottle of brandy, which made him very merry. Like a naughty little boy, he chased Halifax round the cabin, teasing her with a feather and letting her tear up one of his charts. She loved careering off the walls and whirling about in a mock battle. Finally they both fell asleep, Halifax under his knees and purring loudly.

A few days later he woke up to total darkness as usual, but with a terrible migraine behind his eyes. He flipped on a small light to search for a painkiller, but it didn't seem to be working. With his hand he detected the warmth of the bulb and realised he'd gone blind. He felt nauseous and giddy but forced himself to get up and get on with his chores, doing everything by feel. His sense of smell, hearing and touch amplified as he felt his way round the cabin. Eventually, exhausted and sick, he got back into his bag and went to sleep.

Halifax woke him up two days later, by persistently pushing her paws into his face. She wanted her milk and sensed that there was something wrong. For a moment he forgot about his problem, then remembered and reached for the flash light, passing the beam before his eyes. It hurt, but he was relieved to find he could see.

As usual he decided the best cure was a long hike. He was beginning to have delusions again and needed to eradicate the frightening thoughts whirling about in his head. It was 45°C below freezing, but nonetheless he kitted himself up and set out through the moonlight with Halifax on his heels.

They had hiked before at these temperatures and she always loved it. If she got too cold or too tired she'd jump up onto his shoulder and crawl into his hood. But this time she lagged behind, whining. Anxious to keep moving, he was irritated by her slowness. "Come on Puss, don't be such a wimp," he urged as he hiked on, sure she would follow. But she didn't. She sat in his tracks and whined again. Angrily he stomped off up the hill to Thinking Rock to clear his mind. He knew she hated to be too far from him and if he did outpace her she normally turned back to the boat. It failed to signify that they were well past the point of return. Halfway up the hill he looked back and he saw her still sitting as if frozen in the dim moonlight, a little black speck in the snow.

Suddenly frightened for her, he ran back down the hill, where she sat stiffly staring at him and half-frozen to death. As he picked her up and pressed her too hard into his coat, he felt a sickening crack as her frozen right ear snapped in two. He looked and saw it was hanging pitifully down her cheek. My God, what have I done, he asked himself remorsefully as he ran all the way back to the boat, keeping her close to his warm body.

Once below deck, he placed her in the sleeping bag, lit the heater and tried to get her to drink some warm milk. But she lay deathly still. He pulled her ear back, and she felt nothing. Her body thawed slowly but as the warmth returned, the pain started and she howled in agony. His heart ached with guilt and he cursed himself for being so stupid. He should have spotted the signs. The icy wind had freeze-dried her ears. He should have remembered that cats don't belong in the Arctic because they can't drop their ears, like dogs.

"You tried to tell me and I wouldn't listen," he agonised as he hugged her in the sleeping bag, begging her to survive. He promised that, if she did, he would care for her for the rest of her life. He tearfully asked her to forgive him for his cruelty.

Her pain grew worse. Her poor ears puffed up and wept and then scabbed over. The broken ear began to grow back together again, but with a permanent droop. She went crazy when the itching started, and tried to scratch her ears off. Alvah had to hold both her paws as they slept. Slowly she recovered, but her jet black ears turned a permanent, snowy white, acting as a constant reminder to him of his act of stupidity.

In early February the sun came back, very weakly at first but he was able to entertain Halifax by locking his thumbs and spreading his fingers to cause a shadow resembling a raven to fly above her head. Totally taken in, she crouched in a sunken footprint to avoid it and he laughed delightedly.

In March he had visitors, two heavily fur-clad Inuits on a snowmobile. They had privileged government permits to allow them to hunt bears and, knowing he was there, had called in with fresh meat and a letter from Diana to say her father had died and she was on her way home to him from New Zealand. Her journey would take several weeks. The hard part would be finding transport across the icy wastes to the *Roger Henry* .

Concerned for the first time since she left about his appearance, he looked in a mirror and was horrified to see a hairy, unshaven monster staring back at him He washed and shaved and then attempted to clean up the boat.

Excited as he was at the thought of seeing her again, part of him strangely resented her intrusion into their lonely life. To relieve the tension of waiting, he and Halifax went hiking, content in each other's company. As was her habit, Halifax would constantly leap onto his shoulder to warm her paws and hitch a ride when she was tired. Then something like a feather or fox track would lure her down to explore.

One day he noticed Halifax flick her head sideways, her eyes fixed eagerly into the distance as if she could hear something approaching. Alvah couldn't hear a thing. All that was visible to him were miles of ice and snow. Following Halifax's gaze with his binoculars, he spotted a black speck coming towards them and he knew for sure it was the snowmobile bringing his wife home to him.

When the vehicle arrived out stepped three people. Diana was dressed from head to toe in traditional furs she had borrowed from a generous Inuit native and at first he feared he had been mistaken. Then she pulled back her hood and they fell into each other's arms. She had brought a huge can of diesel and 35-lbs of cat food for Halifax.

The still intense cold, after the warmth of New Zealand, was a shock to Diana's system and for two weeks she went into hibernation. Halifax proved himself to be fickle, transferring his affections to her and preferring her sleeping bag to Alvah's. Now a family of three again, they were soon able to enjoy what they had come there to experience together - the peace, the silence, the wildlife, the mystery and the uncertainty of the Arctic plains and mountains.

As the ice began to melt Halifax grew more confident. When a large fox headed for the boat at full trot, it seemed to be going straight for Halifax. Alvah shouted a caution to Diana, but Halifax puffed herself up as a warning to her enemy. The fox stopped and the two locked eyes. Then an unearthly scream came out of Halifax as she sprang up and charged. The fox held its ground until Halifax leapt upon it. The fox whirled around and ran with the cat hot on its heels and they disappeared over the snow dunes. Alvah and Diana waited anxiously, fearing for the cat's life but after an hour she appeared smugly purring in triumph.

Then the ice began to break up more determinedly and, with difficulty, the *Roger Henry* was released from the ice. This meant that Halifax could no longer jump ashore to relieve herself but had to be rowed to the beach. When she felt the need, she took to jumping into the dinghy and meowing demandingly, as if to say: "Free Halifax. Free Halifax". If her calls weren't answered she would jump on passing ice floes and drift off like a shipwrecked sailor. They were forever searching the bay for her ice rafts. When they did find her she would jump imperiously into the dinghy as though she had just ordered herself a taxi.

After much lingering, they reluctantly decided it was time to return south and went on one last hike to say goodbye to Tay Bay. The three of them stood on a rock together and surveyed what had been their territory, shared with the bears, the foxes, the ravens and other creatures. As the fog rolled in they made their way back to the *Roger Henry*. Alvah couldn't bring himself to look back.

Next morning they set sail for Pond Inlet. It was August and the ice floes were crammed with breeding bears. When Diana looked out of the galley porthole one morning, a bear looked back at her unblinking. Not sure whether to be frightened or delighted, they sailed cautiously amongst them and massive males prowled the ice edges as they slid past. By the time they reached Lancaster Sound, huge walruses huffed and puffed around the boat too.

At Dundas Harbour, still reluctant to return, they foolishly lingered on the ice floes, sometimes risking their lives as huge walls of ice threatened to fall on them. Then they headed south to Melville Bay and approached the mouth of Upernavik's harbour, one year to the day since they left.

They sailed south with the wind nipping at their heels, from the Greenland coast on to Davis Strait at Sukkertoppen until, on 20 October, 1995, they laid their lines on the same dock in Maine from which they had begun seventeen months and eight thousand miles earlier.

In his best selling book about their voyage, North to the Night, Alvah acknowledged that Halifax's companionship during his long dark winter in the Arctic had probably saved his life. The Arctic, he wrote, is all about sift and drift and illusion. Halifax kept him sane. Without her, he might not have survived that long, perilous Arctic night.

The Ship's Cat that Became Dish of the Day

On record is the story of the ship's cat aboard an eighteenth century cargo ship, the *Peggy* which, on 24 October 1765, sailed from France to New York carrying fine wines and brandy. After only seven days there were violent storms, which lashed at the ship relentlessly for four weeks. One by one the sails were torn away and the *Peggy* was left with a single mainsail.

The only hope was that a passing ship might rescue them and the *Peggy* floated on helplessly until the food ran out. On board were two pigeons and the ship's cat. First the pigeons were killed and eaten by the starving crew. Then they turned their attention to the ship's cat, whose fate was inevitable.

The men cast lots for portions of the cat. Captain David Harrison was unlucky enough to draw the head. But he'd been without food for so long, that any qualms he had about eating not only cat, but the most dubious portion of the animal, were soon banished.

"I never feasted on anything which appeared so delicious to my appetite. The piercing sharpness of necessity had entirely conquered my aversion to such food and the rage of an incredible hunger rendered that an exquisite regale which on any other occasion, I must have loathed with the most insuperable might."

Another savage storm ripped away the mainsail and their plight seemed even more grim. After finishing up the last of the water, the crew resorted to drinking the liquor from the cargo, which made them drunk and desperate. First they ate their way through the stock of tobacco, candles, bone buttons from their jackets and every scrap of leather they could lay hands on. Still no help had arrived and some of the crew were by now half crazed with hunger. They drew lots again to see who would be next on the menu, and the short straw was drawn by an Ethiopian slave who was part of the cargo. In those days it was considered a legitimate thing to do at sea in such desperate circumstances. On land it was referred to darkly as "the custom of the sea". The poor slave was shot, cooked and eaten with manic relish.

Captain Harrison claimed he refused to eat the human flesh, and he locked himself in his cabin fearing that he might be the next dish of the day. Fortunately a ship arrived just in time and rescued them.

Matthew Flinders' Remarkable Cat Trim who Helped Him Map Out Australia

Trim was born in 1799, aboard HMS *Roundabout*, during a passage from the Cape of Good Hope to Botany Bay. His mother was a cat from Stepney who'd sought refuge on the ship after being savagely assaulted by a London moggy. To her surprise, in the middle of the Indian Ocean she gave birth to a litter of kittens.

These kittens were therefore accustomed from the very start to the rolling of the ship in high winds and the smell of salt air, and were born with a unique sense of balance and an indifference to water.

One kitten stood out from the rest. Playing with his siblings on the deck in the moonlight one night, when the ship was lying tranquilly at harbour, he surpassed himself with his energy and daring and fell overboard into the sea. Apparently undeterred by this unceremonious introduction to the water, he learnt to swim instantly and made it safely back to the ship and climbed up a rope to the main deck with impressive dexterity.

Watching him was Matthew Flinders, a dashing young English sailor with a lust for adventure, born in Donington, Lincolnshire. He'd already had some exciting sea experiences himself, having sailed on HMS *Reliance* from England as far as Sydney. It was his ambition to prove that Australia, which was then considered to be a collection of islands, was in fact one huge continent and the only way to do this was to circumnavigate it. (It was later called Australia at Flinders' suggestion).

Flinders was at first amused by the kitten's antics, then stunned with admiration for his amazing agility and intelligence. He was also fascinated by his markings. The kitten was jet black with the exception of his feet which, he wrote, "seemed to have been dipped in snow". His underlip was also white but particularly distinctive was the white star on his breast, which seemed to indicate that "nature had designed him to be a prince of his race". Flinders was instantly besotted and christened him Trim "the name of my own uncle's honest, kind hearted, humble companion".

Trim became a firm favourite of everyone on the *Roundabout*, officers and seamen alike. So enamoured was he by his cat, that Flinders filled his spare moments writing down detailed notes about Trim's antics.

"Being amongst sailors, his manner acquired a peculiarity which rendered him different from other cats, as the actions of a fearless seaman are from those of a lounging, shame-faced ploughboy," wrote Flinders. "He had no dread of water. When a rope was thrown over to him, he took hold of it like a man and ran up it like a cat. In a short time he was able to mount up the gangway steps quicker than his master, or even the First Lieutenant."

Being so popular, Trim was well fed and as a result "grew fast in size and comeliness" into "one of the finest animals I ever saw!" He was once weighed on

Matthew Flinders' cat, Trim showing
the white star on his breast and his white underlip.

Illustration by Annette Macarthur-Onslow

the ship's "fresh-meatometer" and the scale stood at between ten to twelve pounds. His tail was long, large and bushy and when he was animated by the presence of a stranger he grew in size and "vivid flashes darted from his fiery eyes". At other times he was "candour and good nature itself. I doubt whether Whittington's cat was to be compared to him" wrote Flinders.

Partial as he was to this magnificent cat, Flinders admitted there was one trait of his character which was not to be admired. Trim was "excessively vain" particularly of his snow-white feet. He would apparently place himself on the quarterdeck before the officers, in the middle of their walk and, spreading out his two white paws in the posture of the "lion couchant", oblige them to stop and admire him "although they were critical of his vanity".

"Yet how many men are there, who have no claim either from birth, fortune or acquirements, personal or mental, whose vanity is to be confined within such harmless bounds, as was that of Trim? I will say for him, that he never objected to the pretensions of others," remarked Flinders, ever defensive of his cat.

"Trim, though vain, was not like those young men who, being assured of an independence, spend their youth in idle trifling and consider all serious application as pedantic and derogatory, or at least to be useless. He was, on the contrary, animated with a noble zeal for improvement of his faculties."

He acquired the art of leaping over the clasped hands of a seaman, with astonishing ability. Every man on board took pleasure in instructing him. At length he reached such a pitch of perfection that Flinders said that: "I am persuaded had nature placed him in the empire of Lilliput, his merit would have promoted him to the first offices of state."

Because he was so quick to learn, the crew amused themselves by teaching him all sorts of tricks. One was to lie on the deck on his back, with four feet stretched out as if dead. He remained like this until a signal was given for him to rise, whilst his instructor teasingly walked backwards and forwards. If he was kept in this position for too long, "a slight motion of the end of his tail would denote impatience and his friends never pushed their lesson further".

Flinders was convinced of Trim's interest in nautical astronomy. When an officer took lunar or other observations, the curious cat would place himself by the timekeeper and study intently the motion of the hands and the uses of the instrument, "with much earnest attention". He would try to touch the second hand, listen to the ticking and then had to walk all round the piece to assure himself it was not alive. He would then mew, as if asking for an explanation. The officer, having made his observation, would give the order "Stop!" which animated Trim and, his tail high in the air, he would run up a nearby rope, mewing frantically as if asking for more information about the proceedings.

A musket ball, slung with a piece of twine, and made to whirl round upon the deck by a slight motion of the finger, never failed to attract his notice and give him pleasure. "Perhaps," said Flinders somewhat wishfully, "because it bore a resemblance to the movement of his favourite planet, the Moon, in her orbit round the earth."

Gravity was one of Flinders' own favourite subjects and he spent hours observing and experimenting with gravitational forces. It was he who thought of mounting a bar of soft iron onto a binnacle to compensate for local magnetism causing error to the compass. Today it is called a Flinders Bar. Trim was also fond of making experiments with projectiles and the power of gravity. If a ball was thrown gently along the deck, he would pursue it. When the gravitating principle combined with the friction overcame the impelling power, he would give the ball a fresh impetus, to turn its direction into an elliptic curve.

The seamen, for their amusement, would stand at either end of the deck and trundle a ball backwards and forward from one to the other, which would keep Trim in constant action running after it. "He had an habitual passion for everything that was in motion," wrote Flinders, perhaps ascribing to his cat a passion which in fact was his own.

Having dealt with astronomy and gravitation, Flinders claimed that Trim graduated to basic philosophy. "The replacing of a topmast carried away, or taking a reef in the sails, were what most attracted his attention at sea. At all times, when there was more bustle on deck than usual, he never failed to be present and in the midst of it."

When confused by the frantic haste about him, he would mew and rub his back up against legs of one or another member of the crew, frequently at the risk of being trampled underfoot, until he gained someone's attention.

He was a professional and knew what good discipline required and, on taking in a reef, never presumed to go aloft until the order was issued. But as soon as the officer had given the order "Away up aloft" he jumped up along with the other seamen. He was apparently so active and zealous that none could reach the top before him.

"Yet he never lost his sense of dignity," said Flinders. "He did not lay out on the yard like a common seaman, but always remained seated upon an officer's cap, as if it gave him authority to assume command. This assumption of authority created no resentment amongst the men. For he always found some good friend ready to caress him after the business was done."

Flinders said that when the ship was in harbour, the measuring of log and lead lines upon deck, and the stowage of the holds below, were favourite subjects of Trim's attention. No sooner was a cask moved, than he darted in under it to attack the rodents or *"enemies of his king and country"* at the imminent risk of having his head crushed to atoms, which he very narrowly escaped several times.

"In the bread room he was still more indefatigable. He frequently solicited to be left there alone and in the dark for two or three days together, that nothing might interrupt him in the discharge of his duty. This was one of the brightest traits in my friend Trim's character. In making the following deductions from it, I shall not, I think, be accused of unjust partiality. He had no fear of evil spirits and a conscience above reproach. He possessed a degree of patience and perseverance, of which few men can boast and like a faithful servant, he employed all these qualities in the service of His Majesty's faithful servants and indirectly of His Majesty himself."

Trim was welcomed at the table of every officer and man on the ship. "In the gunroom he was always the first ready for dinner. Though he was usually seated a quarter of an hour before anybody else, his modest reserve was such that his voice wasn't heard until everybody else was served. He then put in his request, but not for a full allowance. Nor did he desire there should be laid for him a plate, knife, fork or spoon, all of which he knew he could well dispense with. But, by a gentle caressing mew, he petitioned for a little, a little bit, a bit of tythe from the plate of each, and few had the heart to refuse him."

Illustration by Annette Macarthur-Onslow

When a coveted morsel was not forthcoming Trim would, with his paw, whip it off the fork of some startled crewman with such dexterity and grace that it aroused admiration rather than anger. He did not, however, leap off the table with his prize as if he had done wrong but, putting the morsel into his mouth and eating it quietly, would then go to the next person and repeat his insistent meow.

"If refused his wonted tythe, he stood ready to take advantage of his skills of dexterity," wrote Flinders whose admiration for his cat knew no bounds. "There are some seamen so inconsiderate as to be talking when they should be eating, who keep their meat suspended in mid-air till a semi-colon in the discourse gives them an opportunity of taking their mouthful without interrupting their story. These ill-mannered men were a dead mark for Trim. When a short pause left them time to take the prepared mouthful, they were often surprised to find their meat gone."

One day Trim missed a fine morsel from the hungry activity of one of the young seamen who dined in the gunroom. Seeing him, talking and eating at the same time, Trim did not abandon hope, though the piece in the fellow's mouth was half-masticated and about to be swallowed. Running up the waistcoat of his unsuspecting victim, Trim placed one paw at each corner of his mouth, and vigorously seized the morsel. The astonished midshipman exclaimed "God damn the cat!" But Trim had got it firmly between his jaws and triumphantly carried it off. Even Flinders felt that this was pushing his luck and recorded that the cat received a reprimand, but not from him. He was too busy admiring the cat's sheer audacity.

William, the gunroom steward, a big burly seaman, was also totally besotted by Trim. Flinders said that, after sitting down with the masters, Trim was not too proud to sit down a second time with the servants. William admired Trim's intelligence so much he talked to him as to a child and Trim seemed to sit listening as if he understood and could give rational answers. Flinders apparently observed them having the following conversation over dinner one day.

"Do you know, master Trim, you have behaved very ill?"
"Me-ew?"
"It is very well to play tricks with them that know you, but you should be more modest with strangers."
"Mew!"
"How dare you say that I gave you no breakfast? Did I not give you all the milk that was left and some bread soaked in it?"
"Mou-wow!"
"No meat! What! You grow insolent. I'll chain you up. Do you hear, sir?"
"Me-ew."
"Well, if you'll promise to behave better, you shall have a nice piece off the cold shank of mutton for your supper, you shall."
"Mew-wew!"
"Gently, master Trim. I'll give it you now, but first promise me upon your honour."
"We-wee."
"Come then, my good boy. Come up and kiss me."

At which Trim leaped to William's shoulder and rubbing his face fondly against the hardy sailor's hairy cheek, received the mutton piece by piece from his mouth, like a sweetheart.

When an expedition was being planned to explore the northern parts of New South Wales, Flinders maintained that Trim put in a request to join the party, "promising to take upon himself the defence of our breadbags". His valuable services were duly accepted. An Aborigine called Bongaree "an intelligent native of Port Jackson" was on board to guide the little sloop and he and Trim formed an "intimate acquaintance" resembling that of a master and servant - and in this case it was Trim who was the master. If Trim wanted a drink, he mewed to Bongaree and leapt demandingly up onto the water cask. If he wanted to eat, he called him down below to the galley and went straight to his kit, "where there was generally a remnant of black swan".

In 1800 the *Roundabout* returned to England by way of Cape Horn and St. Helena and so Trim, besides his other voyages, completed his tour of the Globe. "Many and curious are the observations he made in various branches of science, particularly natural history of small mammals, birds and flying fish, for which he had much taste. These, with his remarks upon man and his manners, I may perhaps give to the world, and from the various seas and countries he has visited, joined his superior powers for distinguishing obscure subjects and talents for seizing them."

Trim was not only a stranger to England but also to homes built on solid ground. Flinders, because he was busy preparing for his marriage to his sweetheart, Anne, placed his precious cat in the safekeeping of a woman in Deptford, who promised to take good care of him and see he came to no harm.

But, said Flinders, she knew not what she had undertaken. Trim, not being used to simply walking out of a door onto land, would go out through the sash window at the top of the house as if it was a ship, so that he could spy out the surrounding country. When it rained, the sash window was naturally pulled down. This would have been an invincible barrier to a normal cat, but not so to Trim. He bolted through the glass like a clap of thunder, to the alarm of his good hostess below. Flinders described what he was told about the landlady's reaction.

"Good Gad, Trim," she exclaimed on entering the chamber. "Is it thee? They said thou wast a strange outlandish cat, and verily I think thou art the divil. I must shut thee up, for if thou go'st to treat neighbours thus, I shall have thee taken up for burglary. But come, I know thy master will pay the damage. Has thou cut thyself?"

One day Trim got into her closet amongst her best china. "Delicate town-bred cats go mincing in amongst cups and saucers without touching them," wrote Flinders. "But Trim! He spied a mouse and dashed at it like a man-of-war. The splinters flew in all directions. The poor woman thought at first an evil spirit was playing pranks in her cupboard. She opened the door with fear and trembling and to her infinite dismay, out jumped Trim onto her shoulder and she nearly died of fright. Seeing how much mischief was done to her treasured china, she seized Trim to beat him soundly. But instead of trying to escape, the droll animal rubbed his whiskers up against her chin purring. She no longer had the heart to strike him but with a sigh, stooped to pick up the pieces."

Flinders had to find alternative accommodation and so took Trim to London on a stage coach to stay with a friend. As there were no fine ladies to be frightened of a cat, he was allowed full liberty. Flinders said he conducted himself admirably, stretching out his white paws to the admiration of the other two gentleman passengers.

But Trim's stay was short. The friend couldn't cope. "I never saw such a strange animal," he told Flinders. "I am afraid of losing him. He goes out into the streets in the middle of the day and rubs himself up against the legs of passers by. Several have taken him up to caress him, but I fear someone may carry him off."

When Flinders made a second voyage to the South Seas, on the *Spyall*, Trim went with him. As on the *Roundabout*, officers and crew made a great fuss of him. He entertained them with his antics and tricks and was soon a big attraction..

There were several dogs aboard, said Flinders, but Trim was the undisputed master of them all. He described how, when they were at play upon deck, he would go in amongst them with his stately air and give a blow at the eye of one, scratch another on the nose and oblige the lot to stand out of his way.

He was as capable of being animated against a dog, as dogs normally are against a cat. "On more than one occasion," recalled Flinders, "I had to send him from the quarter deck to drive a dog off the forecastle. He would run half the way briskly crouching like a lion which has prey in view. But then, assuming a majestic deportment and without being deterred by the menacing attitude of his opponent, he would march straight up to him and give him a blow on the nose, accompanied with a threatening mew."

If the dog did not immediately retreat, he would fly at him hissing. If resistance was still made, he leaped up on the rail over his head and spat menacingly into the dog's eyes, which would send him off howling. Still Trim would pursue him until he took refuge below. At which Trim would return to Flinders "for caresses and treats".

Trim accompanied Flinders on his circumnavigations of Australia in the years 1801, 1802 and 1803. "Trim had frequent opportunities of repeating his observations and experiments in his favourite science, natural history, and exerting his undiminished activity and zeal for the public good."

In the Gulf of Carpentaria, North East Australia, the climate was close and humid and there was a shortage of fresh food. Trim's fur went almost grey and he lost weight and seemed to be threatened with premature old age. But to the joy of his friends, once they reached better climes, his fur recovered its normal rich jet colour and by the time they had returned to harbour he had assumed his usual portliness.

Flinders claimed that Trim was above thievery but described how, one afternoon, he was tempted by a leg of cold mutton in the pantry. Being unable to carry it off by himself, he enlisted the help of a Dutch cat on board, called Van. Between them they managed to get it off the shelf and onto the deck and were dragging it together into the hold when they were caught in the act by the steward. Van slunk off, but Trim remained, arrogantly confident he could get away with it. To his surprise and indignation, the steward seized him and gave him a harsh beating. "He took the blows with philosophical patience," said Flinders, "but no sooner was he set at liberty, than he ran after his false Dutch friend and repaid him with interest with a similar beating."

The *Spyall* was found to be rotten and unfit for the sea. Flinders, with Trim, embarked on HMS *Janty* to return to England. This ship was wrecked upon a coral bank in the Indian Ocean on the night of 17 August, 1803. Trim, Flinders and other survivors swam to safety to Wreck Reef Bank, in the Coral Sea off East Australia. They must have all endured a miserable ordeal, but Flinders was more concerned for his cat than himself and fellow seamen. "The imagination can scarcely attain to what Trim had to suffer during this dreadful night, but his courage was not to be beaten down."

They were there for two long and difficult months. But one of Flinders' favourite books as a child was Robinson Crusoe and it was from reading this he acquired his love of the sea and thirst for adventure. So "roughing" it would have been just one more challenge to him. And, lively as ever, Trim entertained the men and helped keep up their spirits with his amusing antics. When help eventually arrived, Trim preferred to go with Flinders aboard the schooner *Minikin*, instead of joining the rest

Trim seeing off the dogs
Illustration by Annette Macarthur-Onslow

of the ship's company in a larger, more comfortable vessel.

The *Minikin* was very leaky and was obliged to stop at the Isle of France (Mauritius) in the Indian Ocean. Flinders and others were taken prisoner by the French, who accused them of spying, although they had been away so long they had no idea there was even a war going on between England and France.

Trim stayed close to his master and was locked in a room with Flinders and another officer. Flinders commented: "As he possessed more philosophy than we did, he contributed by his gay humour to soften our captivity, but sometimes contrived to elude the vigilance of the sentinel at the door and left us to explore the neighbourhood."

A French lady took a fancy to Trim and insisted on confiscating him "to serve as a companion for her little daughter". Having no option in the matter, Flinders reluctantly let his cat go. After only a fortnight the public gazette of the island announced that he was lost and a reward of ten Spanish dollars was offered for his return.

Flinders said he would rather have given fifty dollars to have had his friend and companion restored to him. Poor Trim was never seen again and Flinders concluded he had been "stewed and eaten by some hungry black slave". If he was, then he joined a long line of sea-going adventurers who met similar fates, such as Captain James Cook, the English navigator.

Flinders was grief stricken, and wrote in his diary: "Thus perished my faithful, intelligent Trim. The sporting, affectionate and useful companion of my voyages during four years. Never, my Trim, shall I see thy like again. But never will thou cease to be regretted by all those who had the pleasure of knowing thee. And for thy affectionate master and friend he promises thee, if ever he shall have the happiness to enjoy repose in his native country, under a thatched cottage surrounded by half an acre of land, to erect in the most retired corner, a monument to perpetuate and record thy uncommon merits."

Flinders remained a prisoner on Mauritius for seven more years. In 1810, when he was 36 he was allowed to return to England and to his wife, Anne. His period in captivity had been harsh and when he was freed, he looked much older than he was. His health deteriorated rapidly and he died in 1814, aged 40.

There is no evidence that Flinders ever did get round to putting up the promised memorial stone to his beloved cat. But a monument with the appropriate wording **was** erected to Trim in Sydney, New South Wales, an area which, Flinders would have insisted, Trim helped him map out.

He kept copious notes on his voyages and when writing his stories about his beloved cat Trim, for some reason Matthew Flinders changed the names of the ships on which he and Trim sailed. For instance, the *Roundabout* was actually the *Reliance*, the *Spyall* was the *Investigator* , the *Janty* was the *Porpois*, and the *Minikin* was the *Cumberland*

Some 200 years later, neither Matthew Flinders nor his faithful companion Trim is forgotten. A bronze statue of Trim by sculptor John Cornwell stands on a window ledge of the Mitchell Library in Macquarie Street, Sydney, Australia, directly behind the statue of his master that was erected in 1925 when his grandson donated Flinders' papers to the library. The cat statue, commissioned by the North Shore Historical Society and unveiled in March 1996 by Rear-Admiral David Campbell, is very popular, and the library café is named after Trim.

This sculpture, by John Cromwell, of a rather haughty looking Trim, can be seen at the State Library of New South Wales, Australia.

The Bewitched Cat on the Doomed *Infanta Maria Teresa*

On 3 July 1898, during the Spanish-American war, the Spanish Admiral Pascual Cervera, and his 497-man crew were forced to leave their burning flagship, the *Infanta Maria Teresa*, in Santiago harbour, Cuba. One hundred and fifty of the crew either drowned or perished in the flames. The ship's cat was left behind on the ship with only dead men for company. The rest of the Spanish fleet was totally destroyed by American naval vessels.

Two weeks later 38-year-old American Naval Constructor Richmond Pearson Hobson arrived in the repair ship *Vulcan* to salvage the magnificent 333ft two-masted Spanish flagship. The flames had burnt themselves out. Miraculously the hulk was still floating although half-submerged. As he walked about the stricken ship, assessing the damage, Hobson was astonished to come across a frightened, half-starved black cat. The cat, it was darkly rumoured amongst the *Vulcan* crew, had managed to survive by feeding on the burnt corpses of dead sailors.

Richmond Pearson Hobson

Hobson was a hero himself. A month earlier he had been given the dangerous task of scuttling America's own collier, ss *Merrimac*, described as being 'old and nothing but trouble so no great loss', in an effort to block the entrance to Santiago Harbour to prevent the Spanish Fleet escaping. Hobson with a crew of six managed to successfully scuttle the *Merrimac* but failed to obstruct the way through and they were taken prisoner by the Spanish. After the battle of Santiago, they were released on 6 July. Hobson was surprised to find himself acclaimed a national hero. Years later, in 1933, he was awarded the Congressional Medal of Honour and later made a Rear Admiral.

Hobson therefore recognised a fellow hero immediately in this hardy little feline. Impressed and moved by the cat's gutsy determination to survive, he gave her food and water and much loving attention. During the following weeks the little black cat followed him everywhere, as Hobson assessed the damage on the huge hulk and supervised the patching of the hull and the pumping out of water. Eventually the crew got the wreck floating and it was securely roped to the *Vulcan* for towing back to the American naval shipyard at Charleston, South Carolina.

Having other business to attend to and satisfied that all was now in order, he left his adopted cat on the *Maria Teresa*, with members of the salvage crew, with strict instructions that the cat should be nourished and cared for until he was able to pick her up at the end of the salvage voyage. The sailors on the *Vulcan* were convinced she was a demon in disguise and insisted the ill-fated black cat stayed on the Spanish ship.

All went well at first, as the *Vulcan* towed the wreck out to sea and then around the eastern end of Cuba and north to Charleston. But just off the Bahamas, a hurricane arose and the Captain of the *Vulcan* became terrified that the 7,000 ton *Maria Teresa* would sink and pull the *Vulcan* down with it, drowning the crews of both ships. In the stormy darkness he imagined he saw the stricken ship sinking and ordered the temporary crew to abandon her.

Before casting off, remembering Hobson's strict instructions to look after the cat, the crew tried to rescue her too. But she ran up the mast and stayed there. So the men hastily transferred to the *Vulcan*. The hawser rope snapped and the two ships were separated, much to the relief of the Captain. Consequently, his ship, the *Vulcan* was able to struggle home through the storm unencumbered.

On reaching Charleston, he reported the total loss of the *Maria Teresa* and sadly told Hobson that the cat had refused to leave the sinking ship, despite frantic attempts to save her. Four days later an American freighter, steaming off the Bahamas, spotted the charred shell of the ravaged Spanish battleship, drifting ghostlike in the ocean with no one aboard. The officer-on-watch was convinced at first he was seeing a bewitched ship, especially when a black "demon cat" was spotted prowling the charred decks.

The sighting of the *Maria Teresa*, with its mysterious phantom cat, was duly reported to Hobson, who was furious with the captain of the *Vulcan*, accusing him of lacking courage and abandoning her in a moment of panic. He was also angry that the cat had been left alone to perish on the doomed ship.

The wreck itself was still of great value and Hobson decided he could only rely on himself to rescue it and the cat. So he set sail on the *Vulcan* to see the evidence for himself. But by the time they reached the *Maria Teresa*, the currents had carried her fifty miles to the west and the waves had dropped her on a coral reef, breaking her back completely, just off the coast of one of the Bahamian islands.

Hobson, approaching from the sea, realised there was no hope of salvaging the *Maria Teresa*, since the two halves of the ship had separated. But there was still a chance that the cat might have survived. So he sent his young Lieutenant Simms to search the twice-wrecked derelict ship. Simms was told firmly not to come back without the cat.

On investigation, Simms discovered that the cat had been taken off the wreck by the Negro natives and given to their chief who, in turn, gave her to his little daughter.

The child by now adored her new pet and refused to part with her. She was offered five and then ten dollars. It was a great deal of money and the chief was tempted but his little girl cried when they tried to take the cat away. Eventually 15 dollars was offered, which was a small fortune in the remote Bahamas, and it was accepted.

So the jinxed cat was brought aboard the *Vulcan* despite objections from the ship's Captain and his crew who were reluctant to take her aboard. The crew were all muttering that she was a witch, a demon or a curse. She was sure to bring them bad luck. But Hobson disdainfully dismissed them as ignorant and superstitious.

Sure enough, though, the sky darkened, the barometer dropped and signs of a severe storm became evident. The Captain swore he would never get his ship home with the Demon Cat aboard. He seized her to throw her into the sea. Hobson managed to tear her from his grasp.

"If anybody goes overboard, it should be you," Hobson told the Captain angrily, "This cat has given us all an extraordinary example of fidelity. She clung close to her ship when everybody else deserted it. She stood guard alone for two weeks while the sea swept over the hulk. She helped me to raise the *Maria Teresa* and we would have got her all the way to Charleston, if you hadn't lost your nerve and set her adrift.

"What is the name of the coral island, to which this brave little cat laid her course? Look at your chart. You will see it is called Cat's Island. Even adrift, all through the hurricane, as captain in sole charge of the *Maria Teresa*, she knew exactly where to go."

Hobson took the "Demon Cat" into his arms and gave her apple-pie and cream and the wind went down and the barometer went up and nobody went overboard. In the summer twilight the two of them climbed to the top deck, where Hobson found a canvas chair. And there, according to one of the crew, the heroine of the *Maria Teresa* curled up on the lap of the hero of the *Merrimac* and together they watched the moon rise out of the sea.

Infanta Maria Teresa

Smuggled Cats on Board
the ss Great Britain

Isambard Kingdom Brunel designed the world's first iron-hulled, screw-propelled ocean steamer, the 3,270-ton ss *Great Britain*, launched in 1845 at Bristol. Before that, long distance sea voyages were made in wooden sailing ships which were dangerous and unpredictable. With the launch of this impressive ship, the world suddenly became a smaller place and ss *Great Britain* slashed the journey time to America and Australia. It became possible to travel to these distant lands to a schedule. On average it took 56 days to sail to Australia.

The ship was 322-feet in length and was able to carry 252 passengers, a crew of 130, and 1,200 tons of cargo. It was the first of the great luxury ocean liners and over the years carried over 15,000 emigrants to Australia. There were sumptuous first class cabins and an exclusive ladies' boudoir for social gatherings. Although the ship carried livestock, pet cats and dogs were strictly confined to the ship's kennel quarters.

In 1875, occupying one of the suites was Anna-Maria Georgina Bright, who boarded the ss *Great Britain* on 27 August, with her three sons, Alfred, Charles and Richard, her baby daughter Georgina, and her personal maid. She was returning to Melbourne to join her husband, Charles Edward Bright, of Gibbs Bright and Co., the shipping and merchant bankers. Her father was the Viscount Canterbury, recently retired as Governor of the Province of Victoria, Australia and was now living in England. Anna-Maria and her family had been home to England for a visit.

In a letter written to her parents on Monday, 30 August, she describes excitedly that she discovered a kitten wandering freely on board the ship, "which little Charlie is mad after".

She was aware of the strict rule on board that pets must be restricted to kennel areas throughout the voyage. Some passengers however couldn't bear being parted from their pets. Others wanted to avoid paying the cargo fee. Consequently, pet cats and dogs were smuggled aboard and hidden in cabins. Cats, being naturally more devious and cunning than dogs, found it easier to escape and wander freely round the huge ship, skulking into corners and niches when in danger of being spotted. Strictly speaking, Georgina should have reported her find to the captain, but the children begged her to let it go.

A week later, on Tuesday, 7 September, she noted: "Last night awoke with someone screaming violently and on going to see what the matter was, found King (her personal maid) at the door of her cabin vowing she had a rat in her berth. I said I knew it was all nonsense and that it was only the kitten we had found. Having said so, I was obliged to show that I believed what I said, by putting my hand in the berth (pitch dark it was) and most thankful I was to find that I had got hold of the poor kitten instead of a great rat. What a bite I should have got. I gave King 'fits' and the sal'-volatile and heard no more of her until morning."

In 1873 seven Presentation nuns from Ireland sailed on the ss Great Britain for Australia to set up a convent school in Melbourne. They had never sailed before and this quaint party naturally aroused the curiousity of their fellow passengers. Their leader was Mother Mary Paul Mulquin, a remarkably down-to-earth lady who kept a day-by-day diary, which revealed a wicked sense of humour.

On Thursday, October 30 she noted that the seven nuns had enjoyed a few pleasant hours in the luxury cabin especially reserved for ladies' gatherings. After retiring to bed, Mother Mary noted that a visitor found its way into their cabin. "We were awakened from our nightly slumber by a strange cat, who came quite uninvited and continues his attentions ever since."

Again, she doesn't mention whether she reported the cat's presence to the Captain. She certainly knew they were forbidden because she notes later: "The Captain tells us droll stories of people smuggling in cats, for which £5 must be paid or an auction is held on deck, the prize given to the highest bidder as all such pets are forbidden. For indeed, we have enough *human* voices – of children – no need of the addition of quadrupeds."

The ss *Great Britain* ended her working life as a store ship in the Falklands, before being beached and abandoned there. In 1970 she was salvaged and brought back to the Great Western Dock in Bristol for restoration. By 2010 she had been completely refurbished and transformed to exactly as she was when she was launched in 1845. There was no electricity then, so even the lights on the ship are made to flicker like oil lamps to make the atmosphere more authentic.

Brunel would undoubtedly have been proud of her as she is now, a splendid Museum Ship. There is even an imitation Ship's Cat called Sinbad. Sinbad's location is changed regularly and he turns up in the most unlikely place, so children invited to hunt for him as they explore with the help of audio guides.

Real cats are forbidden on board, a rule which any cat worth its salt disdainfully ignores.

The launching of the ss *Great Britain* 19 July 1843

The Cat that Stowed Away
On a Ship to America

Early last century, about 1909, a poor family of immigrants was leaving Poland to start a new life in America. Although they were going on a great ocean liner, a modern new steamship with four funnels and electricity, they couldn't afford cabins, not even third class ones, so they travelled steerage, which meant being cooped up in the hold of the ship like animals.

Their few possessions included some gold coins hidden in the heels of their shoes and two silver cups baked inside a loaf of bread. The little girl, Chanah, aged nine, carried a basket with some of her own bits and pieces and a down-filled pillow – the only comfort she was likely to get in steerage, which was the very worst way to travel. The family's home for two weeks would be two hard wooden benches shared between five of them.

As her father was busy buying the tickets for their passage, she noticed a yellow and white striped cat skulking miserably in the gutter. It was weak and thin, its ribs stuck out and its fur was dull and patchy. It looked at her pitifully and immediately won her heart. On impulse she threw away her bulky goose-down pillow to make room in her basket for the starving cat, and quickly covered it up with her shawl.

She knew if she told anybody about the cat, she would have to get rid of it. As an added precaution, she undid the red ribbon from her hair and tied it round the handle of her basket, to protect her new pet from bad spirits. She called her Pitsel, which means small in Polish.

Clutching her basket close to her, praying Pitsel wouldn't meow and give the game away, she followed her family onto the ship and down into the depths of the hull. There were about 900 hundred people down there, and it was so noisy and crowded anybody hearing cat noises might have thought it was a baby or a small child crying.

There was no running water, no sink and no windows, except for tiny portholes high up, which let in very little natural light. There were some lanterns swinging on the beams, which threw strange shadows round the crowded hold. Food each evening would be ladled out from huge kettles. During bad weather, the hatches would be bolted down making the atmosphere stuffy and unpleasant.

Their mother made their wooden benches into something vaguely resembling a home and, for a few days, Chanah managed to keep her secret, feeding the cat on scraps of food left over by the other passengers. They were well into their journey before the stowaway cat was discovered by her brother, Benjamin. He was older than her and rather bossy.

"You won't get away with it. As soon as we get to the next port, they'll send her back," he warned her.

The steerage passengers were free to wander about the lower decks unless chased away by the crew. Chanah always carried her basket with her, wherever she went. When no one was around, she let her out in dark corners to do her toilet.

Then a cousin called Schmuel, who was also travelling to America with his family, found out about Pitsel. He seemed determined to "let the cat out of the bag" so to speak, by deliberately putting his hand in the basket to torment the cat and then teasing Chanah by saying loudly "Did anyone hear anything?"

His younger brother, Yaacov, was deaf and dumb. He wore a scarf around his neck and he was kept very much in the background. Whenever anyone asked why he never spoke, they were told he had a bad sore throat. His mother knew that the American authorities didn't accept children who had problems and might be a burden on the State. She was banking on no one noticing his handicap.

Yaacov was also let in on the secret. He was much kinder than his brother and brought Chanah fish heads for Pitsel and never lifted the basket cover unless given permission.

One night a baby was born in steerage. There were a lot of moans and cries, but Chanah managed to sleep through the birth, occasionally waking up to put her hand inside the basket to stroke Pitsel, who would purr and arch her bony back with pleasure. In the morning, she noticed the red ribbon had gone. Someone had taken it to pin to the newborn baby's shawl, to protect it from spirits, as was the custom.

After breakfast Chanah's mother asked her to help her do some washing. They worked hard all morning and after they'd hung up the clothes, they returned to their bench. Chanah went to her basket and peeped inside. Pitsel had gone!

Trying not to cry, she called the cat softly, searching every nook and cranny in the hold. But Pitsel was nowhere to be found. She asked her arrogant cousin, Schmuel, who suggested sarcastically that she asked the captain.

Chanah felt desperate. Her father and mother knew nothing of the cat. If she told them, they would be cross with her for smuggling the cat aboard. Her father would say they had enough problems without her heaping more upon them. She had to keep her distress to herself.

Her brother was not very sympathetic either. The only person prepared to help was her deaf and dumb cousin, Yaacov. Together they searched the passages and the decks of the huge ship. They went into the engine room, and looked under the canvas covers of the lifeboats. They sneaked onto the third class deck and searched there, but they were soon chased off by the officers.

They'd been away for so long that when they returned, they found that their families in steerage were now searching for them. They'd been as worried about their children as Chanah was about her cat.

"We thought you'd fallen overboard," fretted her mother.

It became colder and that night there were huge waves, and howling winds.

Chanah's mother asked her where her goose down pillow was, which would allow her to sleep more comfortably. She confessed she had thrown the pillow away. Her mother was very cross with her, but Chanah was too worried about Pitsel to care. She feared she might have fallen overboard or was hiding in a dark corner somewhere, frightened and cold. By the end of the second day, she was beside herself with worry. Pitsel had become very dear to her.

Then it began to rain and things got worse in steerage. The hatches were bolted down, lanterns swung on the beams in a menacingly way and the air became steamy and oppressive. The following night water came into the hold and sailors rushed in with pumps and buckets. Everyone was scared the ship was going to sink and they would all be drowned.

Chanah's father turned their benches upside down and tied each one of his family to them. He did the same to Yaacov and Schmuel and their mother, who were travelling without their father because he was already in America.

The ship rolled about so much, that any person or creature walking on the decks would have been swept into the sea. Chanah began to think that there was no way Pitsel could have survived. She started to cry, which was unlike her, and her grandmother thought it was because she was frightened of the storm.

Next day it was calm and the family spent the day drying out their possessions. Chanah went on another search for Pitsel, shadowed by the ever silent Yaacov. Hiding behind a funnel, Chanah thought she heard the sound of a cat. Yaacov, being deaf, couldn't hear, but seemed to understand her signs. He began to climb a mountain of luggage. She followed him. On the top of the pile were the small bones of a mouse, picked clean - a sure sign that a cat had been there. Chanah raised her eyes and chin to the sky, and sighed with relief.

There was a Polish woman on the third class deck, wearing a hat with a feather in it. Chanah approached her and asked cautiously if she had seen anything "unusual" hoping she would say yes, she'd just seen a cat. The woman was quite rude and asked witheringly if the two children were from "steerage". If so, she said she didn't want to be seen associating with them.

They climbed to the first class deck, which was more open than the others. Then Chanah heard dogs barking. They went in the direction of the noise and were stopped by an officer who asked if they were from steerage. They guiltily admitted they were.

"We're just looking for the dogs," she said.

"I'll show you where the dogs are, but don't tell anyone I told you," he said kindly. The officer sketched a little map of the ship and marked where the kennels were.

The children returned to steerage, intending to explore the kennel area later. On their way back they saw the Polish woman again, standing by the railings. Chanah thought she looked sad and wistful. She noticed the woman no longer had a feather in her hat and wondered if this was why she was unhappy.

She pulled out of her pinafore pocket a soft down feather she had been carrying around with her, and offered it to the woman.

"What do I want this for?" said the woman, looking around to make sure no one was watching her talking to these common steerage children.

"To put in your hat," said Chanah.

"I wouldn't dream of it," she said disdainfully.

The Captain himself came into the hold. He and some other officers stood looking at the passengers, which made them feel uneasy. Chanah thought he had come to tell them off for trespassing into first class. But when he spoke he was very friendly and kind, saying he had come to see the new baby he'd been told had been born. He said that, if the parents wished, as Captain he had the authority to christen the baby. So a ceremony was carried out and the Captain gave the mother a carton of eggs as a gift.

He then sprinkled sand on the new baby's feet and said that the sand came from the ballast stored in the hold. Since the sand came from Staten Island, New York, he explained that the little baby was the first amongst them to set foot in America. It was a nice gesture and, although most of the steerage passengers couldn't understand a word he said, it cheered everybody up.

Chanah felt sure that if they found the kennels where the dogs were kept, she would find her cat. Cats liked tormenting dogs, she reasoned, especially ones that were tied up and out of reach.

Both her cousins insisted on joining her to search for Pitsel. They climbed to the top deck so that they would have a better view of the rear of the ship, and spotted the kennels below, a small structure with a fenced run for the dogs. As they slipped under the canvas covers of the lifeboats, something caught Chanah's eye. She held her breath, not daring to believe what she saw.

From behind a ventilator emerged Pitsel. She turned and looked at Chanah. She was scruffy and underfed but seemed to recognise Chanah. She started to walk in their direction. Just as she was almost close enough to touch, Schmuel jumped up and scared the cat off. Chanah ran after her, with the others at her heels.

They breathlessly followed the cat down to the next level. Chanah nearly caught up with her. She could almost feel the fur on her back, she was so close. Then some ship's officers confronted them. Schmuel ran off, but Yaacov stayed loyally with her.

The ship's bell was rung so loudly that they all had to clap their hands on their ears. All except Yaacov who didn't react. The two officers asked if he was deaf, and Chanah hurriedly said no, he just had a cold. They looked at the children suspiciously and told them to go back to steerage.

Chanah felt terrible. They had all managed so far to conceal Yaacov's handicap. Now she had given the game away. She knew it was so serious, she would have to confess all to her mother. Which she did, but they were all too worried about Yaacov to be cross with her about the cat. If the authorities were told about him, he might be returned to Poland. Yaacov's mother sat crying inconsolably.

They were coming closer to land. Instead of the occasional sighting of a ship, there were half a dozen vessels close enough to see their markings. Chanah no longer carried her basket. It made her sad to do so. Her grandmother carried it for her instead. Next morning they woke to an awful din. Everyone was rushing about excitedly. The ship was in a bay, and the passengers could see islands and fields, hills and woods and rivers. About them were tugboats, barges, sailboats, freighters and ocean liners, all blowing whistles or blasting horns.

There was mist but as it cleared, they saw tall buildings and, most amazing of all, out of the mist rose a giant statue of a woman holding aloft a torch in one hand and clutching a book in the other - the Statue of Liberty. They had arrived in New York. The next stage was to go by ferry to Ellis Island, where they would be inspected to see if they were suitable to be accepted as American citizens.

Everyone was excited. With mixed feelings, the steerage folk gathered on the deck with their bundles of possessions, while the passengers on the upper decks patronisingly threw down coins to them. Chanah was not interested in all this. She was looking round the ship, hoping Pitsel would suddenly appear. Once she stepped off the ferry, she would certainly never see her cat again.

It took 15 minutes to reach Ellis Island. They were inspected by doctors, for diseases, nits, and lice and then asked searching questions to establish they were suitable. Her father was asked if he had any money. He knew he had to declare what he had, otherwise he might be turned away as a vagrant. He took his five gold coins from where he had hidden them in his shoe and the inspectors laughed.

Then they questioned Yaacov's mother about her youngest son. The word had got to them that he was deaf and dumb. Yaacov's mother began to weep and wail, frightened she would be told he would be sent back. Then Chanah came forward to defend her cousin, pointing out that he could speak perfectly well with his fingers. Lots of the passengers spoke a strange language, and Yaacov's language was not much different. The inspectors were impressed by her courage in speaking up and decided to bend the rules and accept Yaacov.

As Yaacov's mother was thanking her, Chanah turned and recognised the Polish woman from third class, standing alone in the throng. She was carrying a hatbox and looked worried. She beckoned to Chanah, who approached her timidly.

"There you are. I was going to let it go."

"Let what go?" asked Chanah, thinking she wanted to give her back her feather.

The woman handed Chanah her blue flower-tinted hatbox. Scratching sounds were coming from inside.

"It followed me into my cabin. It's ruined my hatbox," she complained. Chanah lifted the lid and inside was a tired-looking unhappy Pitsel. She picked her up and held her thankfully to her breast.

"I thought I'd never see you again," she said.

Her mother didn't want her to keep Pitsel because she was worried she might catch fleas or some awful disease but, because of the plucky way she'd stood up for Yaacov and probably saved him from being deported back to Poland, her father allowed her to keep the little cat that had stowed away all the way across the Atlantic from Europe to America.

Note: *Evelyn Wilde Mayerson wrote that she used to tell this story to her own children and her grandchildren over and over again. The father in the story was her aunt's grandmother's brother. She calls it a bubbemeiser – a grandmother's tale.*

Naomi James's Cat Boris

Naomi James never intended taking a cat with her on her single-handed voyage round the world in 1977. But a well-meaning friend gave her a kitten, thinking he would be company for her. Having been brought up on a farm, Naomi was more partial to dogs and horses than cats. A cat would be a nuisance, she decided. It meant sacrificing valuable space for a litter tray and enough tins of cat food to last the ten-month voyage. She made up her mind to refuse the gift, until the adorable little kitten was placed in her arms and her heart melted.

She called him Boris and hoped that at least his unique feline "sixth sense" might serve as a sort of "radar" by him meowing or reacting in some way when a ship or unfamiliar object came too near.

"He is a rather pocket-sized radar, no more than five inches long, fluffy and still very attached to his mum. I decided not to take him aboard until the very last minute, so that he would have a chance to grow up a bit first."

On 9 September, 1977 Naomi, a 28-year-old New Zealander and self-confessed "duffer", set sail from Dartmouth in a 53-foot yacht lent to her by her friend and fellow sailor, Chay Blyth, to sail single-handed round the globe via Cape Horn. Chay Blyth had circumnavigated the world, alone and non-stop, in *British Steel* some years earlier and was very encouraging, despite the fact that Naomi had only been sailing for two years, and was openly terrified of falling overboard.

The yacht Chay Blyth lent her was the *Spirit of Cutty Sark* but when Derek Jameson, editor of the Daily Express newspaper, offered to sponsor her he insisted she changed the name to *Express Crusader*. It was the first attempt by a woman to sail round the world alone and non-stop and his newspaper needed to get good publicity in return for their sponsorship.

It was a wrench parting from her husband, Rob James. They'd only been married a few months and hadn't yet had a chance to even set up home together. But Rob was also planning to sail round the world, in *Great Britain II*, captained by Chay Blyth. The two trips would coincide.

On Day One, 27 September, 1977, they set off with the automatic sailing gear doing most of the work. As she and Boris prepared to acclimatise themselves to life at sea, in those first few hours, it all seemed a bit too easy. "It seemed to me, all I had to do was to point the yacht in the right direction and make sure I didn't run into any rocks or boats. Feeling remarkably content I went down below to make myself a cup of tea."

She found Boris was lying on the bunk looking decidedly unwell. He was staring with fascination at the flexible fuel tank lying on the quarter berth wobbling like a waterbed. Naomi drank her tea and scolded him for not being a good sailor. By next day she was unwell too.

Naomi James's kitten, Boris, relaxes in his favourite spot amongst the ropes on the winch of the *Express Crusader,* in which Naomi was the first woman to sail single-handed round the world via Cape Horn, in 1978.

"I am now feeling seasick, which tends to make things appear rather grey, although Boris, I see, after being sick is now eating like a horse. So I should be thankful for small mercies. I've done all I can to make myself happy with the navigation and fixed my position with various landmarks." Next day she noted: "Finally sick and feel better. There are times when being sick is the **only** way to get relief."

By the end of their first day and night on board, both cat and woman were weak and listless. Naomi, still apprehensive about bringing a cat with her, looked at her fluffy, cute-looking "radar set" sleeping blissfully on her bunk and decided it was too early to vote him a failure. He might yet turn out to be useful and if he felt anything like she did after their first day and night aboard, then his listlessness was understandable.

As the two odd shipmates gained confidence they began to relax. By the time they reached the Bay of Biscay, when a sudden big swell made things a little uncomfortable below deck, they had more or less learnt how to control their stomachs.

Naomi wrote in her log: "I don't feel too bad now, propped up here by the chart table, tired but not exhausted. The motion of the boat is steady and I'm getting used to it. In fact this is the fastest recovery from seasickness I've ever made. Boris is playing out of sight in the saloon. I can hear the occasional scratch and spit. He's just had a big feed of my goulash, which he enjoyed. He's a dear little thing, quite affectionate at times and thoroughly able to amuse himself."

They were beginning to bond now that, having both found their sea legs, they had conquered seasickness together. It seemed no problem to either of them, even in the galley. Naomi noted that one morning for breakfast she had left-overs of fried potatoes and peas with two fried eggs and "I had to fend off the cat while I ate. Eventually I gave him some, but he was more interested in climbing on to my plate. He certainly has some perverse habits such as sleeping during the day and playing at night, and sitting on the charts when I am trying to navigate."

She was missing her husband Rob and reflected that he too was sailing round the world, ahead of her. She found that thought immensely comforting. He had taught her how to be a sailor and, each day, she meticulously went through all the routine jobs, checking and rechecking boom, sails, wind indicators, automatic steering etc. Deep down she nursed a fear of failing because of her own inexperience and inefficiency. What other lone sailor, she reflected, was daft enough to take a cat with them on a journey such as this? Alec Rose, Francis Chichester, Chay Blyth – all of them had the sense to leave animals on shore. Most of all she feared drowning. The thought of struggling for breath in the water was horrific.

When the rudder of the automatic steering came off and she saw it was hanging by its safety rope, Boris was amazed to see her lie flat on her stomach and reach out and pull the rudder inboard. He playfully tried to help by clambering on her. When she tried to take off the cylinder link from the gearbox she dropped the vital pin that secured the rudder into the water. It was watching it disappear into the ocean, into infinity, that upset her. It briefly crossed her mind that it might have been her. Or Boris! It didn't bear thinking about.

Her next frightening experience was when the halyard unclipped itself from the sail and wrapped itself round the shrouds, the flag halyard and the aerial. She knew she would have to climb up the mast, which she'd never had the courage to do before, to untangle it. Watched by Boris, up she went, cautiously having secured herself with a safety harness. It was terrifying but she managed the task successfully and returned to the bunk for a lie down and to quieten her thumping heart. Her hands were in a sorry state, rough with the salt water she washed in. There were several cuts that weren't healing well. She relaxed and allowed herself the luxury of a manicure and felt better.

On 27 September she had arranged to rendezvous at the Canary Islands with the Express photographer, to pick up supplies and pose for photographs. As they neared the islands, it became warmer and she was able to wear shorts and T-shirts on deck. Boris too was now venturing on deck and exploring his upstairs territory. He was steady on his feet but Naomi noted that he was too inquisitive for his own good. When the boat was becalmed the sheets would flap up and down as the sail filled with wind and then collapsed. Boris was determined to find out what caused this strange phenomenon.

"He was so taken with it that every time I took him below to try and distract him, he would ignore whatever it was I was trying to interest him in and return to examine the sheets. I would hold my breath as he balanced on the toe rail around the boat's edge and reached up to hit the sheet with his paw.

"I thought of lowering him over the edge into the water, just to let him know there was something nasty down there, but if he'd struggled and got free, I'd never have forgiven myself. I had to let him have the run of the deck in calm weather so that he would get used to it. It would only have made his life a misery if I had harnessed him to anything. I simply hoped that the novelty of the moving sheets would eventually diminish. Meanwhile, the precarious situations he contrived worried me and I got into the morbid habit of coming on deck and first of all looking for him in the wake."

Rob had warned her to grease the steering regularly so she climbed into the aft hatch with the grease pot. She wasn't sure what exactly needed attention so decided to put grease haphazardly on everything within reach. She had forgotten to bring a grease gun, and was obliged to use her fingers. Boris came to inspect her work and got grease all over his paws, which he objected to and she wrote with amusement that he seemed to think she should have told him it wasn't wise.

When they arrived at Lanzarote, to meet up with the Express photographer, Boris revealed his unsociable side. The rendezvous boat drew up alongside the *Crusader* and as soon as he saw the photographer, Boris's hackles rose with resentment. He bolted down below and hid in an empty locker and refused to come out until the boat had gone.

Naomi was totally sympathetic. She too resented her continuity being interrupted. She wanted to get on with her voyage and resented having to slow down just to have her picture taken. Then she remembered she had a duty to the newspaper that was sponsoring her. They had kindly brought her the spare parts she had asked for, so she gritted her teeth and posed accordingly.

After setting sail again, she wrote: "Cape Town, here I come. Gran Canaria is still just visible in the distance. I wouldn't care if I never laid eyes on it again – unless it's on the way home, of course."

Ahead of her lay over 6,000 miles of empty ocean, to her an unknown quantity. She was apprehensive, but excited. She put in a call through her radio to Rob's father and was told that Rob's ship, *Great Britain II*, was furthest south of all the yachts and would probably reach Cape Town in about three weeks. This gave her spirits a much-needed lift.

There is something endearingly bizarre about a rather (at her own admittance) scatter-brained young woman sailing single-handed round the world with only a cat for company and an unwavering and illogical faith in her own ability to succeed. Without a man aboard to scoff at her she was able to cheerfully admit to her own inadequacies.

One day she was annoyed to find she'd carelessly stored some of her stock of potatoes at the bottom of a pile of heavy towels. Unable to breathe, the potatoes had rotted. The result was an evil, sticky mess, which she and Boris had to clear and throw overboard. Male though he was, Boris refrained from criticism, although she suspected he was partly to blame for lying on the towels and adding to the heat which caused the potatoes to rot.

After the job was done, they were both filthy. Boris contented himself with washing fastidiously but Naomi decided to throw away the clothes she was wearing as she hadn't enough fresh water to wash them. She then washed herself sparingly and shook talcum powder all over her, which at least made her feel cleaner and hid the overpowering smell of the rotting potatoes.

In her log book Naomi revealed some of her prejudices, admitting that she didn't have the patience to talk over the trivialities of life with people she found "as uninteresting as their topics of conversation". Nonetheless she found herself talking to Boris, who would sit and listen intently and replied with an occasional, reassuring meow. If it were not for Boris, she realised, she probably would have forgotten how to speak at all.

On 4 October, they sailed passed the Cape Verde Islands. A fine Sirocco dust was blowing from the desert and it was evident everywhere, leaving a coat of orange mess on the deck, on the sails and giving her and Boris a dusty orange tan. It was now very hot.

"I feel too lazy to wash," she wrote. "Boris is languishing in the bows, but every now and then makes a desperate leap in the air to try and catch the foot of the genoa as it flaps inboard. His feet hit the top of the guardrails and he falls back, panting, to the deck. He got into a box of tissues last night, tore up half a dozen and scattered the remainder over the floor. I had previously thrown him off my bunk for chewing my feet, so I suppose he did that to punish me."

Although Boris didn't like the heat any more than Naomi, nonetheless he would loyally accompany her on deck for sail changes. "I discouraged him from lying in the sails on deck because I was afraid the wind might catch them and balloon him over the side. His favourite trick was to climb up the mast a little way and sit on a winch to watch me. Either that, or dangle upside down in the ropes, practicing for the Antipodes. He took to guarding his territory very seriously and, whenever birds or flying fish landed on deck, they would be speedily and noisily evicted. Often Boris ended up with scales lodged in his teeth or stuck to his paws."

It was hotter below deck but at least away from the dazzling glare of the sun. On 5 October, she put a call through to Rob's father and was thrilled to learn that Rob was due to arrive next day in Cape Town, where she would be able to talk to him on the radio. The call was interrupted by a familiar noise through the hull, which meant that the dolphins had arrived to check up on them.

She and Boris went up on deck to say hello. There was no moon but the sea was alive with phosphorescence that glittered and gave each dolphin a fiery tail stream. They put on a magnificent display for the two shipmates, thirty or forty of them suddenly leaping into the air and returning with snorts and mighty splashes which sent a fine spray over the deck.

"Boris didn't approve of this. His fur stood on end and, resembling a cactus, he fled below. He reappeared later looking suspiciously around the hatch and listening to the squeaks and snorts, but obviously resentful."

That afternoon, five small whales passed within twenty yards of the stern, but didn't stop. Fortunately, she said, Boris didn't see them or he would have gone berserk.

Another radio call next day confirmed that Rob had arrived in Cape Town and would be standing by the phone for the next two nights, waiting for a call from her. She excitedly picked up the handset to make the call, but nothing happened. It had gone completely dead. She was desperately disappointed and it dawned on her that she was still thousands of miles from Cape Town and, unless she hailed a passing ship, no one would know whether she was dead or alive. However, although she wasn't aware, the radio breakdown **had** been noted and ships had been alerted to watch out for her.

She tried not to think of her husband hovering by the phone waiting for her call. Nonetheless she felt very down. The winds were feckless and she was making slow progress and all these things were affecting her efficiency. She found herself making careless mistakes. As she tried to snap out of this lethargy, suddenly the weather

Naomi James holds Boris as she waves from the
Express Crusader

turned rough and jolted her into action.

"How it lifted my spirits to see the *Crusader* come alive and gobble up the miles again. It was beautiful to see her surging through the waves and occasionally crashing down and sending mounts of spray to glitter in the sunshine. It was impossible to feel downhearted and I was hardly aware of the discomfort or the constant need to hang on and brace myself against the wild and surging movement."

On 13 October she noted: "I'm thrilled at the way the *Crusader* is sailing. The sail area is just right for the strength of the wind, so long as it doesn't fall under twenty-two knots."

To celebrate crossing the equator, Naomi cooked a three-course dinner of vegetable soup, beef with boiled potatoes, onions, peas and pickled red cabbage, with pineapple slices for afters and a small bottle of champagne. She and Boris sat down to this banquet. The champagne was delicious but Boris declined her offer to share it with her. But, she said, he did enjoy the special dinner, scattering bits of it over the chart-room as was his usual practice.

"Boris looked the picture of a contented cat secure in his own neighbourhood and didn't mind the occasional wild lurch or bank, which was so much part of this strange environment. However, I did shatter his complacency for a moment one afternoon, when I dropped the grill pan on the floor close to him. He gazed at me in horror, with his fur on end and his mouth full of tuna. I broke the spell, laughing, and his hair slowly settled."

On 17 October she wrote that she brought Boris up into the cockpit and held him aloft so he could admire the reef she had just put in the mainsail. Naomi was desperately needing some show of appreciation. She was finding the rough job of reefing easier and she felt much more confident about handling sails generally when the bad weather eventually arrived. Boris obligingly reviewed her work, but eventually objected to the way the wind flattened his ears and went below.

Boris made constant attempts to walk across the flexible fuel tank. "He tries to maintain some dignity, but it is an impossibility while gyrating. I laugh and he looks at me with disdain, then sniffs and stalks off. He doesn't like being laughed at. He has grown fussy about his food of late and has insisted on a change of diet. This morning I weakened and gave him some more tuna, which he condescended to eat."

"One of these days you'll be eating corned dog and beans" she threatened him severely, but he turned his head and pretended not to have heard.

Her main treat for herself was to sit in her comfortable seat by the chart table with an Edith Piaf tape playing her favourite French songs and sipping her favourite drink, sweet martini, with Boris playing about at her feet. She said this gave her a feeling of extreme well being. One of her own philosophies was that when things got bad, they could only get better. Situations never stayed constant and sooner or later one snapped out of black moods and went on to tackle the next problem. Little did she know that she would soon need to put this philosophy to the test. But right now she dwelt complacently on how everything was going so well for her.

On 24 October, she wrote in her log that she was bracing herself for bad weather. Two days later she glanced out of the window and noticed a gigantic wave, which turned out to be a cloud growing up over the horizon like a giant mushroom. She decided to adopt storm tactics, checking that everything was secured and that her survival kit was in order and all loose equipment stowed away.

Then came a period of calm but on 28 October, as she and Boris went on deck they were greeted by a huge dowsing of seawater. Naomi hadn't bothered to put on her oilskins and Boris just shook himself nonchalantly and perched as usual on the jib winch.

"He looked shocked as he shook himself, but he didn't go below as I thought he would. He looks funny when he gallops along the heeling deck with his ears flat and his fur fluffed up, but I'm sure he doesn't mind getting wet now. He spends many hours gazing down the cockpit drain watching the bits of flotsam gurgle up and down. Every now and then he reaches a paw and tries to grab a piece only to find that the water rushes up the drain and all he gets is a wet foot for his pains."

That night she noted that she was threatened by another of those "funny" squalls which looked like cyclones, and spent most of the time sitting in her oilskins and boots waiting for it to pass. But it didn't and finally she decided: "This squall is all bark and no bite. So I'm going to back to bed."

Next morning, at eight o'clock, she recorded bleakly that Boris went over the side.

For two and half senseless hours, she searched the ocean frantically. What kept going through her mind was that, if a creature as agile and alert and sensitive as a cat could fall overboard, how much more likely it was to happen to an inept inexperienced sailor such as herself? All her nightmares about falling overboard came back to haunt her.

Finally she sat down at the chart table and forced herself to write an account of what happened.

"Boris has gone. I feel numb and unable to think straight, but I'm going to write this down so that I can begin to accept that it has happened and there's nothing more I can do. Nothing! Shortly after breakfast I was on the foredeck, getting the ghoster ready to hoist, when I saw him doing his daredevil act of walking on the toe rail around the boat's edge. I reached out to pull him back, but he came voluntarily. Then I must have turned away. A few minutes later, out of the corner of my eye, I saw him lurch as he had done several times before. But this time he went over.

"I saw him hit the water and I rushed to the stern to disconnect the self-steering gear and put the wheel hard over. Then I dashed to the mast and let go the mainsail and staysail halyards. I could see him in the wake about fifty yards away and *Crusader* was slowly turning around towards him. But then I had to go below to start the engine and although it took only a matter of seconds, when I got back to the wheel he had disappeared. When I was past the place where I'd seen him last, I cut the engine and called and listened. There was nothing to be seen or heard. I called and called like a fool and steered the boat round in circles, but it was no use and eventually I told myself to stop. It was so calm and there were barely more than a few ripples on the surface. But Boris was nowhere to be seen."

For a long time afterwards, Naomi sat rigid at the stern, numbed and shocked but dry-eyed. As she stared into the water, her mind was a turmoil of remorse and her thoughts transfixed by the sheer horror of what had happened. "If only I could have found him, " she told herself over and over again. "There must have been something more I could have done."

She forced herself to get on with her chores. Next day, October 30, she wrote: "I've just finished doing something I've been meaning to do since the outset and losing Boris has at last frightened me into action. I've looped long thin ropes down either side of the boat to act as a lifeline. The ends are trailing about twelve feet off the stern, which gives me a fighting chance if I go over. There'll be a certain amount of drag from the ropes that will affect my speed, but they are thin and anyway, it's a matter of deciding on priorities."

That day she spent in a fever of activity, doing anything she could to take her mind off the horror of losing her best shipmate. With studied practicality, she flung overboard the cat litter tray, and all the tins of cat food and used the extra space to store boxes of beer and soft drinks. She swept below decks to get rid of cat hairs, which might give rise to sad thoughts. She knew she could not afford such luxuries. If she was to make progress she had to eradicate from her mind her feelings of guilt and bereavement.

Even so, that night she was reluctant to go to bed, concerned she wouldn't be able to sleep thinking of Boris. Instead she sat watching the water dripping off her oilskins and running in little rivulets over the floor. Losing Boris made her morbidly safety conscious and she had awful visions of falling overboard herself. If the worse happened, how would she clamber back? The sides were too high to climb and even with the aid of a ladder it would be difficult. She rationalised that the important thing was to make sure she didn't go over in the first place. She took to walking round the deck with meticulous care and made a habit of never going up on deck without saying to herself: "Take care and watch what you're doing".

"It would have been easy to have succumbed to the feeling of loss and distress I felt at losing Boris, but I knew I couldn't afford to do that. So I forced myself to think about him while it was still painful.

"Luckily I hadn't depended on him to overcome loneliness. On the whole, I had only noticed he was around when he made his presence felt, although I must say he did that pretty often. He was a dear little cat and he spent his short life onboard very happily. Sadly, his nature proved too inquisitive and too bold for his environment."

She was able to congratulate herself when she succeeded in working out a problem she was having with compass error. She reflected that people might well ask "how on earth can a duffer like her think she can navigate round the world when she doesn't even know the difference between compass error and deviation?" But, on her own in the ocean, she had forced herself to solve the problem. It was a personal triumph. And somehow it helped her to come to terms with the loss of Boris.

She headed into frightening gales. Her self-steering broke down and she had to work hard coping with all the jobs necessary to combat the winds. She read a lot. She cooked and ate automatically. Then it dawned on her that without Boris there to talk to, she had hardly heard the sound of her own voice for days. "Boris always made me laugh, but after he'd gone, I hardly ever spoke aloud."

Fearing that when she reached the coast in a few weeks time she might have lost her voice, she took to singing to herself, the birds and the ocean.

On 8 November, Day 61, she realised she had made a mistake in her navigation and was further south than she had thought. "I am either nowhere near South Africa, or else I'm about to trip over it in the dark."

Then she reached Cape Town. By daybreak Table Mountain was clearly visible. She spent three restless days there, swamped with kind hospitality but eager to continue on her voyage. She needed those three days to get her self-steering equipment and the radio fixed and pick up spares and provisions. Several people invited her to go ashore and stay at their homes, but she said she didn't want to relax too much, fearing she might lose the rapport she had built up with the *Crusader* and the sea. Invited to the yacht club for lunch, she felt very strange sitting at a table talking and listening to people. "It felt very abstract and unreal, as if I wasn't really there at all. I could still feel the motion of the *Crusader* under my feet."

Despite the wonderful hospitality bestowed upon her at Cape Town, she motored out to sea feeling vastly relieved and not at all apprehensive at the thought of spending the next four and a half months in the Roaring Forties entirely alone and facing danger daily. She was just glad to be on her way.

On 26 November at long last she spoke to her husband, Rob, on the radio. He had arrived in Auckland. They chatted for twenty-seven minutes. She told him about Boris and it was a relief to unburden herself. Suddenly he seemed so much closer. She calculated she was only about 7,000 miles from him.

By Christmas Eve she was one-third of the way round the world. Next day she opened parcels. Chay Blyth's wife, Maureen, had thoughtfully prepared a sumptuous Christmas dinner for her, including some white wine and mangoes. That evening she treated herself to a candle-lit dinner and opened presents. Her husband, Rob, had given her an antiques book.

On the last occasion she had prepared a special celebratory meal, when she crossed the equator, Boris had been there to share it with her. Now, any thoughts of Boris she kept to herself. She was feeling cheerful and resourceful and the loss of Boris was still too painful a subject to dwell on. In fact, it seemed, during the ensuing months she managed to eradicate all memory of him from her mind. Only in dangerous situations, aware of the awful consequences of falling overboard, did a distressing image of him struggling in the wake flash before her eyes, almost as a warning. In fact, losing Boris made her more safety-conscious than she might otherwise have been, more alert to danger. Boris's cruel fate taught her to treat the sea with the utmost respect.

In the end she rounded Cape Horn without even setting eyes on it, her first sight of land being Illa Los Estados, well on the way to the Falklands. She was now homeward bound and it seemed all was plain sailing. By 28 June she was sailing towards the finishing line. A message from Rob came over the radio: "Do you want to open the Southampton Boat Show?" Elated and triumphant she found herself emphatically saying yes.

She sailed into Dartmouth and one of the first things she spotted was the dear, familiar face of her husband pointing to what she realised was a gun and the finishing line. It was all too unreal. All she could see from then on was a sea of boats and waving people. Suddenly the gun went off and she knew she had made it. She dropped her sails, as willing hands came on board to help her. "I shut my eyes and turned round and a few seconds later, Rob's arms were around me."

Poor Boris, that he was not there to share in the excitement and triumph. But he probably wouldn't have enjoyed it. Naomi James later reflected that it seemed to her that her trip round the world was a totally separate life from the one she had before and after her voyage. Boris was part of that separate life. He had enriched it and played a huge part in ensuring she returned safely. Even with her indomitable spirit, Naomi James might not have survived without the hard lesson that she learnt from Boris's sad end.

Admiral Lord Nelson's cat Tiddles

Horatio Nelson aficionados have searched high and low for even the slimmest evidence that Nelson might not only have had a cat, but maybe even taken one with him to the Battle of Trafalgar, perhaps to curl up with him in his bunk in place of the lovely Emma. A cat on HMS *Victory*! Surely there must have been a ship's cat to rid that great oak ship of rodents? It was also rumoured that Nelson was an ardent cat lover.

Despite extensive searches, there has never been the remotest suggestion of Nelson having a cat. Then a few years ago a letter came to the author through the post which set the heart fluttering, referring to Admiral Lord Nelson's faithful cat, Tiddles!

The relationship between Lady Emma Hamilton and Nelson has been well documented but, as the writer of the letter pointed out, the relationship Nelson had with his cat Tiddles has been grossly overlooked by naval historians.

Tiddles, according to the letter from a Mr. Guy Evans, printed in the Spectator in December 1990, was discovered as an abandoned kitten in the courtyard of the Palazzo Sessa, the British Embassy in Naples, in March 1797. Pitiful and starving, he was taken in by the kind-hearted Emma Hamilton.

As the wife of the British Ambassador, Neopolitans were enamoured by her beauty and she became famous for her dramatic poses, or still life tableaux, depicting mythological characters and dramatic heroines from history, which became known as "Attitudes". When very young she became the muse of the artist George Romney who was fascinated by Emma's intense physical presence and her ability to hold poses and expressions like a professional model. He painted more than 100 pictures of her.

Once Emma had restored Tiddles' fur to a smooth healthy shine, and fattened him up, she was said to have even used him in one of her "Attitudes" in the fighting role of Nemean Lion, strangled by Hercules as part of his 'twelve labours'.

Soon Tiddles was the favourite of everyone, including the Queen of Naples, Maria Carolina. He was a brilliant mouse hunter and even earned the admiration of King Ferdinand. Emma's husband, the Naples Ambassador Sir William Hamilton, a lover of all graceful and beautiful creatures, was delighted. And it was all good for international relations.

The three of them, William, Emma and Tiddles returned to England in 1800. A few years later, as Nelson prepared to go to sea again, she insisted he adopted the cat as a mascot. He became part of the ship's crew on HMS *Victory*. During the Battle of Trafalgar in 1808, Tiddles remained on deck, unruffled by the noise of gunfire. As a result he earned respect and a reputation for keeping calm in the midst of battle.

When his master was fatally wounded, Tiddles was disconsolate. Captain Hardy arranged for him to be transferred to HMS *Amphion* and the skipper, Captain William Hoste, recognised him as a true hero by promoting him to Boatswain's Mate.

Depiction of Nelson's cat Tiddles!

Tiddles sailed with Hoste on both his successful Adriatic actions, displaying his now legendary coolness under fire at the battle of Lissa, only to fall victim to a stray shot at the siege of Trieste in 1813. A monument was erected in the Protestant cemetery of that city, which survived until 1924, when it was destroyed by Mussolini's army, an act that would not have pleased Il Duce for he, like Nelson, was also said to be a noted cat lover, or as Mr. Evans described, ailurophile.

The dictionary says AILUROPHILE is from the Greek for a cat lover and describes the reference as 'facetious'.

This tale might seem wildly improbable, but Mr. Evans maintained it was the result of diligent research and stuck to his story. The life and death of Tiddles was next aired in the Tenth anniversary of the Nelson Society's journal, the Nelson Dispatch, in 1991, along with an alleged likeness of Tiddles in attendance at Nelson's death bed.

Some readers might reject this tale as fabricated nonsense. This author thinks it is charming and prefers to believe every word.

Matthew, the Lonely Old Ferryman
And his Sixteen Cats

John Thomas Smith, keeper of Prints and Drawings at the British Museum in 1790, described vividly how, when he was young, he used to walk with his sweetheart to Old Matthew Cook's Ferry by the side of the River Lea, near Edmonton.

"Matthew was a very lonely old man and to keep him company, he had sixteen cats, all of the finest breeds and of the best tempers. He taught them all distinct tricks and it was his custom morning and evening to put them through their paces. One after the other, they would leap over his hands joined as high as his arms could reach. This attention to his cats, which occupied nearly the whole of his time, afforded him much pleasure.

"Melancholy as Cook's Ferry is during the winter, it is still more so in the time of flood, when it is almost insupportable. Had not Matty enjoyed the society of his cats, who certainly kept the house tolerably free of rats and mice, at the accustomed time of a high flood, he would have been truly wretched."

One year, during the flooding, John Smith said he decided to travel over the meadows to visit Matthew, partly in a cart and partly in a boat, conducted by his baker and Tom Fogin, his barber.

"We found him standing in a washing tub, dangling a bit of scrag of mutton before the best fire existing circumstances could produce, in a room on the ground-floor, knee-deep in water, whilst he ever and anon raised his voice to his cats in the room above, where he had huddled them for safety.

"The baker, after delivering his bread in at the window, and I, after fastening our skiff to the shutter-hook, waited the return of Fogin who had launched himself into a tub to shave Matthew, who had perched himself on the top of a tall Queen Anne's chair, and drawn his feet as much under him as possible. With the palms of his hands flat upon his knees to keep the balance true, he was prepared to listen to Fogin's tales in the tub during his shave."

Having described this extraordinary scene, John Smith goes on to write of other things and exasperatingly omits telling his readers whether the cats and Matthew survived that miserable wet winter with their wits intact.

Cats that Cruised the Inland Waterways

Orlando was a ginger cat who, for three years, cruised the inland waterways with writer and photographer, Hugh McKnight, who had been commissioned by the Shell Organisation to write the definitive book on the thousands of miles of British waterways. Hugh approached this challenge with the purposefulness of explorers of old, intent on writing about every cruisable stretch of water he could find.

Hugh found a neglected and shabby old 20ft gaff-rigged wooden sloop called *Ricky II* on the Thames at Richmond and lovingly restored it with the intention of earning a living by cruising and writing about the waterways. The first thing he did was paint her green, put in a new engine and change her name to the *Dorymouse*, the West Country name for a small mouse.

"She was a warm, friendly little boat with two portholes that looked like eyes, so the name seemed to suit her," explained Hugh. There was a two berth cabin, a tiny galley and very little else in the way of luxury.

Orlando was given to him as a kitten by June Humphries, whose husband, John, was the chairman of the British Inland Waterways Association at the time. Hugh met them both at a meeting to discuss the 1970 National Rally of Boats at Guildford. When he left the meeting he found he was the surprised owner of one of June's cat's new litter of kittens.

"I never really planned to take Orlando with me on my voyages but, the first time he came aboard the *Dorymouse*, he immediately made himself at home. I took him on one trial trip and he was so affectionate and intelligent and such good company I had to keep him on as my first mate. At first I was nervous of him straying and kept him on a lead, but it soon became obvious that he was not a wanderer. He was quite doglike, following me everywhere and greeting me with enthusiasm whenever I returned from an outing."

One minor drawback was that Orlando hated the sound of the boat engine and whenever the *Dorymouse* was on the move, he would curl up in the bilges where it was marginally quieter. Despite this, for three years he faithfully travelled with Hugh on the *Dorymouse* all over England and Wales. On one trip, to Llangollen, North Wales, from Shepperton-on-Thames and back, they covered a total of 2,000 miles.

Each time they moored, Orlando would jump ashore and play on the towpath. At night he would go hunting but always returned in the early hours of the morning. "Usually he had a little gift for me, a field mouse or tiny water vole, which he would kindly deposit on my bunk," said Hugh. Exhausted by his nightly forages, he would curl up fast asleep at the bottom of the bunk, at Hugh's feet.

There was only one occasion when Orlando didn't return, when the *Dorymouse* was moored at Market Drayton on the Shropshire Union Canal. Hugh spent half a day searching frantically for him. Just as he was about to give him up for lost,

Cat, of the narrow boat *Crane*, on the Grand Union Canal, May 1961, tethered to the cabin top by his owner, Ray White - the traditional method of preventing the ship's cat jumping ashore while on the move.

(By kind permission of Hugh McKnight)

Orlando came back, looking a bit worse for wear after a night on the tiles.

After his book, "The Shell Book of Inland Waterways", was published, Hugh went on to write about, and cruise, the French waterways (Slow Boat through France) and the waterways of Western Europe and Germany, this time on his narrowboat *Avonway*. Sadly, Orlando didn't accompany him on these trips. After surviving three years on the British canals, he was killed by a car outside Hugh's home in Shepperton, when he was only four years old.

Hugh McKnight's travels took him to many canal boat rallies. He said it was always a fine sight to see assembled on the water dozens of brightly painted pleasure-cruising narrowboats, either converted from old working coal and freight carrying vessels or modern, custom built versions. Usually to be seen also, were the owners' pet cats on leads, tied to the chimney or one of the handrails in the traditional manner. Often they would be exercised up and down the towpath, like dogs.

Present day narrowboat owners, who now cruise for sheer pleasure and love of the canals, are dedicated traditionalists. They take pride in trying to be as authentic as they can. They will go to extreme lengths to imitate the original born and bred boat people who would often spend their entire lives in a tiny cramped cabin at the tiller end of their working narrowboat where, miraculously, there was space for bunks for the whole family, a comfortable area for eating and a sturdy iron stove for warmth and cooking, in which they burnt wood or coal.

Living in such cramped conditions didn't stop the family from keeping ferrets and maybe a lurcher, for hunting rabbits and wild fowl. There was usually a pet cat which, when it wasn't curled up in the warmest spot beside the stove, was kept on a lead and tied to the chimney.

Today, of course, narrowboats are fitted out with a superb galley and a luxury bathroom or shower and double beds. Despite the fact that the boats are so narrow, usually only 7ft wide so that they can cope with the restrictive widths of the canals and locks, there is still space for the owner's family to spread themselves around in comfort.

Hugh McKnight remembers in 1961 cruising the Grand Union and the Northern Oxford Canals with that legendary, professional boatman, Ray White. Ray was a former bus conductor who took to commercial canal carrying for the Willow Wren Canal Carrying Co., of Brentford and Braunston (Northants) who were making a brave attempt at the time to bring back canal-carrying on a moderately large scale. He travelled in two narrowboats, the motor boat called *Crane* and the unpowered butty called *Dunlin*.

An idyllic sight, the two traditional boats would, side by side, work their way along the miles of canals, with Ray at the tiller. Ray would tell how once, as he was steering his narrowboat past a waterside factory near King's Langley, a girl factory worker leaned out of a mill window and cheekily called down to him: "That looks like a nice life. I wouldn't mind joining you."

Being a single man, Ray replied hopefully: "All right then!" At which she promptly did. The girl, Margaret, took to river life with sheer joy. They married and raised a family on the narrowboat. After their first child was born, the happy couple acquired a black and white cat which, being an unpretentious sort of guy, Ray called simply Cat. Cat spent most of its time on top of the cabin – tied to the chimney or hatch in the traditional manner.

Canal boatman Ray White aboard his narrow boat pair *Dunlin* and *Crane* with his cat, Cat, on the cabin roof with a lead.

(Picture by kind permission of Hugh McKnight)

Bengy the Canal Bargey

Children's story writer, Cicely Fraser-Simson was married to the composer who set to music a dramatised version of Kenneth Grahame's 'Toad of Toad Hall' and consequently to Ratty's immortal words: "There's nothing, absolutely nothing half so much worth doing as simply messing about in boats."

In the 1950's, after her husband died, she settled in London beside a tree-lined stretch of the Regent's Canal, where narrowboats passed her window every day. One day she came upon a stripey black cat with a family of kittens, in the garden of an empty house beside the canal. The writer became fond of them and each day would leave out scraps of food and saucers of milk.

She christened the mother Mrs Stripey-Black and was inspired to write a story about her. Mrs Stripey-Black, she decided, was descended from a grand old sea cat called Admiral who had sailed the seven seas and was reputed to have caught mice in every port in Europe.

Mrs Stripey-Black, abandoned by her owner and left to her own devices, falls in love with a cat called Spitty. The relationship produces four kittens – three female, stripey like their mother and called Faith, Hope and Charity, and one male called Bengy, all black except for a white nose and a white tip on his tail.

Mrs Stripey-Black tells her kittens stories about the old Admiral and lulls them to sleep with a song he used to sing.

Oh, the life of the sea
Is the life for me
And I leave the land,
For them that can't stand
The sway and swinging.
The clutching and clinging.
They haven't a notion
How grand is the ocean.
I travel and roam
But the ship is my home,
A sea-cat, that's me,
Born and bred by the sea.

Spitty's owners move house and, naturally, he goes with them. To feed her family, Mrs Stripey-Black is obliged to go out to work hunting mice on behalf of a fat elderly cat called Marmalade, who seriously lacks hunting skills but whose owners expect her to keep their home free of mice. In return Marmalade allows Mrs Stripey-Black and her kittens to share her food.

The three female kittens grow up learning all the proper feline skills. But Bengy is a worry, showing signs of being a true sea cat and having the old Admiral's salt blood in his veins. Instead of learning how to hunt, he prefers to sneak down to the canal to watch the barges go by. Recklessly, he jumps aboard boats moored on the bank, enjoying the thrill of balancing himself in precarious places at the risk of falling into the water. His sea legs come naturally to him and he gets quite nifty at jumping on and off boats and running along the decks.

After a few months, Spitty returns to inspect the kittens. He tells Mrs Stripey-Black that now they are almost grown, she must find them homes and suggests several. New owners are easily found for Faith, Hope and Charity, who have been taught by their mother to be good mousers. But nobody seems to want Bengy.

One day he notices a pair of narrowboats, side by side, one towing the other. They are so close to the bank, he easily leaps aboard. After a few minutes the boats drift into the middle of the canal, a stretch too wide for him to jump off without getting wet

Frightened, he goes down below and curls up in the middle of a coil of rope. Running away to sea doesn't seem such a good idea any more and suddenly he wants his mother. The chug-chugging of the engine soon lulls him to sleep. When he wakes up the narrowboat speaks to him in a chugging language they both seem to understand. Bengy is advised by the wise old boat that it would be foolish to try to jump ship because they'd already travelled for so many miles and he'd never find his way back to his mother. The best option would be to stay aboard until the narrowboat turned round and came back. It might take a few months, but at least he'd be sure of seeing his family again.

The kindly narrowboat sings a song to him, in a deep, oily baritone voice.

I follow the waterways,
Up and down the land.
Through the town and through the country,
It's a life that's grand.
Calm and peaceful, free and happy,
Never a tie to bind.
Off for a voyage on the breast of the water
Worries left behind.

The two narrowboats, brightly painted with flowers and castles, are work and home to a fat, rough-diamond of a man and his wife, who is even fatter than her husband and never gets off the boat because she finds it too difficult. They have a daughter called Elsie and, in their two narrowboats, the family travel the waterways transporting goods such as coal and timber from one end of the country to the other.

When they find the very hungry stowaway cat, Elsie's father wants to chuck him into the canal. Elsie begs to be allowed to keep him and her father reluctantly agrees. Suddenly Bengy is Elsie's cat and she is feeding him on delicious, freshly cooked kippers and cool milk. That night he curls up in Elsie's bunk, in the cabin, close to her feet. He is happy. At last he is, if not a sea cat, at least a canal cat and he falls asleep singing to himself:

> I'm a bargey, that's me,
> My name is Bengy.

Mrs Stripey-Black is meanwhile beside herself with worry. She fears Bengy has fallen into the canal and drowned. All her kittens are gone and she is sad and lonely. Luckily a nice lady comes to live in the empty house beside the canal, takes a liking to her and gives her a home. But every day, Mrs Stripey-Black goes down to the canal, hoping that Bengy will turn up.

After several months, Bengy's narrowboat **does** return. Swaggering like a true sailor, he steps niftily off the barge onto the river bank and there is his mother waiting for him. She is very proud of her bargey son even though she knows the visit will be short and soon he will be away again on his travels on the British waterways.

Manx Cats that Charm Away Storms

Sailors believed cats had magic in their tails and were capable of attracting storms by erecting their tails. Cats were needed on board to control the rats, but had to be kept content and malleable with kind words and treats. An angry, unhappy cat was more likely to raise its tail and bring bad luck to the ship.

Therefore a cat which had no tail was considered lucky and brought good fortune to ship and crew as well as warding off storms. Although tail-less cats are fairly common in China and Japan, in Europe they are rare and found mainly on the Isle of Man. In fact the Manx cat-without-a-tail is the emblem of the Isle of Man and is featured on the local currency.

There are many different stories about how they came to lose their tails. One is that it is the result of mating between domestic cats and rabbits.

Legend has it that the cat was the last creature to enter *Noah's Ark*. A pair of them insisted on one final mousing trip before the flood water rose and kept putting off the moment when they would have to board the *Ark*. When the rain began to fall really heavily, they rushed up the gangplank just as Noah was closing the hatch. As they squeezed through, the heavy hatch slammed shut on their beautiful bushy tails and severed them. So although the cats were saved from the flood, their tails were lost forever.

Another theory is that a ship from the *Spanish Armada* was shipwrecked in 1588 on rocks off the coast of the Isle of Man, in the extreme south west of the island. Aboard was a family of seven cats born by chance without tails, who managed to find shelter until the low tide when they were able to clamber ashore at a location now known as Spanish Head. Finding themselves isolated from other cats on this small island, they began to reproduce and established themselves as the distinctive tail-less Manx cat.

There is also a story that the Manx cat was originally a temple guardian in Tibet, who travelled on a ship to Spain, and boarded a Spanish galleon. This galleon was part of the Armada and was sunk near the Isle of Man. The cat swam ashore and settled on the island where it produced a large number of kittens. They all had long bushy tails. Because these tails were so beautiful they were repeatedly cut off by Irish soldiers who coveted the cats' tails as lucky mascots. To discourage this, the mother cats would bite off the tails of their kittens at birth. A variant of this story describes

how the tails of the cats were sliced off by Vikings who rather liked them for decorating their helmets.

And there is the unlikely myth about Samson swimming the length of the Irish Sea. As he swam rather close to the Isle of Man he was caught by a cat that nearly drowned him with his long tail. In retaliation, Samson bit his tail off and from that day onwards the cats on the island had either only stumps for tails (these are called Stumpies) or no tails at all (these are called Rumpies).

Manx cats have helped to make the Isle of Man famous but the Manx cat population has been dwindling. It is rumoured that some owners have been so unscrupulous as to have had the tails of normal cats chopped off at birth to perpetuate the myths and help attract tourists.

In the 1950's Doolish, a proper Manx tail-less cat, landed the glamorous job of promoting holidays in the Isle of Man to the people of South East England. He was treated like a film star, travelling to London in style in his own executive cabin on the Isle of Man's Steam Packet Company Ferry. The Manx Information Centre meticulously worked out the cost of supplying him with milk and tinned cat food, allowing for inflation and the expected increase in Doolish's appetite as he became accustomed to rich living. Whether Doolish was successful in attracting more holiday makers to the Isle of Man is not recorded.

The Night the RNLI Rescued Freddy
From the Wrecked *Hawksdale*

On 22 January, 1899, the *Hawksdale*, a sleek three-masted commercial sailing ship, of 1,723 tons net, from Liverpool, was on her way from Hamburg with a cargo of 500 German-made pianos on board, heading for Melbourne, Australia. Amongst the twenty-seven man crew was a 17-year old apprentice sailor, Aubrey Chaplin, of The Firs, Rugby, England. It was the young Aubrey's second voyage and this time he was likely to be away from home for many months.

The master, Captain William Steele, had kindly allowed Aubrey to take with him his pet cat, Freddy, to keep him company and rid the ship of rodents. The marmalade coloured cat soon became a favourite amongst the crew.

Freddy was devoted to Aubrey and would follow closely at his heels up and down by the hour, as he paced the deck when on watch. He liked to curl up at the bottom of Aubrey's bunk and seemed to spend much of his time lulled to sleep by the constant swaying of the ship, neglecting his duties as rodent controller.

After leaving the Elbe, off the German coast, the *Hawksdale* met up with violent winds and rough weather and by mistake went off her course for Australia and on 26 January ran aground on the Long Sands between Margate and Clacton-on-Sea, off the English coast. She lay there helplessly, tossed about ruthlessly by the savage winds and waves.

The crew clung to the ship in terror, fully expecting her to break up. The sails had already been torn to shreds by the gale and the massive masts were in danger of crashing down on top of them. Things looked bleak. A disastrous attempt was made to launch one of the ship's lifeboats but it capsized and three of the crew, including the pilot, drowned. Then a second lifeboat broke from its fastenings and was lost. For six hours the remaining men on board the *Hawksdale* were at the mercy of the elements, in mortal fear.

At last the distress signals they had sent out were observed and the Royal National Lifeboat Institution at Clacton and Margate prepared to rescue the stricken men. Undaunted by the foul weather, the valiant lifeboat crew launched their boats and headed for the wrecked ship.

It took several hours to get to her. With seawater lashing viciously at their faces so that they could barely see what they were doing, the lifeboat crew got as near as they could to the wreck, seriously risking their own lives in their efforts to save others. As the lifeboats were lifted by the waves to the same level as the ship, the men on board were urged to jump over and clutch the ropes on the rescue boats as best they could. It took many attempts, and incredible displays of courage, to haul the men aboard the two RNLI Lifeboats.

Aubrey, soaked and frightened, was on the deck of the *Hawksdale*, clinging for dear life to anything he could lay his hands on as he waited for his turn to jump. Suddenly he remembered with horror that Freddy, the ship's cat, was still below. To the amazement of his fellow crew members, he disappeared down the hatch to search for him. He found Freddy was still curled up in his bunk, sleeping soundly and totally unaware of the danger. When Aubrey woke him he was indignant at being so rudely disturbed and struggled ungratefully.

Aubrey dived into the storeroom and found a sack, into which he unceremoniously stowed the surprised cat. Then he clambered back onto the deck. The lifeboat captain was furious. His boat was in danger of capsizing and here he was waiting for some foolhardy apprentice sailor who for some inexplicable reason had dived back below decks. When he saw the sack he presumed Aubrey was trying to retrieve some valuable possession and shouted angrily at him that he was only allowed to bring "live cargo" on board.

However, when told that there was a cat in the bag, Aubrey was allowed to fling it from the ship into the bottom of the lifeboat, where it immediately became saturated in the deep water that had collected in the hull. Then Aubrey struggled to haul himself in too and in doing so struck the side of his head a heavy blow as he splash-landed beside Freddy.

It was a savage struggle to get back to shore as huge waves came into the boat and soaked the men. The sack with the cat inside was now under water. Wet and cold, and half stupefied by the blow to his head, nonetheless Aubrey realised that the cat was in real danger of drowning. He dragged the sack from the water and lifted it onto his knees. By now the contents of the bag were alarmingly still and Aubrey feared Freddy might be dead, but couldn't risk opening the neck of the sack to see, in case he jumped out. With frozen hands, he clutched the sack tightly to his knees for three to four long and sickening hours, as the RNLI Lifeboats struggled back through heavy seas to Clacton – a distance of over fifteen miles, having successfully saved 24 men from the *Hawksdale*.

Luckily, Freddy survived his ordeal. After arriving safely on shore, he was pulled out of the sack half conscious and gently resuscitated. After being tenderly dried and fed warm milk he was laid by a comforting fire to sleep it off. It was decided that after such a terrifying adventure his career as a ship's cat should end, and Aubrey's parents took him home to Rugby with them to spend the rest of his life on firm, solid ground.

The wrecked ship was pounded by heavy seas for four days. The tug *Merrimac* was sent with three other tugs, *Challenge*, *Goole* and *Revenge*, to try to tow her off the Sands, but their attempts were unsuccessful. Apparently most of the pianos and some other cargo were salvaged by numerous small vessels. The *Merrimac* reported that the *Hawksdale's* hull finally broke in half and became submerged.

It appears that Peter Iredale & Porter, of Liverpool, the proud owners of the 270ft steel-hulled *Hawksdale*, which had been built in Londonderry and launched only nine years earlier in May 1890, laid the blame for the disaster and loss of lives on Captain William Steele. He was suspended for six months but later went back to sea and died in 1925.

Aubrey was not put off his sea career and probably learnt a great deal from his horrific experience. Some months later, Aubrey was given leave from his ship in Liverpool, to travel across the Irish Sea to Dublin. There, at the Mansion House and in the presence of the Lord Mayor and other very important people, he was presented with an impressive silver medal from the Dublin Home for Starving and Forsaken Cats, in recognition of his bravery.

The inscription read:

"Presented to Mr Aubrey F.Chaplin by Miss Alice M.Swifte, founder of the Dublin Home for Starving and Forsaken Cats, in remembrance of his brave conduct in saving the life of a cat, at the risk of his own, in time of shipwreck".

On the other side was an embossed wreath with an engraving of a cat and the name "Freddy".

The Hawksdale

Footnote: *Prior to her unfortunate end, the **Hawksdale** unsuccessfully attempted to beat the **Cutty Sark** on a voyage to Australia. On board the **Hawksdale** was Apprentice Dowman who later became a ships master. In 1922, on a trip to Falmouth Dowman recognised a Portuguese ship with the name **Ferreira**, in Falmouth for repair, as in fact the **Cutty Sark** and was responsible for her purchase and eventual preservation as the famous Museum ship at Greenwich.*

Stray Cats that Live on Dutch Barges

In Amsterdam there are three barges permanently moored alongside the Singel Canal, one of the famous waterways in the city centre. Thousands of stray cats live aboard, depending on charity for their survival.

The first barge, known as the *De Poezenboot* (The Pussycat Boat), was bought in 1969 by cat lover Henriette van Weelde to provide a home for the orphaned, stray, sick and rejected cats of Amsterdam. It quickly became a tourist attraction. Originally she offered her own house as a sanctuary for the strays, but soon there were too many. The barge provided the answer and also enabled visitors to see the animals and provide much-needed funds to support her work. By 1971 she was forced to expand and bought a second barge.

The original boat now holds about 60 elderly and sickly cats that will spend the rest of their lives on board. The second boat houses the younger and healthier cats, waiting adoption. Since no stray cats are ever turned away (and it has been estimated that altogether there are about 50,000 stray cats in Amsterdam) it is not surprising that there is now a third barge, as the city's feline problem continues to escalate.

Henriette, who is now elderly, is assisted by five volunteers but receives no financial aid from the city authorities and has to rely on donations from tourists and visitors. Her feline *Noah's Ark* is open to the public every day.

The *Poezenboot* (pussycat boat) on the Singel canal
in Amsterdam provides a home to hundreds of stray cats.

William the Seafaring Cat
With a Huge Ego

William was a self-centred cat with a huge ego, who features in a story by James Thurber, entitled "Cat in the Lifeboat" (1956). William imagined that he was the Will referred to in "Last Will and Testament".

Taken on a round-the-world voyage, he encountered a terrible storm and, as the ship was sinking, he thought he heard the cry "William and children first" and immediately leapt into the lifeboat, only to be thrown out by an irate sailor. When he eventually swam ashore to a remote island, he was so shocked he couldn't remember his name.

The Shipwrecked Cat that
Climbed Aboard a Rum Barrel

One distinguished seafarer who was so passionate about cats he eventually, in his old age, became convinced he resembled one, was the Vicomte de Chateaubriand Francois René (1768-1848), the French writer, politician and ambassador.

His own cat originally belonged to Pope Leo XII and after his death, Chateaubriand adopted him and named him Micetto, although he was always referred to as the Pope's Cat.

As a young man of 23 years, Chateaubriand sailed across the Atlantic to North America. Because of his passion for cats, he became attached to the resident cat on board the ship, who he described as "a greenish tabby with a hairless tail and bushy whiskers".

"He was firm on his paws, able to bring back-balance and side-balance to play against the pitching and rolling of the ship. He had been twice round the world and saved himself from shipwreck by climbing on board a rum barrel. Tom has the privilege of sleeping where he pleases, but prefers the second mate's fur coat."

How Dick Whittington's Cat Earned Him a Fortune by Going to Sea

About 1370 a poor orphan boy called Dick set out for London to seek his fortune. He'd been led to believe that the streets there were paved with gold. When he arrived he was disappointed to find that they were made of stone, like everywhere else.

Totally destitute, he slept on the hard pavement amongst the rats and mice, and begged for food. Seeing the starving child in the gutter, a rich merchant called Ivor Fitzwaryn rescued him. He was washed and fed and given a place to sleep and work in the merchant's kitchens.

Dick's sleeping area was infested with rats and mice and to get rid of them he bought a cat for a penny from a little girl he met in the street. The cat proved to be a champion rat catcher, and soon got rid of the vermin. Dick was well pleased and became very fond of his cat.

Fitzwaryn was impressed when he heard about how good the cat was at getting rid of mice and rats. His merchant ships were swarming with vermin, so he asked Dick if he could borrow this marvellous cat to take with him on one of his trading vessels, the *Unicorn*. Dick reluctantly agreed.

The ship was away for many months and there was no news of it. During this time, Dick was badly treated by the cook in the merchant's kitchen. Soon he could bear his cruelty no longer and, thinking he would never see his cat again, decided to run away. Just as he was leaving the city, on Highgate Hill (where today there is a bronze statue of the cat) he heard the pealing of Bow Bells and they seemed to say to him: "Turn again, Whittington. Three times Lord Mayor of London." He decided to return to the city.

Meanwhile, the ship on which his beloved cat was sailing reached its destination on the Barbary Coast. The Moorish court was overrun with rodents and, when the ruler heard how excellent Dick's cat was at getting rid of rats, he offered to pay ten times as much for him as the price offered for the whole of the rest of the cargo. A bargain was struck and the cat was let loose at the court where he got rid of the vermin with admirable efficiency.

When the merchant returned from his voyage he handed over to Dick the fortune he had received for the cat. Dick prospered rapidly and was soon able to marry Alice, the merchant's lovely daughter. The words he thought he heard the Bow Bells pealing out soon came true. He became Lord Mayor of London three times – from 1397-1399, 1406-1407 and 1419-1420.

In 1416 he also became a Member of Parliament and was made a Knight and became known as Sir Richard Whittington. He died in 1423, but never saw his cat again, although he owed his fame and fortune to him.

Illustration from an 18th century song sheet telling the story of Dick Whittington & his cat

Picture of Queen Tiyi and her daughters, on a papyrus canoe
with her cat beneath her seat

Ancient Egyptian Cats on Nile Barges

The Egyptians revered and respected cats and used them as hunting companions, training them to travel with them on boats in the marshlands of the Nile, in the pursuit of fish and river birds. Several Egyptian scenes, painted on walls of tombs and temples, depict this type of pastime. One shows a cat on a barge impatiently pawing his master's clothes as the man hurls a stick at a cluster of birds on the shore.

Another, carved on the back of her daughter, Princess Sat-amen's chair, shows a scene with Queen Tiyi, of the XVIII Dynasty, on a papyrus canoe in the marshes of the Nile. The Queen is sitting in a high-backed chair with arms. Beneath her seat is a cat with tail erect. In the prow of the canoe Princess Sat-amen is offering her mother a bunch of lotus flowers.

Another scene shows Nebamun, "the scribe who kept account of the grain" hunting on a canoe on the Nile with his cat. The cat catches birds as they fall. This illustration, painted 3,000 years ago, is in bright colours and the colouring of the long tapering tail reveals that the cat is *felis maniculata* from which our domestic breeds are derived.

Cats were so venerated by the ancient Egyptians that they took special care to preserve and embalm them, concealing amongst the colourful bandages jewel encrusted trinkets to amuse them on their journey to the next world. Special cat cemeteries were set aside and over the years thousands of cats were entombed. It was felt they would repose in greater peace and security if they were in large numbers. Above the tombs, temples were built in their honour.

The Greek historian, Herodotus, mentions the concern Egyptians felt at the loss of a cat and the general mourning that ensued in a house when a cat died. If a cat became ill it would be watched and attended to with the greatest solicitude and if any person purposely or even involuntarily killed one of these revered animals, it was deemed a capital offence.

Mummified Egyptian Cats Shipped to Liverpool by Victorian Merchants.

In January 1890 ss *Phou* and ss *Thebes* steamed out of Alexandria, Egypt with 180,000 mummified Egyptian cats on board. The cats had been dead for at least 4,000 years and had been unceremoniously dug up by local labourers from a sacred cat cemetery in Beni Hassan, about 100 miles from Cairo, on the East Bank of the River Nile.

Guano and bone merchants, Messrs. Leventon and Co., of 16 Hackins Hey, Liverpool, bought 19½ tons of the embalmed cats from an Alexandrian merchant with the intention of converting the lot into a fertiliser rich in phosphate of lime and ammonia, at their bone mills in Liverpool. It was expected they would get £3.13s 9d per ton for them – in those days a princely sum.

An auction was planned for "trade only" but news of what was in the consignment got out and members of the public, as well as distinguished Egyptologists and Museum Curators, turned up. The individuals made no secret of the fact that they just wanted to add one of these ancient curiosities to their private collections. The Egyptologists and curators sanctimoniously expressed their distaste at the proceedings and said the whole affair was appalling vandalism. They pointed out that these animals were sacred to the goddesses of the Nile and venerated by ancient Egyptians who were grateful to them for destroying the vermin that did serious damage to their stored grain, which was essential to the economy of their country. Nonetheless, they too made their bids in the interest of science.

In fact there were very few complete specimens of embalmed cats. The local labourers who had found the tombs had unraveled thousands of the mummies as they searched frantically for valuables traditionally concealed within the colourful linen bandages. As a result of being so rudely disturbed the mummies broke up into fragments and it was in this dusty condition that most of the bodies were bagged and shipped to England.

At the auction samples of the embalmed cats were held up for inspection. A genial atmosphere prevailed and one newspaper reported that "the auctioneer thought it amusing to knock down the lots using one of the pussies' heads as a hammer".

Amongst the powdery bones there were some complete mummies and these were the ones disposed of first. One perfect specimen with what the auctioneer called a "sweet face" went for 3s. 3d. Another not-so-handsome mummy, but in better condition, went for 4s. 6d. Yet another the auctioneer described as having "a human look" to which some of the more hypercritical bidders murmured: "Don't insult the animal". It still went under the hammer - for half-a-crown.

The rest of the remains were knocked down at £3. 13s. 9d per ton and were transported in bags to the bone mill and converted into fertiliser to contribute to the fruitfulness of English soil.

Mark Twain claimed his trip up the Nile was fuelled by mummified cats.

Sacred mummified cats being auctioned in Liverpool

In his book, *The Innocents Abroad* (1869) Mark Twain wrote: "The fuel (Egyptian railroaders) used for the locomotive is composed of mummies 3,000 years old, purchased by the ton from the graveyard for that purpose. Sometimes one hears the profane engineer call out pettishly, 'D--n these plebeians, they don't burn and aren't worth a cent--pass out a King!'"

Newspapers all over the country gave columns of space to the story. The curious shipment incited a wealth of excitement and curiosity. The shipping firm, Messrs. Leventon and Co. received daily letters from people asking if they could buy specimens. In fact, so successful was the sale of the 19½ tons of embalmed cats, that the merchant's two steamships raced back to Alexandria for more and was lucky enough to buy another ten tons of cat mummies.

On February 8, 1890, the Liverpool Echo announced that there was to be another auction sale of mummified cats at Gordon's Sale Room, Romford Street, at 12 noon. One of these was bought by F.S.Moore Esq., Curator of Liverpool Museum. Today's modern visitors can see it there on display. So for sure, one cat at least was saved, after 4,000 years of peace in its sacred tomb, from a fate worse than death.

Three Intrepid Cats that Sailed the World With a Teenage Dropout

Dinghy was a timid, black and white kitten born, not to the roar of the sea but to the wail of city traffic, who had the dubious honour of being chosen by an 18-year-old New York dropout from a broken home to keep her company during her rash attempt to sail around the world alone.

He was not yet weaned when, on 28 May, 1985, his new mistress Tania Aebi set off from New York in *Varuna*, a cramped little 26ft sloop which her father had bought her. Tania was disappointed her new "buddy" was still too young to be taken from his mother but her sister promised to personally deliver him to her as soon as she reached St. Thomas, in the Caribbean. Still very much a child herself and desperate for affection, at various points of her two-and-a-half-year voyage Tania acquired three ship's cats as "crew".

What little she knew about sailing she learnt from her eccentric father, and **he'd** only been sailing for two years. It was the first time she had ever sailed alone. Her engine was faulty, her navigational knowledge limited, she was inexperienced and *Varuna*, a Contessa 26, would have to cope with horrific storms on huge oceans. But her father was ambitious for her. He wanted her to be the youngest ever single-handed circumnavigator. Tania accepted the challenge, not fully appreciating what was involved.

They had estimated it would take nearly two weeks to sail the 751 miles to Bermuda, her first landfall. Terrified and lonely and wishing she had her new kitten to share her fears with, she battled against seasickness, huge squalls, a flooded hull and engine failure. She frantically changed sails, changed tacks and changed direction as her fragile little boat heeled in cruel seas. She pored over meteorology books and charts, trying to understand navigation and weather systems. Awed by the sea and missing New York, miraculously she arrived in Bermuda on 12 June, and made straight for the nearest telephone booth to tell her father she had arrived safely.

"Daddy, I'm wet and cold. I want to go home."

"You'll be fine" he told her brusquely. "Hang in there."

He flew to Bermuda to sort her out, hiring a mechanic to fix her engine and after a week pushed her on her way to St. Thomas, a 900-mile voyage leading into the Bermuda Triangle. This lap too was full of problems, but somehow she made it. There waiting for her was her sister, Jade, clutching the bewildered-looking kitten she had fallen in love with in New York.

It was a relief to have a warm body to snuggle up to at night. Dinghy was to become her cuddly toy, her "buddy". On coming aboard, he immediately fell off the dock into the water, and learnt the hard way that he loathed swimming. He had two weeks to get used to his new home before Tania tentatively set sail for Panama.

The home that up to now had seemed so stable suddenly started sloshing around like a washing machine and Dinghy went frantic. Seasick and in a state of panic, he hid inside the cabin meowing, his legs splayed out in all directions as he tried to minimise the motion.

"It's OK, Mr Dinghy," Tania assured him. "This is how it's supposed to be." He hesitantly ventured out of the cabin and sniffed the air but every little wave sent him meowing back inside.

She felt more relaxed with another living being to lavish attention on. Now she could talk aloud without feeling ridiculous and when she felt tearful, which seemed to be often, she felt better sobbing into his soft fur. Before leaving New York she'd been told that her mother was terminally ill with cancer and the news was still sinking in.

Meals were no longer a lonely affair. She shared what was on her plate with Dinghy, playfully teasing him with titbits. On July 19 she wrote: "With his black and white coat, Dinghy looks like a dinner guest in tie and tails. I'm finding little fish stranded on deck and offer them to him, but he turns up his nose. I awoke this morning to find him in good spirits, mutilating rolls of toilet paper."

With the gentle trade winds filling her sails, *Varuna*'s motion became steady and swift and they fell into a comfortable domestic routine. Every morning Dinghy woke her up by prodding her with his nose and prancing all over her, anxious for his breakfast. When a school of whales came to visit, she tried to get him to share in her excitement but he showed no interest. After their evening meal, they would sit together outside admiring the sunset and then, in her cramped little bunk they'd bundle up cosily as *Varuna* rocked them gently to sleep.

Two days before estimated arrival at Panama, a storm blew up. Tania battened things down and closed hatches, and then huddled below for nine hours, holding a quivering Dinghy in her arms, crying and praying that the mast wouldn't be struck by lightning. Despite this they arrived safely in Panama where she met Luc, a romantic Frenchman with film star looks. He was 15 years older than her, sailing on his pretty French ketch *Thea* with Jean Marie as his crew. Tied up beside *Thea* was another Frenchman, Rene, from Brittany, on his yacht *Saskia*.

A close friendship was formed. They ate together, talked idly for hours in the sun, explored the town and generally helped each other out. Within no time the naive young New York teenager had fallen in love with the smooth talking Luc, who she described as "a romantic dreamer, a poet, a gardener of imagination".

Her heart fired with her first love, she was lulled into a false sense of security. Invited to have dinner with Luc, Jean Marie and Rene on board *Saskia*, she forgot to check the tides and rowed across to the other boat leaving the hatch open and Dinghy wandering freely on the deck. As they sat drinking from Rene's good French wine store, huge waves arrived from nowhere and started smashing over *Varuna*. She could hear Dinghy on board meowing in fear, but it was too dangerous to try to get to him. For six hours they watched helplessly as the boats pitched and rolled. As soon as the tide rose, she rowed back over the calmed waters and climbed on board to hug her buddy and clean up the mess.

On 20 August the three boats headed in convoy to the Galapagos. As the wind filled *Varuna*'s sails, Tania thought constantly of Luc. He was planning to spend the hurricane season in Tahiti. In her head she composed a letter to her father justifying why it was a good idea for her to do so as well.

Varuna, Dinghy and Tania had to beat into the wind the whole way to Cocai. For a while the three boats managed to stay in radio contact and Tania's day revolved round the radio. She was at least able to chat to Luc. Then the radio died and she was cut off from her friends. Before they had departed Luc had told her: "Tania, you are the bravest person I know." When she insisted she was a coward and terrified he replied: "Bravery is confronting something you are **really** afraid of."

Alone in the middle of the Pacific after weeks of being in warm social company, she became weepy and scared. She tried to keep herself occupied by reading a lot, doing her daily chores and playing with Dinghy. Her family had given her presents to open when she reached the Equator. To celebrate she made a festive meal of macaroni cheese, which she shared with Dinghy, and then opened presents. While she ate gifts of candy, Dinghy cheerfully chewed up balloons and that evening they both drifted into a contented slumber.

She often found Dinghy dragging in a scaly flying fish or squid that had become marooned on the deck. At first she was amused, pleased that he had fended for himself and saved her from opening another can of sardines from the dwindling supply. Then she complained to him about the mess his snacks left behind. "Flying fish hold so much gluey substance to their scales that it wouldn't be surprising if rubber cement was made from it," she grumbled. "The squid invariably leave behind a smelly inkspot on the fibreglass deck or my bed and Dinghy never cleans up after himself."

At last the jagged islands of the Galapagos rose like "ebony pyramids" from the sea and, at 8.30 am they sailed into Wreck Bay, San Cristobel, and moored up beside *Thea* and *Saskia*. After the euphoria of their reunion, her spirits quickly fell when she discovered that *Varuna*'s engine had packed up again. It meant she would have to make the long haul to Tahiti under sail alone. There was absolutely no option since no one was qualified to fix it on the tiny island of San Cristobel.

After stocking up supplies she wearily set sail. As she raised the mainsail and pulled up *Varuna*'s anchor, she warned Dinghy that it was the last piece of land they would see for three and a half weeks.

Being without an engine as an emergency back-up scared her. For the first two days she felt tired and dizzy and cried often as she thought of the daunting 3,000 miles before the next landfall. Before she set off, Luc had admitted that he had a wife and child who he loved and would never leave. The news had broken her heart and made her feel like a vulnerable little child. Which, of course, she was.

"Nowhere but in my minuscule *Varuna* with my buddy, Dinghy, in the middle of the ocean, could the enormity of the planet Earth make me feel so little, a mere speck of nothingness."

She kept busy, studying charts and plotting her course. Her navigation was improving and using the sextant had now become almost second nature. Dinghy would help by playfully attacking the end of her pencil as she pored over the charts. But as they sat each night eating whatever stew she had cooked, tears spilled out into the food and onto Dinghy's fur. At night she had "whoppers" of dreams that were so vivid she said she had trouble differentiating between them and reality.

October 7 was her 19th birthday. The sun came out like a gift from God, and she felt much happier and grateful for life. She was now making good progress – 936 miles in eight days. Only 2,020 miles to go! That day, determined to have a good birthday, she read and worked around the boat, adjusted sails and played games with Dinghy and in the evening cooked herself a Chinese birthday meal. Dinghy was treated to a can of sardines smothered in tomato sauce.

Luc's present was a cassette with a romantic note. "Today is your birthday and I come with the my friends, the wind, the skies and the sea. You are 19-years-old today and you are alone on a sailboat in the middle of the ocean. I think you feel very lonely with Dinghy but close your eyes and feel the vibrations from all the people who love you." Weeping, she curled up with Dinghy in the crook of her arm, puffed up her pillow and fell asleep.

Apart from the fact that she was alone at sea, she was very much a typical teenager, who liked playing popular music all the time and very loud. After all, there was no one out there to complain. She stuffed herself with chocolates and cookies and made herself mountains of popcorn in her pressure cooker, cramming them greedily into her mouth as she sat on deck with Dinghy. Dolphins visited in their hundreds, putting on fantastic displays, as though saying: "We're giving a party and everyone's invited." They usually came in the evening, announcing themselves with playful whistles and she said they made her want to scream aloud with joy. Everything was now so beautiful and tranquil, she truly appreciated how privileged she was compared to friends in New York suffocating in city pollution.

On 24 October the three boats met up and sailed together into Traitor Bay. After mooring they climbed aboard each other's vessels to share food and drink and laugh and joke. She rang her father to report and he immediately wanted to know what her plans were for leaving. She told him two or three weeks. When he urged her to go on, she reminded him wearily that she had two years to do the trip. She reflected later how he always made her feel like a child causing her to seriously question her own decisions. As she put the phone down she decided to follow her own inclinations and spend "refit time" in Tahiti.

Then she rang her mother. Her mother, a nurse told her, was too weak to come to the phone and was fading fast. Filled with remorse, Tania immediately made up her mind to return to New York to say a final goodbye. When she rang her father to tell him, he advised her against it. "You knew she was dying when you left New York. You said goodbye then. If you come back, you'll just make it harder for yourself."

Still vacillating with herself, Tania sailed the 750 miles to Tahiti, which took ten fraught days. There she met up with Luc, who urged her to go to her mother, and assured her he would look after *Varuna* and Dinghy. His own family were joining him in Tahiti where he had a job fixed up. He said his wife wanted to meet her. But there was no time. She secured *Varuna* alongside *Thea* and flew home to spend Christmas with her dying mother.

She stayed a month in New York, trying to comfort her mother in her last weeks, but she seemed to be lingering on indefinitely so Tania returned sadly to Tahiti to continue her journey.

It had been a traumatic four weeks and now she was desperate to be back on *Varuna* with her dear buddy Dinghy. Luc had promised to meet her at the airport, but when she arrived he wasn't there so she took a taxi to the harbour, where she found *Varuna* moored between two unfamiliar boats, her dinghy upside down and no cat. Feeling miserably let down, she unlocked the companionway, pulled out the slats and stepped into her dark damp little home which hadn't been aired for weeks. Completely drained, she threw her luggage down, curled up and went to sleep.

Next day Luc arrived apologising for not meeting her. He said he'd expected her the previous day. He brought Dinghy, who'd been staying with him on *Thea* and also his wife, Fabienne who immediately gave her a warm, motherly hug. She knew about Tania's affair with her husband and told her she was sorry she had to meet up with a creep like Luc. When the phone call eventually came that her mother had died, Fabienne was the first to comfort her.

Tania moored near a boat called the *Katapoul,* and acquired some good new friends in the captain, Claude, a spry Frenchman and his girlfriend, Margot, who was twenty. It was a relief to have a friend the same age as herself. They latched on to each other like long lost sisters. Her new friends helped her refit *Varuna* by enlarging the bunk to make sleeping more comfortable. They bought new sheets and pillows made from colourful Tahitian cotton fabrics and the *Varuna* took on a more homely look.

She was writing articles for a cruising magazine and letters from readers had been forwarded to her. Some said her father was a raving maniac for putting his inexperienced teenage daughter on a boat and letting her loose on the ocean.

Four idyllic months were spent in Tahiti. Friends and relatives came to visit her and she almost forgot what it was like to sail alone on the ocean. Then the hurricane season passed and departure day inevitably dawned. Before leaving, she decided to take on a stray grey tabby she'd fallen in love with and who she'd been feeding and playing with whenever she went on shore. Each time she returned to *Varuna*, the cat would sit watching her forlornly, with a look of abandonment which tore at her heart.

To justify adopting him she persuaded herself that Dinghy needed the company for, whenever she returned from ashore, he would be pacing the deck, meowing with wild delight as he recognised her rhythmic pattern of rowing. As soon as she climbed aboard, he'd purr and glue himself to her as if he'd been lonely. She called her new 'buddy' Mimine. Dinghy took to her immediately.

Before tackling the next long haul there was first a twenty-mile trip to Morea. The two young girls were reluctant to part, so Margot came with her on this short hop. For two days they gossiped and explored then said tearful goodbyes and Margot returned on the ferry to be with Claude. Tania stayed on another two weeks finding every excuse not to continue her voyage.

Finally, on Friday, 9 May 1986 she set sail, deciding to ignore an old marine superstition never to set sail on a Friday. Her next landfall would be Pago Pago, American Samoa, 1,200 miles to the west north-west. After four months of frantic social life, she was desperately lonely but the antics of her two little "buddies" playing below were a comfort and kept her amused. The two cats got on well together and Mimine was adapting to her new lifestyle.

At first there was little wind and it was frustrating bobbing about on the ocean without making much progress Then she developed a severe earache and her nerves began to fray. Trade winds returned erratically from astern, waning and waxing and driving her mad and squalls attacked from every way, unleashing rainstorms. The ear infection was bad enough without obnoxious weather pecking away at her spirits. She noticed that the mainsheet she'd piled up in the cockpit was covered in cat poop and, when she saw both cats peeing on her bunk she lost her sense of humour and let rip at them: "I hope you guys get reincarnated as bathroom attendants at the Grand Central Station men's room".

Now absorbed in each other's company, the cats showed little interest in what was happening around them. When she fell heavily onto her wrist and it became hugely swollen so that she couldn't even lift her toothbrush to clean her teeth, neither of them were sympathetic and she felt childishly rejected.

The wind remained constant for five days until 22 May when it dwindled to a flat, tedious calm. The last straw came when she discovered she had head lice, which filled her with self-disgust. "My ear is still pulsing, my head itches and my wrist aches, there are still 300 miles to go and there's no wind," she wrote in despair.

Suddenly a monstrous squall got up and they went flying. Rain crashed down into the cabin and the cats freaked out. As she struggled to mop up the water she spotted Dinghy taking a leak on her fresh pillow.

"This is a nightmare," she screamed at him and, feeling sorry for herself, she started to cry. The squall lasted a terrifying five hours before everything was back to normal. Exhausted and emotional, she crawled into her bunk and went to sleep on her urine-stained pillow.

As soon as she arrived in Pago Pago harbour she went to a doctor who assured her that her wrist was only sprained, prescribed ear drops for her ears and gave her medicated shampoo for the lice.

Next lap was to Apia, West Samoa. She met a young girl called Colleen who begged for a lift. It was only 80 miles and it seemed churlish to refuse. Someone in the sailing fraternity heard she'd had "crew" aboard for the trip, which might jeopardise her bid for a record. An anonymous note fixed to her lifeline when she returned to *Varuna* one night warned her to go back to Pago Pago and do the 80 mile trip again, by herself. But her heart was heavy and she wasn't even sure she would ever complete the trip. She decided to ignore the note.

On 3 July they sailed for Efate, Vanuatu, 750 miles to the west southwest, for a while in perfect sailing weather before savage storms raged again. Below deck Dinghy and Mimine huddled together and only moved or perked up their ears when they heard the sound of a can of sardines being opened. Dinghy seemed to find this trip particularly uncomfortable. Tania had noticed in Tahiti that he often went into the litter tray, crouched and came out with no sign of having relieved himself. Concerned, she had taken him to a vet who had told her to feed him more wet food.

Vanuatu turned out to be both lucky and unlucky for her. Invited to another boat for a meal, she met and fell in love again with a blonde-haired French/Swiss called Olivier, who was sailing single-handed on *Akka*, a rusty old 32-foot steel boat. It was a lovely evening and she returned to *Varuna* with her heart singing, to find Dinghy bleeding from his genitals.

"Oh, my God, no," she cried. "Not Dinghy, please." She tenderly wiped him clean and gave him a favourite snack and he lay there limply meowing his pain. Mimine meowed too, as she circled his body, nosing him to respond. Feebly, he tried to move but was too weak.

Crying inconsolably, Tania scratched his ears in his special place, thinking how small and helpless he looked. He lapped a little water from a bowl and seemed to perk up. "All that sleepless night I spent trying to push away the thought that something could alter the one precious relationship that had sustained me for months."

First thing next morning she and Olivier took him, bundled in a towel, to the vet, who laid Dinghy on a stainless steel table and then he ticked her off for bringing the cat ashore, saying there were strict quarantine rules. After examining Dinghy, he softened and, looking grim, said he would have to operate. Tania went outside to wait with Oliver, thinking remorsefully of the times she had got cross with her "little buddy" for missing his litter box, not realising he was ill.

"Dinghy was my first pet, my closest companion for half the world. He'd been right there, living through all the bad times and the good. He alone had tolerated my cursing and screaming, watched me laugh and talk to myself and shared my meals. Whenever life had got me down he was my only comfort with his gentle little face rubbing mine before curling up in my arms. My handsome, snuggly buddy who'd shared those memories of endless days in the sea warp."

The vet came out with bad news and she wept on Olivier's shoulder. They paid the bill and returned to a strangely empty boat. When she called her father to tell him about Dinghy, he said it was a bad stroke of luck but not the end of the world, and pointed out briskly that she was behind schedule.

As Tania prepared for departure, Mimine rubbed herself round Tania's legs and then nosed into the cabinets and all the favourite spots she and Dinghy liked to curl up in together. She reflected sadly that Vanuatu brought her Olivier but it was here she lost her precious buddy.

Before leaving she bought a replacement, a fuzzy tabby which Mimine immediately took under her wing. Clawing his way up the wall hangings, belts, Tania's legs and the table whenever it was meal times, she thought he looked like something from the jungle and called him Tarzoon.

Despite her father's objections, she decided not to sail round South Africa but to rendezvous with Olivier on Akka and sail through the Suez Canal and into the Mediterranean in convoy. On 21 August 1986 *Varuna* and *Akka* motored out of the harbour at Vanuatu and set sail for their next destination – Cairns in Australia. Tania reluctantly waved Olivier goodbye and, with the mainsail and genoa booming out in a feeble breeze, they slowly drew apart and she was on her own again.

Immediately Tarzoon became sea sick, all over her nice clean bedding. "Bravo, Mr T," she scolded him cheerfully. "Are you going to join the ranks of those who bear a complete disregard for my sleeping quarters?" Not caring, he crawled weakly into the crook of her arm for comfort.

Like any teenager in love, she couldn't get Olivier out of her mind. She wasn't even sure she would ever see him again. But there was a 1,300-mile voyage ahead and she decided philosophically that whatever would be would be. She just had to concentrate on getting to Australia, which would not be an easy task.

Thirty-five miles off the coast of Australia was the Grafton Lighthouse. It was vital she found it, otherwise she risked her vessel being smashed to bits on the Great Barrier Reef. The first nine days were comparatively calm, and she made use of this time making sure her navigation was better than perfect. By the tenth day she calculated that they had passed 15 miles north of Willis Reef on the chart and, if her navigation was accurate, soon the lighthouse should appear.

Then a storm blew up and huge waves picked up *Varuna* and ruthlessly threw her down. She noted that it was like being the first car of a roller coaster. She still hadn't spotted the lighthouse and suddenly felt frightened and insecure. Anxious though she was to reach land and meet up with Olivier again, she decided to take heed of some advice a fellow sailor passed on to her: "When in doubt, seek sea room until your mind clears. Never make a hasty decision for the sake of an anchorage or a shower."

So she headed back to sea, and waited until it was light. To her relief, at 9am she saw the lighthouse base emerging like magic through the mist and she grabbed Tarzoon and pointed his head in that direction. But he was not enjoying the storm and outside it was rainy and cold, so he dug his claws into her arm and jumped back to the safety of the cabin.

More squalls arrived. She found herself being pulled away from the lighthouse and towards the reef. Wearily heading again for the safety of the open sea she noted in her logbook: "On Tuesday, September 2, 1986, all I knew was that I was a very scared nineteen-year-old who wanted to quit."

September 3 dawned warm and sunny and by now she and the boat were at least familiar with the area. They retraced their steps, found the lighthouse and everything was suddenly all right with the world. The sun shone on the decks and dried out the sails and brought the colour back to Tania's ashen face. Even Tarzoon and Mimine were prepared to come out to sit on the drying wood of the cockpit, and watch her steer cautiously past the lighthouse, running the length of the Barrier Reef to the safety of Cairns.

As soon as she spotted *Akka* in the harbour, her heart leapt and Olivier appeared on deck, signalling her to pull up alongside him. It was the start of summer. Ahead of them lay several weeks of quiet exploration, enjoying the sights and each other. All thoughts of quitting fled and she forgot about the horrors she had just endured.

Nevertheless she was behind schedule and knew that her father would soon be urging her on. He would not like her plan to sail home with Olivier, via Sri Lanka, up the Red Sea to the Mediterranean. Olivier intended staying in Malta, leaving her to sail on to Gibraltar and cross the North Atlantic to New York.

They met more old sailing friends and spent time socialising before *Varuna* and *Akka* continued their voyages on September 19. For eighteen days the two boats comfortably wove in and out of an idyllic latticework of coral heads for 400 miles, up to Thursday Island and the Torres Strait. Each night they tied up alongside each other. Tania noted romantically that in her view, *Varuna* and *Akka* were like a perfect couple, floating on the blue lagoons together – a dainty little scarred lady next to the rough and rusty adventurer.

It was good to celebrate her twentieth birthday on 6 October, with someone she loved and hoped to spend the rest of her life with. A year earlier, on her nineteenth birthday, she'd been in the South Pacific alone except for her beloved Dinghy.

On reaching Thursday Island they used drastic means to rid themselves of the head lice that plagued them both, by saturating their hair in straight kerosene and then washing it off with washing up liquid. The kerosene burnt their scalps as well as the lice, and they suffered head sores with lumps of hair falling out, but the relief they felt at getting rid of the lice made it all worth while.

Mimine reminded her painfully of Dinghy and, perhaps sensing this, had now become attached to Olivier. So when they next set sail, Mimine stayed aboard *Akka* and Tarzoon remained with Tania on *Varuna*. There was a journey of 1,800 miles across the Arufura Sea, to Bali. It was very hot and there was not much wind. The two boats sometimes tied up together in mid-ocean and Tania would swim across to *Akka* for a meal and company. Even Tarzoon, anxious to meet up with Mimine, managed to jump across to the *Akka*. On another occasion, when Olivier was in the water tying the boats together, Mimine accidentally jumped in too and found, to her surprise, she could swim.

One sweltering hot day, an Australian Coast Guard cutter sliced through the water and offered them ice cream, flinging across to them a green rubbish bag containing a huge block of ice and half a gallon of vanilla ice-cream which they all, including the cats, licked up greedily.

When they finally arrived on the doorstep of the Indian Ocean the wind picked up and the *Varuna* began to heel. Tarzoon, who wasn't used to the heeling, poised himself to jump up and join her at the helm. Hearing him, she turned round to pick him up and give him a cuddle and found he wasn't there. He had gone overboard. Looking back into the wake behind the boat, she saw his little head, a picture of terror, bobbing up and down in the waves. She disengaged the automatic steering, and backwinded the sails, pushing the tiller over so that *Varuna* would back down on the spot where she had seen Tarzoon. Tarzoon swam frantically towards the boat and she managed to lean over and scoop him up.

She had already formed a strong bond with Tarzoon which had never quite developed where Mimine was concerned. "Torturing myself with the thought that one day, alone at sea, he could very well be lost, I picked up his soaking body and hugged him close, swearing I would always do my best to protect him."

At Bali they stayed for four days, stocking up with fresh fruit and vegetables before continuing to Christmas Island, a tiny speck in the middle of the Indian Ocean and 660 miles away. But there was no time to linger there for long. The hurricane season had already started and they had to get to Sri Lanka 1,800 miles away, through the doldrums and over the equator. On 8 December they set off, having decided it was too difficult to try to stay together and they would both sail independently. Nevertheless, Tania found herself constantly climbing up several mast steps to see if she could sight *Akka*. Her engine started playing up again and, after dismantling the engine, she discovered two tiny holes in the fuel tank and hardly any fuel left. She managed to bung up the holes, but faced the fact that she could only use the engine in an emergency.

As well as dolphins, the ocean now was full of garbage drifting from India. One week, three baby Dorado used *Varuna*'s shadow for shelter, along with flip-flop sandals with families of fish attached. There were floating logs, plastic bags and bottles and barrels which Tarzoon watched float by with curious interest.

One night she was awakened by drops of water on her face. Hearing no rain on the deck she turned on the light and there was a soaking wet Tarzoon shaking himself over her. She concluded he must have fallen overboard and somehow managed to clamber back unaided. He was a real survivor, just like herself.

On Christmas Day she cooked a special meal of sauerkraut and hotdogs and boiled potatoes and opened Olivier's present, a coral necklace he had made himself, and she fell asleep dreaming about him, with Tarzoon in the crook of her arm.

New Year's Eve came and went almost without her realising it. She talked constantly to Tarzoon, telling him their exact position and assuring him and herself that they would soon arrive at their destination. By 7 January they approached a serious shipping lane and were dazzled by endless streams of lights from enormous tankers, carriers and freighters. The *Varuna* seemed very tiny and invisible amongst them. Fearing that one of these monsters would hit her, she made plans to grab her passport, Tarzoon and some vital boat papers, before abandoning ship.

Then Sri Lanka emerged, like a jewel in the ocean. It had taken her thirty-one days, her longest trip ever at sea. As she gingerly approached land a boat came out of the harbour, motored up to her and a friendly voice asked if she was Tania. "Everybody's been worried sick about you. You're late."

On shore Olivier was there to meet her, and they threw their arms round each other. Her father, he said, was already on the phone.

"Where the hell have you been?" he ranted.

"Daddy, I didn't have any wind or engine," she said apologetically.

Two days later her father arrived in Sri Lanka to see for himself what she'd been up to and, she suspected, to check out Olivier. She hadn't seen him for eighteen months. As he entered the room she said his energy seemed to radiate and everyone turned their heads as he swooped on her like a dynamo. For two whirlwind weeks, the three of them went sightseeing and her father experienced some of the discomfort she had suffered at sea, by staying on the cramped *Varuna* with her.

Finally, satisfied she was capable of looking after herself and Olivier could be trusted with her, he booked his flight home. "Remember," he told her before he left, "this is not a vacation. It's a job."

They prepared their boats for the 3,100 mile trip across the Arabian Sea and halfway up the Red Sea to Port Sudan, again loading up with fresh fruit and vegetables, and set sail on Tuesday morning, February 10, 1987.

Tania was beset by her usual problems such as engine failure and huge, unexpected waves but as long as *Akka* was close by, she felt confident she could cope. Then, one evening, she made herself a meal, which resulted in a vicious stomach upset. Doubled up on her bunk in terrible pain, she didn't keep a proper watch and by next morning *Akka* had disappeared and she was once more alone. Ill and weakened by her bellyache, she began to cry like a child. Life seemed so unfair. Her kerosene and food store began to dwindle and Tarzoon used her vegetable box as a litter tray and then became averse to eating sardines in oil.

On 8 March, after twenty-six days at sea, she arrived at Djibouti Harbour at the entrance to the Red Sea. Some of her sailing friends were there already, but Olivier didn't turn up until the next afternoon. At sea they had formed their own little sailing community and their VHF's were permanently tuned to Channel 78, the radio waves positively buzzing with social chit chat.

The convoy of little ships sailed through the Red Sea, *Varuna* and *Akka* coming last, towards Suez. Everywhere there were huge ships and they had some harrowing near misses. Tanya found herself flying into rages at the stupidity and ignorance of these huge vessels that threatened constantly to mow her down. As she ranted and raved, Tarzoon would watch her with a perplexed expression on his face and then she would see the funny side of the situation. "After I'd lost control, I would relax completely and cuddle up with my buddy until the aggravation accumulated all over again."

When they got to Suez two large boxes were waiting from her father, with a new mainsail, a masthead light, a new steering device, food, chocolates, books and a flashlight. In Port Said they met a couple on a Swiss boat who were heading for the Philippines in the other direction. Morris, the captain, and Ursula, his girlfriend, fell in love with Mimine and asked if they could adopt her. Reluctantly Tania agreed and, feeling a bit of a traitor, handed her over.

After that, her worst fears materialised. One night a blaring horn and the rumbling churn of ship's propellers awoke her. She rushed up on deck and looked up. Twenty feet away, the towering hulk of an immense cargo carrier barrelled down on her. Its bow passed 10 feet in front of them and *Varuna* bounced around in the side wash of thousands of tons of displacement. Her mast was jerked back and the steel forestay was sliced away and the jib left hanging from its head, only saved from complete loss by the attached halyard and sheets. She grabbed her "buddy" protectively and held him to her.

Olivier on *Akka* stayed close and nursed *Varuna* along until they arrived at Loutros, on the southern coast of Crete. After repairing the damage to the *Varuna* on 18 July they set sail for Malta, 580 miles west, separating soon after leaving. They both arrived safely in Malta on 24 July to be met by her brother, Tony. Two weeks were spent exploring the island and then Tony worked on the *Varuna*, repairing her ready for her final big trip across the Atlantic and home.

Leaving *Akka* and Olivier in Malta, Tania and Tarzoon were soon alone again at sea. There was 1,000 miles to go before Gibraltar and shipping of every variety clogged the Mediterranean all the way to the one natural exit at the Strait of Gibraltar. For the first few days Tarzoon sat in his corner, watching her alternate between crying, talking into a recorder to Olivier, playing solitaire and changing sails. She felt more intimidated by the 4,000 miles left to go until home, than the entire voyage.

When the weather got bad she wedged herself miserably in a corner of the bunk and like a little girl, snuggled up with Tarzoon beneath the blanket. *Varuna* rolled about in huge Mediterranean waves and one big spray drenched the boat inside and out. Again she considered abandoning ship but that would mean leaving everything behind, including Tarzoon, which she knew she could never do. As long as they were still floating she'd stick it out.

They still hadn't reached Gibraltar and she was cold and weak and had to struggle to cook a meal of rice and tomato paste, sharing it with Tarzoon. Feeling she had reached the end of her tether, she headed in desperation to the closest town on her chart, Almeria. It was a nightmare but she finally managed to eventually tie up in the marina and immediately sought the nearest telephone box to call her father. "Daddy, I'm so scared," she cried into the phone, "you can't possibly imagine how horrible it is. I lost so many important things overboard. I need so much stuff and don't have any money."

He ordered her to stay put until she had recovered herself and then head for Gibraltar, where he would meet her and take care of everything. For two days she lay most of the time in her bunk as Tarzoon jumped ship and freely roamed the marina sniffing out the Spanish cats. She tried to fatten herself up with calamari and steaks and salads and fruit. Then she replenished her fuel supply, scooped up Tarzoon and headed down the coast to Gibraltar. It was night when *Varuna* made it into the harbour and anchored safely. Next morning, her father arrived in a dinghy, overjoyed to see her. But his main concern still was to make sure she accomplished what she set out to do. The ultimate goal, he said, was in sight.

He arranged for repairs to the boat and stocked her up with provisions. Knowing it was going to be cold on the Atlantic crossing, he bought her warm clothing and packed her light summer things and souvenirs to take home with him on the aeroplane.

She relaxed as *Varuna* became ship-shape again. She had new pots and pans, new bedclothes, new tools and Tania felt quite houseproud. Tarzoon was meanwhile enjoying Gibraltar immensely. He took to jumping across to the dock, sometimes falling in and, much to the amusement of onlookers, calmly swimming up to the steering gear of another boat, clambering aboard and then shaking himself vigorously.

On the last night she and her father went over the charts one more time and finalised her route. It looked daunting and Tania's fear of the passage increased as she visualised the hazards of the 3,000-mile trip. They decided she should take a straight path from Gibraltar to New York, passing south of the Azores to avoid the

Gulf Stream and the higher risk of storms. Finally, having bid farewell to her father, she undid *Varuna*'s ropes for the last time, shuffled Tarzoon below to the safety of the cabin and set sail on the final leg of her voyage.

She noted in her logbook. "Ever since Australia, the journey has seemed long and hard and the truth is that the ocean can still terrify me. Most of the time I think about things that a girl my age doesn't think about and I'm bugged with thoughts of my future."

They finally passed Portugal and forged into the Atlantic heading straight for New York. It was calm and one evening, as she was sitting on deck eating a cookie, a yellow canary landed on the boom. She called out to it and it responded and hopped closer. Then, showing no fear, it hopped right on to her head, filling her with wonder. After a few minutes, fearing it might mess on her hair, she gently shooed it on to the deck and gave it some crumbs from her biscuit and went below for a few minutes. Hearing a crunching noise she rushed back on deck in time to see Tarzoon munching away, with a bloody mess of feathers sticking from his mouth.

"Oh, my God," she screamed in anger. "You murderer!" Except for a couple of feathers and bloodstains on the deck there was nothing left of the pretty bird. "In my eyes, that heartless scoundrel had been soiled and I couldn't bear the thought of touching him for the rest of the day."

On her tenth day at sea she opened a letter from her father. He was not one for showing his feelings, but now he wrote: "You are on the ocean alone, with *Varuna* and Tarzoon. This is just to tell you that more than ever, I know how you feel. I'm proud of you and I love you."

With tears rolling down her cheeks, she reflected that in accepting the challenge and leaving New York she had been searching for the golden apple of his approval, feeling that it had been lost beyond hope during her rebellious teenage years. "What I had been searching for was his love and now I knew I needn't have gone round the world to get it."

The journey was turning into a real battle. They were in the Azores and in the throes of calm, having barely made 900 miles in two weeks. In her logbook she noted: "Tarzoon and I are going crazy. I've almost finished the sweater I'm knitting and don't know what to do with myself. I just want to get home." Tarzoon amused himself unravelling balls of wool and chasing the ends of toilet paper, and the dolphins glided by to see what they were doing.

As the winds changed and storms lashed at the little boat, she noted: "The ocean is coming in everywhere. Tarzoon and I have the slats closed up tight, making the cabin air stale, and we scrunch up together watching Father Time march on."

October 6 arrived and it was her birthday again. She was 21 and had come of age. "I don't feel any different except I have to cook my own birthday dinner and then do the dishes." Other twenty-one-year-olds were having big parties, balloons, dancing the night away with friends and family wishing them well. She was alone at sea with Tarzoon.

As her big adventure drew to an end she began to savour the unique solitude. It was the end of a beautiful story and life would never be the same. She spent those last weeks reading, keeping the cabin immaculately clean, cooking, properly folding the sails - and marvelling for hours at a time "how wonderful nature was to create such an exquisite creature as Tarzoon".

Then her mood changed and the cloudless sky began to annoy her. She wanted to move the sails and prayed for wind and a good old-fashioned squall. Instead a little canary plopped into the cockpit and, just as Tarzoon pounced to make a meal of it, Tania shooed it off the boat for its own safety.

By 19 October her prayers were answered and violent weather arrived with a vengeance. Aside from trips into the cockpit for horizon checks and sail changes, Tarzoon and Tania stayed huddled together on their sodden bunk. By 25 October the waves were 25-ft high.

"My heart is thumping so hard with fear, and I can't stop the tears. I am huddled in bed with Tarzoon as we listen to the noise and pray. I think we are about 880 miles from home. Not like the Med where after a storm there is a calm. Here it is just one giant, non-stop storm."

The waves seemed to grow to the size of Alps. Thundering waterfalls flooded the cockpit and then slowly funnelled out by way of the drain. There followed gentle winds and clear blue skies. By October 28 they reached the longitude of Bermuda and crossed their outward track of two and a half years before. Her round the world odyssey with *Varuna* was drawing to a close and these last days at sea were to be treasured.

She had set off as an eighteen-year-old, scared and apprehensive. Living at sea had taught her the importance of taking each new dawn in her stride and doing the best she could with whatever confronted her.

Thirty miles from the Ambrose Light that indicated the approaches to New York, a powerboat with a film crew appeared, waving and screaming congratulations. They said they had been searching for *Varuna* since dawn. After taking pictures they headed back to land to relay their story.

By 1pm on 5 November she could see the outline of the World Trade Centre. She sat below with Tarzoon, crying over what they were leaving and savouring their last minutes alone together. At last she went on deck clutching Tarzoon and saw a blur of people, microphones and TV cameras. Then she spotted her father.

"Daddy! I made it," she screamed triumphantly. He screamed back: "I'm so proud of you."

Behind him, blowing her loving kisses, stood Olivier - the man she hoped would replace her father as the major influence in her life.

She reflected: "It was the beginning of the end of the life I had come to know. I would soon have to play the role of an adult in New York."

Tania didn't achieve the world record for being the youngest person to sail alone round the world. She was disqualified because of the 80 mile "lift" she had given a 19-year-old girl in the South Pacific. Her father was miffed but Tania was happy with her own, personal achievement.

Note: *Tania and Olivier got married the following May and, with plans to buy a 60ft yacht for chartering, went to live in Rhode Island with their "buddy", Tarzoon, who'd proved himself such a plucky ship's cat. Tania wrote a best selling book entitled "Maiden Voyage".*

Joshua Slocum's Low Opinion Of Cats on Boats

Joshua was a rather grumpy, unsociable sailor, whose ambition was to sail single-handed around the world. A friend offered him an old ship, warning him that it "wants some repairs". Slocum gratefully accepted only to find that it was a rotting old 37ft oyster sloop named *Spray*, propped up in a field. Nonetheless he painstakingly rebuilt it, determined to be the first to sail around the world alone. He set off from Boston on 24 April 1895, and became the first person to succeed in such a voyage despite the fact that it took him three years to reach Newport, Rhode Island in 1898.

His friends and relatives couldn't understand how he managed to put up with just himself for company. Suggestions were made that he should have taken a dog with him. To which he replied: "I and the dog wouldn't have been very long in the same boat, in any sense."

When they next suggested a cat his reply was equally curt: "A cat would have been a harmless creature, I dare say. But there is nothing for a puss to do on board and she is an unsociable animal at best." One suspects they would have got on very well indeed, totally ignoring each other.

The *Spray* was lost with Captain Slocum aboard in 1909, while sailing from Vineyard Haven, Massachusetts, on the island of Martha's Vineyard, to South America.

The Accident Prone Indian Cat

Charles Lane, the Victorian writer, in 1901 mentions an Indian Cat called Indischer Fürst, who belonged to a Mrs H.C.Brooke and appeared to have the typical markings of an Abyssinian Cat. His owner described to Lane how the cat was stolen from a hotel in Bombay by an English sailor who boarded a ship for England with the cat smuggled in his rucksack.

The cat was accident prone and apparently twice fell overboard and each time was rescued. He was then shipwrecked and rescued again and then mysteriously disappeared. After several days absence he was discovered in the bowels of the ship, black as the coal in which he had been fast asleep. Arriving in England, he fell out of the ship into the docks, where the sailor gave him to a shoemaker in Leytonstone. Mrs Brooke, hearing of the cat's unusual history, was attracted to the strange creature and adopted him as her pet, and called him Indischer Fürst.

Pussy Willow Legend

An early Polish legend explains how the Pussy Willow that is found along riverbanks, got its name. There was once a grey mother cat whose kittens were thrown into the river by a farmer who felt he already had enough cats to worry about. Their mother wept so loudly that the willows agreed to stretch themselves down into the water to rescue the drowning kittens. The kittens grabbed hold and were saved from a watery death. Ever since, each spring in memory of that event, the Pussy Willows grow soft, grey furry buds which, to the touch, feel like the fur of the new born kittens.

Swimming Cats that Sailed in Noah's Ark

The city of Van, in Eastern Turkey, lies on the edge of Lake Van in the foothills of Mount Ararat. Legend has it that, after the floods receded, *Noah's Ark* came to rest on top of the mountain. Noah let down the gangplank and a pair of distinctive looking cats, with white fluffy fur and handsome auburn tails, emerged from

Van Cat wading through the water

the hold. As they left the *Ark* the cats were blessed by Allah and the patch of auburn hair at the top of their foreheads is said to be the place where the Lord placed his hand.

The two cats made their way down the mountain-side to the ancient settlement of Van. A community of them soon developed and, living near a lake, it became natural for the cats to wade, fish and swim in the water.

In 1955 a couple of British photographers visiting the Lake Van region of Turkey, were struck by the unique markings and characteristics of small colonies of these beautiful half-wild creatures and arranged for a couple to be shipped to England. Viewers were astonished when the cats were shown on television, swimming in a pool. From then on the breed became known as the Turkish Van Swimming Cat.

Because of their ability to adapt to water, which most cats by nature dislike, these fascinating cats have, as a result, become popular amongst live-aboard boat owners. The breed looks like an Angora, with the same long silky fur but with an auburn tail and forehead and amber eyes, sometimes each of a different colour – one blue and one amber.

Richard and Yvonne Stone lived aboard their yacht the *Astina* moored at Bristol docks, with two Turkish Van kittens. Their plan was to one day sail round the world and they decided it would be sensible to acquire kittens that could not only swim but enjoyed travel. The kittens, Kirsty and Morwenna, quickly became adept at leaping about on the deck of the small vessel but showed no inclination to swim.

The author lived on a houseboat on the Thames with her husband, Lynn Lewis. They had a Van cat called Princess Heidi. One winter, when still a kitten, she fell into the fast flowing Thames but valiantly swam upstream until she found a low bank to crawl onto.

Despite having 11 acres of land to explore, she was a bit too inquisitive for her own good and wandered off onto a busy road, chasing a rabbit, and was killed by a car. Needless to say, we were heartbroken.

The author's cat, Heidi

The Cat O' Nine Tails

This, of course, is not a cat but a nautical implement of torture whose design and title were influenced by the idea that a cat has nine lives. It was a whip with nine cords, each cord having nine knots tied in it. As a result every stroke inflicted a large number of small marks, giving a general impression of a body that has been clawed and scratched repeatedly by a savage cat.

It was the authorised instrument of punishment in the British Navy from the 17th century until it was finally banned in 1881. Its use was particularly brutal in the 18th century when victims were given as many as 300 lashes, virtually flaying them alive.

The 'cat' has given us the popular expression of 'no room to swing a cat' meaning cramped quarters. Some people imagine that this saying alludes to swinging a live cat around by its tail. In fact, the truth was that the cat o' nine tails was too long to swing below decks. As a result sailors condemned to punishment with a whipping had to be taken above, where there was room to swing a cat.

The cat o' nine tails is featured in the Gilbert and Sullivan comic opera, HMS *Pinafore*. The hero, Ralph Rackstraw, an able seaman on the ship, and Josephine, the Captain's daughter, fall in love but she is betrothed to the First Lord of the Admiralty, Sir Joseph Porter. The lovers plan to elope, helped by the rest of the crew except the villain, Boatswain Dick Deadeye who, in Act II, reveals their plan to the Captain who hints menacingly that the crew and the lovers should be threatened with punishment by the cat o' nine tails.

Capt:	Good fellow, you have given timely warning,
	Sing hey, the thoughtful sailor that you are.
	I'll talk to Mister Rackstraw in the morning:
	Sing hey, the cat o' nine tails and the tar.
	(He sinisterly produces a "cat")
Both:	The merry cat o' nine tails and the tar!
	The Captain dons a boat cloak, which amply disguises him.
	Meanwhile, Ralph and Josephine and the crew enter the
	stage on tiptoe.
All:	Carefully on tiptoe stealing,
	Breathing gently as we may,
	Every step with caution feeling,
	We will softly steal away.
	(But the Captain stamps his foot.)
ALL	*(much alarmed):*
	Goodness me! Why, what was that?
Dick:	Silent be, it was the cat?
All	*(reassured thinking he means a real cat):*
	It was – the cat!
	(At which the disguised Captain produces a cat o' nine tails.)
Captain:	They're right, it was the cat..
All:	Pull ashore, in fashion steady,
	Hymen will defray the fare,
	For a clergyman is ready,
	To unite the happy pair.
	(At which the Captain stamps his foot again.)
All:	Goodness me, why what was that?
Dick:	Silent be, again the cat!
All:	It was again that cat!
Capt:	They're right, it was the cat.
	(Then he throws off his cloak, revealing himself.)
	Hold, pretty daughter of mine,
	I insist upon knowing
	Where you may be going,
	With these sons of the brine.

It is finally revealed that the Captain is of low birth and the Admiral is therefore no longer prepared to marry his daughter, leaving her free to marry Ralph. So in the end there is no need to use the dreaded cat o' nine tails on the crew or the lovers. All ends well.

Gavroche, the Cat that Sailed to Guernsey to escape Napoleon

Gavroche was the pet cat that Victor Hugo, (1802-1885), the French novelist and dramatist, took with him when he left France in 1851 and sailed to the island of Guernsey, in the Channel Islands, to escape Napoleon II.

Hugo became was instantly captivated by the island and set up home at Hauteville

House, in St. Peter Port, with his wife, mistress, his children and his cat while waiting for the war to end. During his time there he wrote some of his most famous works.

The German philosopher Friedrich Nietzsche included Hugo in his list of 'impossible people', describing him as 'a lighthouse in a sea of absurdity'.

His sense of absurdity became apparent when he refurbished Hauteville House in a distincly Gothic style with idiosyncratic touches.

He loved his cat and once remarked: "God has made the cat to give man the pleasure of caressing the tiger".

The Genius who invented Catflaps and Bounced Pebbles on the Ocean

Isaac Newton (1642-1727) loved cats and loved the sea. When his cat had kittens, he invented catflaps to make life easier for them, by having a door cut in his study for his cat and a smaller one for the kittens.

"I do not know what I may appear to the world but to myself I seem to have been only like a boy playing on the seashore and diverting myself now and then finding a smoother pebble or a prettier shell than ordinary, while the great ocean of truth lay all undiscovered before me."

The Cat that was her Master's Scapegoat

Admiral Andrea Doria (1466-1560) was Commander of the Genoese Fleet and conqueror of the Turks and Barbary pirates. He served as a mercenary for Rome, Naples, Genoa, France and Spain during his 76 year career

He was one of the most successful entrepreneurs of violence, a fierce young man who lived to be a fierce old man, dying at the grand old age of ninety-four.

A favourite cat always accompanied him on all his voyages and took part in all his actions. When he was very old, one was painted sitting beside him 'like a well conducted person'.

Despite his love of cats, it seemed that he didn't always treat them well. He had a foul temper and was used to getting his own way. He had shown, to the end, indomitable energy and ability both in fighting his enemies on sea and land and in defeating conspiracies at home against his house and person.

Even when he was old, he liked to keep a cat near him to remind him of his victories and failures. When a fit of rage came on him he would mercilessly beat his cat with his stick, by way of symbolising the punishment he would visit on his foes.

The old oil painting in his splendid palace of Fazzuolo, painted shortly before the Admiral's death, representing old Andrea in his ninety-third year, still hangs in his own private room, A meagre, worn out old man, with scarce a gleam of fire in his sunken eyes, by his side sits the cat he used as a scapegoat. He and the unresentful cat are sitting together in placid companionship.

The Little Chinese Slum Cat

Pierre Loti, (1850-1923) was the nom de plume of Julien Viaud, the French Naval Officer and author, who had several cats, named Moumouth Blanc, Moumouth Grise, Le Chat, Belaud and Ratonne.

Moumouth Grise was a little Chinese slum cat who crept into his boat and would not be dislodged until, after months of lurking under his bunk, she came out and 'crept into my heart'.

His description of the mangy cat is painfully graphic. The tortured animal, abandoned and diseased and tormented by dogs and children, was determined to cling to life despite her wretchedness. But Loti began to realise that she was doomed anyway with a fatal disease.

Not wanting her to suffer unduly, Loti finally lured her into his house and there, painfully aware of the cat's reproachful eyes, he gently chloroformed her to death, believing the poor creature better off put out of her misery.

The Cat that Lept into the Sea and Was Rescued by a Skiffe

John Locke, who the following year was himself captain of a ship that sailed to Guinea, embarked on the *Fila Cavena* on July 17th 1553 from Venice, bound for Jerusalem. On August 19 of that year, being not far from Jaffa, he recorded the following incident in his diary.

"Sailed west along the coast with a fresh side-winde. It chanced by fortune that the shippes Cat lept into the sea. She kepte herself very valiantly above water, notwithstanding the great waves. The master caused the Skiffe with half a dozen men to go towards her and rescue her.

"Then she was almost halfe a mile from the shippe, and all this while the shippe lay on staies. I hardly believe they would have made such haste and means if the company had bene in the like perill. They made the more haste because it was its patrons cat.

"This I have written only to note the estimation that cats are in, among the Italians. For generally they esteeme their cattes, as in England we esteeme a good Spaniell. The same night about tenne of the clocke, the winde calmed and because none of the shippe knew where we were, we let fall an anker about six miles from the place we were at before, and there we had muddie ground at twelve fathome."

Henry Fielding's account of The Kitten That Fell into the Ocean and Upset the Captain

Author's Note: *While researching at the British Museum Library I found in a reliable collection of stories, an improbable tale about the rescue of a kitten at sea. At the time it seemed far-fetched, but too intriguing not to use. Narrated by a Seaman Fielding, there was no clue as to the name of either the ship or the Captain, or the true identity of Fielding. I'm ashamed to say I slipped the story into the first edition of my Ships' Cats book almost as an afterthought, without further research. Then a reader, Mr. Bob Blackburn, recognised the description as being taken from a book, "Voyage to Lisbon" by the celebrated eighteenth century writer, Henry Fielding, author of Tom Jones.*

Henry Fielding and his younger blind half-brother Sir John Fielding, were magistrates at No. 4 court in Bow Street. Both famously founded London's first professional police force, the Bow Street runners, in an effort the clean up crime on the streets of London. However there is no truth in the legend that they brought to justice the infamous Sweeny Todd, the Demon Barber of Fleet Street, who slit the throats of his customers and made them into meat pies. Sweeny Todd was a fictional character who first appeared in a penny dreadful story entitled "String of Pearls" in 1846.

Desperately ill and hardly able to walk, Henry Fielding decided to voyage by sea to Lisbon in the hope that a warmer climate might restore his health. He was only 47 and suffering from dropsy, jaundice, gout and asthma and fatigued by over-work. Accompanied by his second wife, Mary, and his eldest daughter, Amelia, on 26 June, 1754 they boarded a Spanish ship, the *Queen of Portugal*, at Rotherhithe.

As a magistrate used to dealing with shifty characters, Fielding felt uneasy about the Portuguese skipper's competence. Captain Veal was an old sea-dog type swaggering arrogantly on deck in a cockade, scarlet coat and with an outsize sword but surprisingly in his cabin he kept a mother cat with four kittens, on whom he seemed to dote.

It would be a precarious trip and a risk to his already weak state of health, but Fielding was courageous and determined, although friends feared he would die before he arrived. As a precaution before sailing, Fielding sent for a Mr. Hunter, a surgeon and anatomist, to come aboard and 'let out ten quarts of water to relieve his dropsy'. He also stocked up on wine, spirits and food to sustain him during the voyage.

After four days delay, the ship finally set sail and Fielding was resolved to keep his mind alert during the cruise, by writing a daily journal, in which he recorded some strange and often alarming incidents. At first all went well, despite his wife and daughter being confined to their cabins with seasickness. His only source of conversation was with a Portuguese friar who was travelling with them, and with the unsavoury Captain Veal. Fleming's initial opinion of him, that he was unstable, became strengthened.

Anchored at Ryde for the night, Fielding wrote: "While the ship was under sail, but making no great way, a kitten, one of four of the feline inhabitants of the Captain's cabin, fell from the window into the water. An alarm was immediately given to the captain who was then upon deck and received it with utmost concern and bitter oaths. He immediately gave orders to the steersman in favour of the poor thing, as he called it. The sails were instantly slackened and all hands employed to recover the poor animal.

"I was extremely surprised at this, less indeed at the captain's extreme tenderness than at his conceiving any possibility of success. For if the puss had had nine thousand instead of nine lives, I concluded that it had been lost. The boatswain, however, had more sanguine hopes for, having stripped himself of his jacket, breeches and shirt, leapt boldly into the water and to my great astonishment in a few minutes returned to the ship bearing the motionless animal in his mouth. Nor was this, I observed, a matter of such great difficulty as it appeared to my ignorance and possibly may seem to that of my freshwater reader.

"The kitten was now exposed to air and sun on the deck, where its life of which it retained no symptoms, was despaired of by all. The captain's humanity did not so totally destroy his philosophy as to make him yield himself up to affliction on this melancholy occasion. Having felt his loss like a man, he resolved to show he could bear it like one and, having declared he had rather have lost a cask of rum, or brandy, betook himself to a game of backgammon with the friar.

"The kitten at last recovered, to the great joy of the captain and to the disappointment of the sailors, who asserted that the drowning of a cat was the surest way of raising a favourable wind."

Fleming noted in his journal that by 26 July the ship had still not made much progress and lay at anchor frequently. A month after they boarded the weather was tempestuous and they were wind-bound still in the same harbour. The crew, anxious to be home with their families in Lisbon, grew restless and fearful. How right they were.

At this time Fielding's opinion of the captain began to change. He saw that his imperious and impetuous temper, enforced with 'rough manners and a violent voice', contrasted with his bravery, solicitude for his men and ship and tenderness for his kitten.

"He was in fact one of the best natured fellows alive" wrote Fielding. "He acted the part of a father to his sailors and expressed great tenderness for any of them when ill. He even extended his humanity to his animals; even his cat and kittens had a large share in his affections."

But the following day the kitten that could not be drowned was found mysteriously suffocated under a feather bed in a cabin. Suspicions were directed towards some members of the superstitious crew who were so keen to get home. The captain was beside himself with grief and sat in his cabin and howled - "his lamentations were grievous and seemed to have some mixture of the Irish howl in them."

Despite this, lack of wind continued to delay them throughout the rest of the trip. The *Queen of Portugal* eventually arrived, much overdue, at Lisbon on Wednesday, 7 August 1754. While standing on the deck, waiting for a boat to take him to shore, Fielding marvelled at the beauty of the city. He breathed in the warm air and felt convinced that at last he would begin to recover.

Sadly, his delight was to last but a few months. By October that year, his health had deteriorated and he died on 8 October, 1754 aged only 47. *Voyage to Lisbon* was published posthumously.

When Henry died in 1754, his brother continued the work they had begun together, and refined the Bow Street Runners into the first truly effective London police force, later adding officers mounted on horseback.

John Fielding becoming renowned as the "Blind Beak of Bow Street", allegedly being able to recognise 3,000 criminals by the sounds of their voices. He also continued to develop his ideas on crime prevention and youth employment. He was knighted in 1761.

Sir John Fielding, the Blind Judge

The Cat that jumped into
The Devil's Arms

In 1936 Irish writer James Joyce wrote a story for his grandson, Stephen, called 'The Cat and the Devil'. The poor townsfolk of Beaugency, in France, desperately needed to build a bridge over the River Lire, but hadn't the funds to do so. The Devil himself promised to build a bridge for them. All he asked for in return was that the first person to cross the new bridge would become his slave for eternity. The Mayor of the town agreed to the deal, but deviously tricked the devil by sending over a black cat instead of a person. When he found out he had been hoodwinked, the Devil was furious and contemptuously called the townspeople Les Chats de Beaugency - The Cat People.

However, he took a liking to the poor cat that was made to cross the bridge, after it jumped trustingly into his arms. The Devil decided to take him as his own and the two became inseparable companions. Which is one of the reasons why it is believed that black cats are associated with the Devil.

The Cat that Saved a
Dog from Drowning

Not only do most cats not like water, but normally they positively hate dogs and wisely keep well away from both. One Los Angeles tom cat called Thug found himself in an awful predicament when he spotted a Labrador dog struggling for his life in the sea under a pier. Naturally, Thug was reluctant to jump in to rescue a dog which might not only result in getting his paws wet, but also risk a few misunderstood bites from his sworn enemy. But, being a compassionate sort of creature, he instead began to meow frantically drawing the attention of a passer-bye, who immediately jumped into the water and pulled the dog out. The Los Angeles Society for the Prevention of Cruelty to Animals, gave Thug an award for saving the life of a dog.

Ricci whose Feline Intuition
Saved a Drowning Woman

Ricci was an intuitive ship's cat whose mysterious sixth sense saved the life of a drowning woman. The ship he was on, an Italian cargo vessel, the *Fortuna*, was alerted by radio mid-voyage and asked to help search for survivors from a small aircraft that had plunged into the Mediterranean. The *Fortuna* went round in circles, hunting for any sign of life. But, as the hours went by, hope dwindled. Then it became too dark to be able to see anything and the Captain decided he had no choice but to abandon the search and to continue on their way.

Suddenly Ricci, the ship's cat, seemed to go berserk. He sprang from out of the darkness on to the deck and dashed frantically to the prow of the ship, meowing in a loud, spine-chilling manner. Nothing the ship's crew could do would calm him down. The hackles on the back of his neck rose ominously as he ran to and fro as if demanding some sort of action.

The Captain eventually ordered the searchlights to be projected into the sea. There, desperately clinging for life to a piece of wreckage from the plane, was one woman survivor. The ship's lifeboat was immediately launched and the woman was rescued. If it hadn't been for Ricci the cat, she would not have survived the night.

Pootie the Cat Who Came Creeping Up the Gangplank (from nowhere)

Daphne Trumper and her husband Peter and two children, were living on a converted Brixham trawler in Millbay Docks, Plymouth. One freezing cold night, as they sat cosily round their coal stove, to the family's amusement and astonishment, a small black and white cat appeared through the curtain covering the gangway entrance, with a large bloater in its mouth, as if to say: "I wonder if you'd mind if I came in and ate my supper with you? It's cold outside."

The cat settled down in front of the stove and delicately ate the bloater, leaving only the tail and the head neatly arranged on the mat. After fastidiously cleaning her paws, and wiping her mouth, she coolly sprang up the gangway and disappeared into the night.

In the morning Daphne left a saucer of milk on the deck. That same night the cat appeared again, with a bloater for its supper which she ate with relish before disappearing. This happened two nights running.

Daphne did a bit of detective work and in the dock yard found a truck, partly covered with a tarpaulin, with an open box of bloaters in it, which solved the mystery of where the cat was getting her free suppers.

On the fourth night she appeared again, but this time without a bloater. The truck had obviously moved on and so had the free suppers. Nonetheless, she came in and settled on the mat by the fire as if it was her rightful place. Daphne opened up a tin of sardines for her, which she ate, neatly licking every scrap from the plate.

The family weren't sure whether the cat adopted them or vice versa. But, since it was clear she felt thoroughly at home with them, they decided to give her a name. There was a popular song on the radio at the time: "I though I saw a Pootie cat, creeping up on me....". So the mystery cat became Pootie.

Pootie was not the handsomest of cats. She had a flat white face with a black splodge on its nose, rather bandy legs and scars on both ears, evidence perhaps of being involved in a few fights. But Pootie had a strong personality, and the whole family were thrilled to have her on board. Daphne took the precaution of asking round the dock yard to see if anyone had lost a cat, and was relieved when she was told that she might have belonged to a circus that had set up near the docks and then moved on without her.

Pootie had an endearing habit of climbing into Daphne's bunk and waking her up by gently tapping on her nose. As she became more proprietorial, she took to showing off; swaggering down the gangplank often carrying some gift, such as a live mouse which she insisted should be appreciated by bringing it into the cabin. The mouse of course disappeared behind the lockers. On another occasion Pootie arrived with a dead pigeon. The water in the basin had been lowered and as a result the boat was way down the wall. Pootie jumped off the side of the jetty with the pigeon in her mouth and fell twelve feet into the water.

Panic stations. The skipper on the next yacht and sent out his boys in a dinghy to try find the cat, and they were beginning to fear she had drowned. Then a wet and bedraggled Pootie was seen crawling along the deck from the stern. By some miracle she had managed to climb up the rudder post to safety through a small opening at the top.

Pootie must have felt it was well worth while losing one of her nine lives, because suddenly she was the centre of attention, being dried tenderly with warm towels by the children. The skipper on the next boat sent his wife to get the fish they were due to have for dinner, and served it to Pootie on a silver dish – only the best for this cat.

In the Spring the family moved from the docks across the River Tamar to Mashford's boatyard, at Cremyll and tied up along the outer wall. It was only a short journey but Pootie disgraced herself by being seasick. The move was worth it. In place of a busy dockyard, Pootie had fields and woods to hunt in.

The family were entertaining Daphne's husband's Captain and his wife to tea on board and were anxious to make a good impression. Daphne made a cake and just before the guests arrived, Pootie found it and licked the icing off the top. Then as they were sitting down to tea and scones, Pootie appeared at the top of the companion way with a live rat in her mouth which she dropped in the cabin. The visit was rapidly terminated as everyone scurried around in a panic looking for the rat.

Pootie brought shame to his adopted family by destroying a nest of young wagtails, as well as the parents. There were protests from neighbours who insisted the cat had to go. Rather than give up Pootie, the Trumper family moved to a converted stable in the country, where Pootie lost yet another of her lives by being bitten on the back by a weasel. An abscess developed on the wound. She was taken to the vet, who lanced it and said she had a 50/50 chance of survival as long as she was kept indoors. He warned it was essential she was kept in doors until the wound healed. Within days Pootie had escaped but despite this the wound healed and she survived.

Pootie had now been part of the family for five years. But sadly she developed kidney trouble, lost weight, lost her teeth and, worst of all, her joy of living.

Eventually Daphne was obliged to take Pootie to the vet in Plymouth. She carried her in and gently placed her on the examination table. After examining her, the vet said there was no hope and it was better to put her out of her misery.

"I was choked. I stroked Pootie for the final time, and whispered a word or two of comfort, before walking out the door, clutching the basket in which I had brought her on what we hadn't realised would be her last journey. It was like losing a child".

The Cat that Nearly
Wrecked a Sailor's Manhood

In Istanbul in 1971 a group of very merry and rather drunken sailors on shore leave from their ship, HMS *Bulwark,* came across a half-starved stray ginger kitten who attached himself to them. Purring appealingly, he rubbed against their legs and followed them around town as if begging them to let him join the crew.

One of the *Bulwark*'s stokers, nicknamed Ginge, eventually picked up the kitten and let him nestle in his jacket for comfort. As they waited for the boat to come to take them back to their ship, the other sailors teased Ginge for being soft and challenged him to smuggle the kitten aboard. Ginge took up the challenge and the cat came aboard without anyone noticing.

Next morning, with sore heads and in the cold light of day, the men realised they might be in trouble since cats were forbidden aboard as a result of new Admiralty rules. The ginger tom was kept hidden for a week before the crew decided to come clean and report Cat to the Captain.

Captain D.H.Notley was quite fond of cats and because they were now far out at sea, he agreed that the cat could stay aboard with permission to roam the ship as long as he didn't go ashore. The kitten was named Able Seaman Cat and issued with his own ID card, but not a Station Card, which would have entitled him to shore leave.

According to Leading Marine Engineer Francis Clark, the new recruit became a firm favourite with the entire crew and soon grew fat on the many titbits fed to him. He went off Ginge and attached himself instead to Leading Stoker Beamish Seaton. Beamish was a large, wide man who, despite his size, had been allocated a bunk close to the bulkhead in a particularly tight space. Despite this Able Seaman Cat insisted upon sharing his sleeping bag, his favourite warm spot being between the sailor's legs, cosily nestled in his crotch. One night Cat woke up and decided to have a stretch and inadvertently dug his claws into Beamish's genitals. In struggling to free himself, he only succeeded in wedging himself between the bulkhead and the bunk with the cat's claws still firmly embedded.

The pain was excruciating and the sailor gave an agonised yell which woke up his shipmates. At first the other men thought he was having a nightmare. Despite his acute pain, he managed to explain his problem and immediately the comical side of the situation struck them and it was some minutes before, between with helpless sniggers, they managed to free both cat and sailor. Beamish hobbled to the sick bay for a quick examination and was assured by the medical officer that his manhood was still intact. The incident was the subject of much hilarity amongst the crew, especially as for some weeks Beamish walked about the decks with a particularly pronounced sailor's gait!.

Able Seaman Cat served on the *Bulwark* for about 18 months. After his recruitment, a severe fire broke out in the boiler room. Cat stayed below decks while the crew fought to get the fire under control. They were just off Trieste, on their way back from Istanbul. The damage was so bad that the ship was ordered to return home for repairs. Two officers were awarded British Empire Medals for their bravery. The *Bulwark* was scrapped in 1981.

It was eventually decided that Able Seaman Cat should be retired to a home in Plymouth to live with the family of one of the crew. But, as often happens with ship's cats who find themselves on dry land, he found it difficult to accustom himself to the heavy city traffic and was run over and killed by a car.

Mark Twain's Splendidly-Named Cats

As a young man, Mark Twain (1835-1910) spent much of his time on the Mississippi river. At one time he was a pilot on one of its steamers. His real name was Samuel Langhorne Clemens and he derived his pen name Mark Twain, from the well-known call of the man sounding the river in shallow places (mark twain meaning "by the mark of two fathoms").

Once when sailing on a long voyage on the ss *Oceana*, Mark Twain watched each day, with keen interest, the antics and habits of the three adult ship's cats and their basket of kittens.

He observed with amusement that during the voyage one particularly handsome male cat regularly went ashore at every port and was not seen again until, just before the ship was about to sail, he would come rushing aboard looking rather worse for wear as if he'd had a night on the tiles. In his diary Mark Twain wrote that he could only conclude that this rather rakish cat had a "wife in every port" and was probably going ashore "to see how his various families were getting along".

The prolific writer of many well loved novels, such as Huckleberry Finn and Tom Sawyer, he loved, admired and respected cats and said he couldn't imagine life without at least one. During his lifetime he owned a number of them, all with outlandish names such as Sour Mash,

Appollinaris, Zoroaster and Blatherskite, explaining that the idea was to encourage children to practise large and difficult styles of pronunciation. He was not a talented artist, but an ambitious and imaginative one. He drew a hilariously manic sketch of his own cats with the intention, perhaps, of amusing both children and adults.

He once wrote: "If man could be crossed with the cat it would improve man, but would deteriorate the cat."

Fishing Cats

According to an old proverb, "the cat would eat fish but would not wet her feet", and there are many stories of how a cat will overcome a dislike of water for the sake of a tasty fish meal. At Devil's Point naval battery in Plymouth, one local cat was notorious for plunging each day into the sea and swiftly emerging to settle on the quayside as she delicately ate her catch. When she was well satisfied she would even dive in again and present her catch as gifts to the sailors in the guard room.

The Russian composer and scientist, Alexander Porphyrevich Borodin, had a tabby cat named Rybolov (meaning Fisherman) who skillfully learnt to fish through holes in the winter ice. In Paris, France, there is even a street called the rue du Chat qui Peche (the street of the fishing cat) named after a seventeenth-century cat who was famous for catching fish from cellars after the River Seine flooded one winter.

The Cat that Drowned
In a Goldfish Bowl

But perhaps the most famous fishing cat ever was Selima, belonging to the eighteenth century British politician, Horace Walpole. He was a close friend of Thomas Gray, famous for his poem, the Elegy. On 1 March 1747, Walpole wrote to Gray and told him sadly that his favourite cat, Mademoiselle Selima, had died in a rather extraordinary way. In attempting to scoop some fish out of a goldfish bowl she fell in and died of exhaustion trying to climb out. Gray promptly wrote a poem about the incident, perhaps as a dry warning that arrogant cats shouldn't venture too close to water. He called it "Ode to the Death of a favourite Cat, Drowned in a Tub of Gold Fishes".

'Twas on a lofty vase's side,
Where China's gayest art had dy'd
The azure flowers, that blow;
Demurest of the tabby kind,
The pensive Selima reclin'd,
Gazed on the lake below.
Her conscious tail her joy declar'd,

The fair round face, the snowy beard,
The velvet of her paws,
Her coat, that with the tortoise vies,
Her ears of jet, and emerald eyes,
She saw; and purr'd applause.

Still had she gaz'd; but 'midst the tide
Two angel forms were seen to glide,
The Genii of the stream:
Their scaly armour's Tyrian hue
Thro' richest purple to the view
Betray'd a golden gleam.

The hapless Numph with wonder saw:
A whisker first and then a claw,
With many an ardent wish,
She stretch'd in vain to reach the prize.
What female heart can gold despise?
What Cat's averse to fish?

Presumptuous Maid! With looks intent
Again she stretch'd, again she bent,
Nor knew the gulf between.
(Malignant Fate sat by, and smil'd)
The slipp'ry verge her feet beguil'd
She tumbled headlong in.

Eight times emerging from the flood
She mew'd to eve'ry watery God,
Some speedy aid to send.
No Dolphin came, no Nereid stirr'd;
Not cruel Tom, nor Susan heard.
A fav'rite has no friend!

From hence, ye Beauties, undeceiv'd,
Know, one false step is ne'er retriev'd,
And be with caution bold.
Not all that tempts your wand'ring eyes
And heedless hearts, is lawful prize;
Nor all that glitters, gold.

The Cat that Went to Sea
In a Pea-Green Boat

Foss belonged to Victorian artist and humorist, Edward Lear. Lear was very fond of his cat and used him as a model for his drawings, despite the fact that he appeared to be extremely ugly, with a bloated body, a startled expression and a badly cropped tail. A striped tomcat, he arrived in the Lear household in Italy as a kitten. His tail was cut off by a servant called Giorgio, who believed it would prevent the cat straying.

It was Foss that inspired the seafaring cat in Lear's "The Owl and the Pussy Cat". When the cat died in 1887 he was given a full burial with a grave in Lear's Italian garden, topped by a large tombstone, which claimed the cat was 30 years old.

"Whoever has known me for 30 years has known for all that time my cat Foss has been part of my solitary life," wrote Lear. However, his memory was deluding him. The cat was actually 17 when she died. Lear died two months later, aged 76.

The Owl and the Pussy Cat

The Owl and the Pussy-cat went to sea
In a beautiful pea-green boat.
They took some honey, and plenty of money,
    Wrapped up in a five-pound note.
The Owl looked up to the stars above,
    And sang to a small guitar,
"O lovely Pussy! O Pussy, my love,
    What a beautiful Pussy you are,
You are,
You are,
What a beautiful Pussy you are!"

Pussy said to the Owl, "You elegant fowl!
  How charmingly sweet you sing!
O let us be married! Too long have we tarried:
  But what shall we do for a ring?"
They sailed away, for a year and a day
  To the land where the Bong-tree grows,
And there in a wood a Piggy-wig stood,
  With a ring at the end of his nose,
His nose,
His nose,
With a ring at the end of his nose.

Edward Lear.
æt 73.½

His cat Foss,
æt 16.

"Dear Pig, are you willing to sell for one shilling
  Your ring?" Said the Piggy, "I will."
So they took it away, and were married next day
  By the Turkey who lives on the hill.
They dined on mince, and slices of quince,
  Which they ate with a runcible spoon;
And hand in hand, on the edge of the sand,
  They danced by the light of the moon,
The moon,
The moon,
They danced by the light of the moon.

T.S.Eliot's Mystery Cats

T.S.Eliot was infatuated by cats and owned many, all with eccentric names. He believed that all cats have three names. The first name is the familiar one that friends and family are allowed to use. The second name is his particular name, the one he uses when he wants to look dignified and behave in a superior manner. And the third name is the one the cat thinks up for himself - his deep and inscrutable singular name which he never reveals to anyone.

Eliot wrote that whenever a cat appears to be in deep and mysterious meditation and you wonder what he is thinking about so seriously, he is sure to be contemplating the name that no one else knows about except himself and which gives him such pleasure to know that others don't know it.

Eliot's famous Old Possum's Book of Practical Cats, contains two poems about ship's cats. One is about a pirate cat who has retired to be a door keeper at an establishment in Bloomsbury Square, and the other is about a barge cat who terrorised everyone on the river from Gravesend to Oxford.

Growltiger's Last Stand!

Growltiger was a Bravo Cat, who travelled on a barge,
In fact he was the roughest cat that ever roamed at large.
From Gravesend up to Oxford he pursued his evil aims,
Rejoicing in his title of "The Terror of the Thames".

His manners and appearance did not calculate to please;
His coat was torn and seedy, he was baggy at the knees;
One ear was somewhat missing, no need to tell you why,
And he scowled upon a hostile world from one forbidding eye

The cottagers of Rotherhithe knew something of his fame;
At Hammersmith and Putney people shuddered at his name.
They would fortify the hen-house, lock up the silly goose,
When the rumour ran along the shore: GROWLTIGER'S ON THE LOOSE!

Woe to the weak canary, that fluttered from its cage;
Woe to the pampered Pekinese, that faced Growltiger's rage;
Woe to the bristly Bandicoot, that lurks on foreign ships,
And woe to any Cat with whom Growltiger came to grips!

But most to Cats of foreign race his hatred had been vowed;
To Cats of foreign name and race no quarter was allowed.
The Persian and the Siamese regarded him with fear-
Because it was a Siamese had mauled his missing ear.

Now on a peaceful summer night, all nature seemed at play,
The tender moon was shining bright, the barge at Molesey lay.
All in the balmy moonlight it lay rocking on the tide
And Growltiger was disposed to show his sentimental side.

His bucko mate, GRUMBUSKIN, long since had disappeared,
For to the Bell at Hampton he had gone to wet his beard;
And his bosun, TUMBLEBRUTUS, he too had stolen away –
In the yard behind the Lion he was prowling for his prey.

In the forepeak of the vessel Growltiger sat alone,
Concentrating his attention on the Lady GRIDDLEBONE.
And his raffish crew were sleeping in their barrels and their bunks –
As the Siamese came creeping in their sampans and their junks.

Growltiger had no eye or ear for aught but Griddlebone,
And the Lady seemed enraptured by his manly baritone,
Disposed to relaxation, and awaiting no surprise –
But the moonlight shone reflected from a thousand bright blue eyes.

And closer still and closer the sampans circled round,
And yet from all the enemy there was not heard a sound.
The lovers sang their last duet, in danger of their lives –
For the foe was armed with toasting forks and cruel carving knives.

Then GILBERT gave the signal to his fierce Mongolian horde;
With a frightful burst of fireworks the Chinks they swarmed aboard.
Abandoning their sampans and their pullaways and junks
They battened down the hatches on the crew within their bunks.

Then Griddlebone she gave a screech, for she was badly skeered
I am sorry to admit it, but she quickly disappeared.
She probably escaped with ease, I'm sure she was not drowned – But a serried ring
of flashing steel Growltiger did surround.

The ruthless foe pressed forward, in stubborn range on rank;
Growltiger to his vast surprise was forced to walk the plank.
He who a hundred victims had driven to that drop,
At the end of all his crimes was forced to go ker-flip, ker-flop.

Oh, there was joy in Wapping when the news flew through the land;
At Maidenhead and Henley there was dancing on the strand.
The rats were roasted whole at Brentford, and at Victoria Dock,
And a day of celebration was commanded in Bangkok.

T.S.Eliot

Cat Morgan Introduces Himself

I once was a Pirate what sailed the 'igh seas
But now I've retired as a com-mission-aire:
And that's how you find me a-takin' my ease
And keepin' the door in Bloomsbury Square.
I'm partial to partridges, likewise to grouse,
And I favour that Devonshire cream in a bowl;
But I'm allus content with a drink on the 'ouse
And a bit o' cold fish when I done me patrol.

I ain't got much polish, me manners is gruff,
But I've got a good coat, and I keep meself smart;
And everyone says, and I guess that's enough;
"You can't but like Morgan, 'e's got a good 'art."
I got knocked about on the Barbary Coast,
And me voice it ain't no sich melliferous horgan;
But yet I can state, and I'm not one to boast,
That some of the gals is dead keen on old Morgan.

So if you 'ave business with Faber – or Faber –
I'll give you this tip, and it's worth a lot more:
You'll save yourself time and spare yourself labour
If jist you make friends with the Cat at the door.

T.S.Eliot

The World's Great Explorers

Cats don't swim, so why do they brave
A dangerous life on the ocean wave?
Why leave the safety of solid earth
To sail in a ship on the billowy surf?

Rats, that swarm beneath the decks,
Are first to swim from sinking wrecks.
But cats can't bear to wet their paws
And will stay below to guard the stores.

Life's hard at sea, with the ship always rolling
Waves high as hills, sky black and squalling,
There's many a home cats could be curled up at,
Licking up cream or snug on a lap.

It's maybe because a cat has nine lives,
Plenty to spare if the ship he's in dives;
If the mast falls off and the hull lets waves in,
A cat knows **something** will mysteriously save him.

Cats don't swim, they're not really sailors,
Yet you'll find them at sea on battleships or whalers,
They'll travel the oceans on cruisers and trawlers,
For cats are like that, they're the world's Great Explorers.

Elaine Procter
(also known as Val Lewis)

My family insist I should confess myself the author of this poem,
since it was so well received in previous editions.

Bibliography

Animals in War, Jilly Cooper

Antarctic or Two Years on the Ice, Nordenskjold & Andersson,

At One with the Sea, Naomi James.

Battle and the Cat, Richard Halliburton

Cats in the News, Martyn Lewis

Cat Who Went to Heaven, Elizabeth Coatsworth.

Cat World, Desmond Morris

Count Luckner, The Sea Devil, Lowell Thomas.

Dictionary of Cat Lovers, Cristabel Aberconway.

John Worsley's War, John Worsley & Kenneth Giggal

Little Book of Cats, Susan Fever

Maiden Voyage, Tania Aebi

Mrs Chippy's Last Expedition, by Caroline Alexander

North to the Night, Alvah Simon

Old Possum's Book of Practical Cats, T.S.Eliot.

Rescue of Capt. Scott, Don Aldridge.

Roald Amundsen's Belgica Diary, Hugo Decleir

Scott's Last Expedition, Robert Falcon Scott

Shackleton's Boat, Harding McGregor Dunnett

Silent Heroes, Evelyn Le Chene

Southern Lights (Graham Land) John Rymill

The Cat Who Escaped from Steerage, Evelyn Mayerson Wilde

Thomas Benjy, the Bargy Cat Cicely Fraser-Simson

Through the First Antarctic Night, Frederick Cooke

Trim, by Matthew Flinders.

Voyage of Discovery, James Clarke Ross

Voyage of Discovery, Robert Falcon Scott

Voyages of Discovery, Ann Savours

Voyages of the Morning, Gerald S. Doorly

Voyage to Lisbon, Henry Fielding

War Animals, Robert E Lubow

Index

Ships

202

People

Places

Intrepid Ships' Cats™

Mrs. Chippy of ss *Endeavour*
Simon of HMS *Amethyst*
Freddy of ss *Hawksdale*

Nauticalia **Intrepid Ships' Cats** models are based on three of the ships' cats featured in this book. They are remarkably realistic looking and, particularly for those who long for the comfort of a pet but aren't able to keep one, they provide soothing companionship.

The advantages are:
- ► **No need to feed them**
- ► **They don't pee on the carpet**
- ► **They don't scratch the furniture**
- ► **They can be left at home with a clear conscience while the owner goes on holiday**

As Mr VT of Salisbury said of Simon, purchased for his mother: "He makes the ideal companion for the elderly. Never wants to go out, never wants feeding etc… Not one visitor has noticed that the cat is not real until it is pointed out to them!"

On a more ingenious note, one customer uses her Mrs Chippy as a 'chair saver'. She has one very delicate antique chair which can't take the weight of some of her visitors. So she puts the cat on the chair as a more diplomatic way of making sure her heavier friends don't use it. For who would be so cruel as to disturb a cat from his peaceful repose in a chair, in order to sit down themselves?

"Freddy has gone down so well with everyone, especially my neighbours' youngsters, I thought I'd get him a companion, so I'm ordering Simon!" Mrs. E.G., Southampton.

Each **Intrepid Ship's Cat** is portrayed sleeping, with an engraved name tag around his neck and a history label attached to his underside. They are made from shaped cardboard coated with dyed rabbit fur, a welfare-approved by-product of sustenance farming in Shandon Province, China. They are £29.95 plus £4.95 for UK mainland postage and packing. For readers of this book, prices will remain the same until December 2012.

Freddy, the shipwrecked marmalade cat rescued by the RNLI. Ref: 4695

Mrs Chippy, the tabby cat that sailed with Shackleton. Ref: 4690

Able Seaman Simon, black and white Hero of the Amethyst. Ref: 4692

Order by post with a cheque, or online or by phone with a credit card, from:

Nauticalia Ltd., Ferry Lane, Shepperton-on-Thames, TW17 9NU, England.
Tel: 01932 235550   email: sales@nauticalia.com   www.nauticalia.com.

Nauticalia also publish a mail of order catalogue of maritime heritage and practical boating accessories, clothing and gifts, which they will be pleased to mail a copy on request.